Inequality and Tax Policy

Inequality and Tax Policy

Kevin A. Hassett
and
R. Glenn Hubbard,
editors

The AEI Press

Publisher for the American Enterprise Institute
WASHINGTON, D.C.
2001

Available in the United States from the AEI Press, c/o Publisher Resources Inc., 1224 Heil Quaker Blvd., P.O. Box 7001, La Vergne, TN 37086-7001; call toll free 1-800-629-6267. Distributed outside the United States by arrangement with Eurospan, 3 Henrietta Street, London WC2E 8LU England.

Library of Congress Cataloging-in-Publication Data
Inequality and tax policy / Kevin A. Hassett and R. Glenn Hubbard, editors.
    p. cm.
    Papers presented at a conference held at the American Enterprise Institute.
    ISBN 0-8447-4143-4 (cloth) — ISBN 0-8447-4144-2 (pbk.)
    1. Tax incidence—United States—Congress.   2. Taxation—United States—Congress.   I. Hassett, Kevin A.   II. Hubbard, R. Glenn.
  HJ2322.A3 I54   2001
  336.2'94'0973—dc21   2001046364

1 3 5 7 9 10 8 6 4 2

THE AEI PRESS
Publisher for the American Enterprise Institute
1150 17th Street, N.W., Washington, D.C. 20036

Printed in the United States of America

Contents

Preface

The public debate over tax policy frequently turns on distributional issues. Tax reform proponents, for example, argue that the long-run growth effects of lower marginal tax rates benefit citizens situated throughout the income distribution, while opponents argue that, by starting from a progressive tax structure, marginal tax rate reductions often benefit the wealthy the most. However, many important questions lurk behind the political aspect of the debate. How do taxes affect the distribution of income when all dynamic effects are accounted for? Does an equalization of the income distribution have important economic effects? Do changes in inequality lead to changes in progressivity? Is entrepreneurial activity especially sensitive to attempts to redistribute income?

This volume features six essays originally presented at a conference at the American Enterprise Institute. Each author was asked to focus on what he believed to be the key questions concerning inequality and tax policy. The resulting lively contributions summarize the extensive existing literatures, highlight consensus, and often break new ground.

In the first chapter ("Inequality, Growth, and Investment") Robert Barro explores the relationship between inequality and economic performance. After surveying the sizable literature and providing new evidence of his own, Barro finds scant evidence that inequality significantly affects overall economic growth. He does find, however, an interesting disaggregated pattern, with inequality generally retarding growth in poor countries and encouraging it in rich countries.

Most people feel that a fair tax system treats equals the same. Surprisingly economists have been unable to proceed from this intuitive notion to an explicit measure of horizontal equity that would be useful for policy analysis. In the second chapter ("Tax Policy and Horizontal Equity") Alan Auerbach and Kevin Hassett present just such a measure based on an extension of Atkinson's social welfare–based measure of vertical inequality. They demonstrate that their measure overcomes many problems that plagued past measures because it is based rigorously on an explicit mathematical formulation of social welfare. The authors then document a striking increase in horizontal inequality over the past decade, as various tax credits have increased the complexity of the fairly pristine tax code that emerged from the 1986 tax act

In chapter 3 ("Entrepreneurial Saving Decisions and Wealth Inequality") R. Glenn Hubbard studies the increasing inequality of wealth in the United States in recent years. He finds that most of the runup in inequality reflects the high saving rate and return on saving of entrepreneurs. Hubbard argues that this concentration of wealth likely reflects an imperfection in capital markets; apparently the best way to raise money to start a business is still to save it oneself. Hubbard's results suggest that policies targeted toward increasing entrepreneurship might effectively combat inequality.

In "The U.S. Fiscal System as an Opportunity-Equalizing Device," Marianne Page and John Roemer argue that fairness dictates equality of opportunity. They propose an appropriate measure that holds agents accountable for their efforts but not their original circumstances. A simple example illustrates their measure. Roemer and Page would say that a tax system equalized opportunity if the post-tax and transfer incomes of a white and black worker with identical IQs and efforts were identical. The authors assess the degree to which the current U.S. tax system equalizes opportunities. They find that the system does equalize opportunity well if one defines circumstances to mean socioeconomic status but does poorly with respect to race. Roemer and Page's optimal policy would require that the tax system offset racial discrimination more than it actually does.

Much of the benefit of a consumption tax comes from the reduction in the tax on capital. In "Balanced-Budget Restraint in Taxing Income from Wealth in the Ramsey Model" Edmund S. Phelps investigates the sensitivity of theoretical results that argue for a zero tax on capital. Phelps finds that the result can be overturned if the government faces a balanced-budget rule that precludes it from hoarding large surpluses. He goes on to explore the forces that could reverse his own conclusion, providing invaluable intuition about sources of optimal tax results.

In chapter 6 ("Growing Inequality and Reduced Tax Progressivity") Joel Slemrod and Jon Bakija explore the recent shift in the burden of taxation as the pretax income distribution has become more unequal. Using optimal tax theory, they also probe the link between higher income inequality and higher progressivity. They document a sharp rise in recent years in the income share at the top of the income distribution, and they discuss the sources of this trend and the implications for the desirability of a more progressive tax system.

In addition to these authors, a distinguished group of discussants present commentaries on each chapter.

Although the subject of inequality is an especially difficult one, the contributions presented here should provide a useful guide to the current literature and a roadmap for future research.

Kevin A. Hassett and R. Glenn Hubbard

Contributors

ALAN J. AUERBACH is the Robert D. Burch Professor of Economics and Law and the director of the Burch Center for Tax Policy and Public Finance at the University of California at Berkeley. He had been the chairman of the Economics Department there and at the University of Pennsylvania. Mr. Auerbach is a research associate of the National Bureau of Economic Research and a member of the advisory panels of the Congressional Budget Office and the Department of Commerce's Bureau of Economic Analysis. He was the deputy chief of staff of the Joint Committee on Taxation in 1992. He was a consultant to the Treasury Department, Organization for Economic Cooperation and Development, International Monetary Fund, World Bank, Swedish Ministry of Finance, and New Zealand Treasury.

JON M. BAKIJA is an assistant professor of economics at Williams College. He was a researcher at the University of Michigan's Office of Tax Policy Research and at the Urban Institute. His recent research includes empirical studies of the effects of taxation on charitable donations, portfolio choice, and income inequality. Mr. Bakija is the coauthor of *Taxing Ourselves: A Citizen's Guide to the Great Debate over Tax Reform* (with Joel Slemrod) and *Retooling Social Security for the Twenty-first Century* (with Eugene Steuerle).

ROBERT J. BARRO is Robert C. Waggoner Professor of Economics at Harvard University and a senior fellow of the Hoover Institution of Stanford University. He has written extensively on macroeconomic topics; recent research has focused on the determinants of economic growth and the role of dollarization. Recent books include *Determinants of Economic Growth* and *Getting It Right: Markets and Choices in a Free Society*. Mr. Barro is a columnist for *Business Week* and a frequent contributor to the *Wall Street Journal*.

ALAN S. BLINDER is Gordon S. Rentschler Memorial Professor of Economics and the codirector of the Center for Economic Policy Studies at Princeton University. He is the vice chairman of the G7 Group. At Princeton Mr. Blinder chaired the Department of Economics from 1988 to 1990, and he founded Princeton's Center for Economic Policy Studies. He was the vice chairman of the board of governors from June 1994 until January 1996. Mr. Blinder was a member of President Clinton's Council of Advisers from January 1993 until June 1994. He was briefly the deputy assistant director of the Congressional Budget Office when that agency was created in 1975. Mr. Blinder is a governor of the American Stock Exchange and a trustee of the Russell Sage Foundation. He is the author or coauthor of twelve books, including the textbook *Economics: Principles and Policy* (with William J. Baumol).

ROGER H. GORDON is a professor of economics, University of California, San Diego. He had been the Reuben Kempf Professor of Economics at the University of Michigan. Mr. Gordon had been on the technical staff of Bell Laboratories from 1980 to 1983 and an assistant professor of economics at Princeton University from 1976 to 1980. He is the co-editor of the *Journal of Public Economics*, a research associate of the National Bureau of Economic Research and the Center for Economic Policy Research, and a fellow of the Econometrics Society. His published work explores theoretical and applied topics in public finance, including work on the effects of the Social Security program on individual savings behavior and retirement decisions, the effects of capital income taxes on corporate behavior, tax policy in an open economy setting, and economic reform issues in centrally planned economies.

KEVIN A. HASSETT is a resident scholar at AEI. He had been a senior economist at the Board of Governors of the Federal Reserve System and an associate professor of economics and finance at the Graduate School of Business of Columbia University. Mr. Hassett was the chief economic adviser to

Sen. John McCain during the 2000 presidential campaign and a policy consultant to the Treasury Department during both the Bush and Clinton administrations. He has published in the *Economic Journal*, *Quarterly Journal of Economics*, *Journal of Public Economics*, *Atlantic Monthly*, *USA Today*, *Investor's Business Daily*, *Wall Street Journal*, and *Weekly Standard*. He is the coauthor, with James K. Glassman, of the best-selling book *Dow 36,000: The New Strategy for Profiting from the Coming Rise in the Stock Market*.

R. GLENN HUBBARD is the chairman of the Council of Economic Advisers. He was a visiting scholar at AEI and the Russell L. Carson Professor of Economics and Finance at the Graduate School of Business and the Department of Economics at Columbia University when was completed. He was the deputy assistant secretary of tax analysis at the Treasury Department during the previous Bush administration. Mr. Hubbard was also a visiting professor at the University of Chicago and Harvard University and a John M. Olin Fellow at the National Bureau of Economic Research, where he continues to be a research associate in programs on public economics, monetary economics, corporate finance, economic fluctuations, and industrial organization. He has been a research consultant for the Federal Reserve Board, Federal Reserve Bank of New York, Internal Revenue Service, Social Security Administration, Treasury Department, U.S. International Trade Commission, National Science Foundation, and World Bank.

LOUIS KAPLOW has been a professor at Harvard Law School since 1982 and was the associate dean for research from 1989 to 1991. He is a research associate for the National Bureau of Economic Research and is on the editorial boards of the *Journal of Public Economics*; *National Tax Journal*; *Journal of Law, Economics and Organization*; and *Legal Theory*. Mr. Kaplow has been a consultant to the Department of Justice, state antitrust departments, Legal Reform Project of the Russian Federation, and the controller of restrictive trade practices, Israel.

N. GREGORY MANKIW is a professor of economics at Harvard University and a research associate of the National Bureau of

Economic Research. He was an adviser to the Congressional Budget Office, Brookings Panel on Economic Activity, and Federal Reserve Bank of Boston. Mr. Makiw has written two best-selling textbooks, *Macroeconomics* and *Principles of Economics*.

CASEY B. MULLIGAN has been an assistant or associate professor at the University of Chicago's Department of Economics since 1994. His research interests include political economy and non-pecuniary incentives to save and to work. Mr. Mulligan's recent book, *Parental Priorities and Economic Inequality*, models the formation of altruism by deriving and testing implication of the theory for patterns of intergenerational mobility.

MARIANNE PAGE has been an assistant professor of economics at the University of California, Davis, since 1996. She had been an assistant professor at Santa Clara University. Her research interests include poverty, racial inequality, and education. She is analyzing the incentive effects on welfare programs, determinants of school equality, and the effect of neighborhoods on socioeconomic outcomes. Ms. Page's recent publications include papers on the link between wages and the quality of teachers.

EDMUND S. PHELPS was appointed professor of economics at Columbia University in 1971 and was named McVickar Professor of Political Economy in 1982. Recent research, which includes benefits of capitalism, both for employment and productivity growth, and causes and cures of joblessness and low wages among disadvantaged workers, produced *Rewarding Work*. He is a senior adviser to the Brookings Institution panel on economic activity and was an adviser to the European Bank for Reconstruction and Development during the early years of the transition in eastern Europe. He has been a consultant to the Italian government, Treasury Department, Senate Finance Committee, and Federal Reserve Board. Among his many books are *Studies in Macroeconomic Theory*; *Political Economy*; *The Slump in Europe*, with J. P. Fitoussi; and *Seven Schools of Macroeconomic Thought*.

JAMES M. POTERBA is the Mitsui Professor of Economics at the Massachusetts Institute of Technology, where he has taught since 1982. He is also the director of the Public Economics Research Program at the National Bureau of Economic Research, the associate head of the MIT Economics Department, and a fellow of the American Academy of Arts and Sciences and of the Econometric Society. Mr. Poterba was a director of the American Finance Association. He edits the *Journal of Public Economics* and is an associate editor of the *Journal of Finance* and a member of the advisory editorial boards of the *Journal of Private Portfolio Management* and the *Investment Management Consultant's Association Journal*. Mr. Poterba is a member of the Congressional Budget Office's Panel of Economic Advisers.

JOHN E. ROEMER is Elizabeth S. and A. Varick Stout Professor of Political Science and Economics at Yale University. His fields of interest include political economy, distributive justice, and the theory of socialism. Mr. Roemer was a member of the executive board of the American Economic Association and the Society for Social Choice and Welfare and is a fellow of the Econometric Society. He also serves on the editorial boards of professional journals in economics and philosophy. His latest books are *Political Competition: Theory and Applications* and *Equality of Opportunity*.

JOEL SLEMROD is the Paul W. McCracken Collegiate Professor of Business Economics and Public Policy at the University of Michigan Business School and is a professor of economics in the Department of Economics. He is the director of the Office of Tax Policy Research. Mr. Slemrod was the senior staff economist for tax policy on the President's Council of Economic Advisers from 1984 to 1985. He was a consultant to the Treasury Department, Canadian Department of Finance, New Zealand Treasury Department, World Bank, and Organization for Economic Cooperation and Development. Mr. Slemrod was the editor of the *National Tax Journal* from 1992 to 1998.

1

Inequality, Growth, and Investment

Robert J. Barro

A substantial literature analyzes the effects of income inequality on macroeconomic performance, as reflected in rates of economic growth and investment. Much of this analysis is empirical and uses data on the performance of a broad range of countries. This chapter contributes to this literature by using a framework for the determinants of economic growth that I have developed and used in previous studies. To motivate the extension of this framework to income inequality, I begin by discussing recent theoretical analyses of the macroeconomic consequences of income inequality. Then I develop the applied framework and describe the new empirical findings.

Theoretical Effects of Inequality on Growth and Investment

Many theories have been constructed to assess the macroeconomic relations between inequality and economic growth.[1] These theories can be classed into four broad categories corresponding to the main feature stressed: credit-market imperfections, political economy, social unrest, and saving rates.

Credit-Market Imperfections. In models with imperfect credit markets, the limited ability to borrow means that rates of return

This essay was presented at a conference at the American Enterprise Institute. The research has been supported in part by a grant from the National Science Foundation. I am grateful for excellent research assistance from Silvana Tenreyro and for comments from Paul Collier, Bill Easterly, Jong-Wha Lee, Mattias Lundberg, Francisco Rodriguez, Heng-fu Zou, and participants at a seminar at the World Bank.

1

on investment opportunities are not necessarily equated at the margin.[2] The credit-market imperfections typically reflect asymmetric information and limitations of legal institutions. For example, creditors may have difficulty in collecting on defaulted loans because law enforcement is imperfect. Collection may also be hampered by a bankruptcy law that protects the assets of debtors.

With limited access to credit, the exploitation of investment opportunities depends to some extent on an individual's levels of assets and incomes. Specifically, poor people tend to forgo investments in human capital that offer relatively high rates of return. In this case a distortion-free redistribution of assets and incomes from rich to poor tends to raise the average productivity of investment. Through this mechanism a reduction in inequality raises the rate of economic growth, at least during a transition to the steady state.

An offsetting force arises if investments require a setup cost, that is, if increasing returns to investment prevail over some range. For instance, formal education may be useful only beyond some minimal level. One possible manifestation of this effect is the apparently strong role for secondary schooling, rather than primary schooling, in enhancing economic growth (see Barro 1997). Analogously, a business may be productive only if it goes beyond some threshold size. In the presence of credit-market imperfections, these considerations favor a concentration of assets. Hence this element tends to generate positive effects of inequality on investment and growth.

If capital markets and legal institutions tend to improve as an economy develops, then the effects related to capital-market imperfections are more important in poor economies than in rich ones. Therefore, the predicted effects of inequality on economic growth (which were of uncertain sign) would be larger in magnitude for poor economies than for rich ones.

Political Economy. If the mean income in an economy exceeds the median income, then majority voting tends to favor the redistribution of resources from the rich to the poor.[3] These redistributions may involve explicit transfer payments but can also appear as public-expenditure programs (such as programs for education and child care) and regulatory policies.

A greater degree of inequality—measured, for example, by the ratio of mean to median income—motivates more redistribution through the political process. Typically the transfer payments and the associated tax finance will distort economic decisions. For example, means-tested welfare payments and levies on labor income discourage work effort. In this case more redistribution creates more distortions and therefore tends to reduce investment. Economic growth declines accordingly, at least in the transition to the steady state. Since a greater amount of inequality (measured before transfers) induces more redistribution, inequality would reduce growth.

The data typically refer to ex post inequality, that is, to incomes measured net of the effects from various public interventions. These interventions include expenditure programs—notably, education and health—transfers, and nonproportional taxes. Some data refer to income net of taxes or to consumer expenditures rather than to income gross of taxes. However, even the net-of-tax and expenditure data are ex post to the effects of various public-sector interventions.

The relation of ex post inequality to economic growth is complicated in the political economy models. If countries differ only in their ex ante distributions of income, then the redistributions through the political process tend to be only partly offsetting. That is, the places that are more unequal ex ante are also those that are more unequal ex post. In such a case the predicted negative relation between inequality and growth holds for ex post, as well as ex ante, income inequality.

The predicted relation between ex post inequality and growth can change if countries differ by their tastes for redistribution. In this case the countries that seem more equal ex post tend to be those that have redistributed the most and hence have caused the most distortions of economic decisions. In this case ex post inequality tends to be positively related to growth and investment.

The effects that involve transfers through the political process arise if the distribution of political power is uniform—as in a literal one-person/one-vote democracy—and the allocation of economic power is unequal. If more economic resources translate into correspondingly greater political influence, then the

3

positive link between inequality and redistribution would not apply.[4] More generally the predicted effect arises if the distribution of political power is more egalitarian than the distribution of economic power.

In addition, the predicted negative effect of inequality on growth can arise even if no transfers are observed in equilibrium. The rich may prevent redistributive policies through lobbying and buying votes of legislators. But then a higher level of economic inequality would require more of these activities to prevent the redistribution of income through the political process. The lobbying activities would consume resources and promote official corruption. Since these effects would be adverse for economic performance, inequality could have a negative effect on growth through the political process even if no redistribution of income occurs in equilibrium.

Sociopolitical Unrest. Inequality of wealth and income motivates the poor to engage in crime, riots, and other disruptive activities.[5] The stability of political institutions may even be threatened by revolution, so that laws and other rules have shorter expected duration and greater uncertainty. The participation of the poor in crime and other antisocial actions represents a direct waste of resources because the time and energy of the criminals are not devoted to productive efforts. Defensive efforts by potential victims represent a further loss of resources. Moreover, the threats to property rights deter investment. Through these various dimensions of sociopolitical unrest, more inequality tends to reduce the productivity of an economy. Economic growth declines accordingly, at least in the transition to the steady state.

An offsetting force is that economic resources are required for the poor to cause disruption and threaten the stability of the established regime effectively. Hence income-equalizing transfers promote political stability only to the extent that the first force—the incentive of the poor to steal and disrupt rather than to work—is the dominant element.

Even in a dictatorship, self-interested leaders would favor some amount of income-equalizing transfers if the net effect were a decrease in the tendency for social unrest and political instability. Thus these considerations predict some provision of a social safety net regardless of the form of government. Moreover the tendency for redistribution to reduce crimes and riots provides a mechanism whereby this redistribution—and the resulting greater income equality—would enhance economic growth.

Saving Rates. Some economists, perhaps influenced by Keynes's *General Theory*, believe that individual saving rates rise with the level of income. If true, then a redistribution of resources from the rich to the poor tends to lower the aggregate rate of saving in an economy. Through this channel a rise in inequality tends to raise investment (if the economy is partly closed). In this case more inequality would enhance economic growth, at least in a transitional sense.

The previous discussion of imperfect credit markets brought out a related mechanism by which inequality would promote economic growth. In that analysis setup costs for investment implied that the concentration of asset ownership would be beneficial for the economy. The present discussion of aggregate saving rates provides a complementary reason for a positive effect of inequality on growth.

Overview. Many satisfactory theories can be used for assessing the effects of inequality on investment and economic growth. But these theories tend to have offsetting effects, and the net effects of inequality on investment and growth are ambiguous.

The theoretical ambiguities do in a sense accord with empirical findings, which tend not to be robust. Perotti (1996) reports an overall tendency for inequality to generate lower economic growth in cross-country regressions. Benabou (1996, table 2) also summarizes these findings. But some researchers, such as Li and Zou (1998) and Forbes (1997), have reported relationships with the opposite sign.[6]

My new results about the effects of inequality on growth and investment for a panel of countries are discussed in a later section. I report evidence that the negative effect of inequality on growth shows up for poor countries, but that the relationship for rich countries is positive. However, the overall effects of inequality on growth and investment are weak.

5

The Evolution of Inequality

The main theoretical approach to assessing the determinants of inequality involves some version of the Kuznets (1955) curve. Kuznets's idea, developed further by Robinson (1976), focused on the movements of persons from agriculture to industry. In this model the agricultural-rural sector initially constitutes the bulk of the economy. This sector features low per capita income and perhaps relatively little inequality within the sector. The industrial-urban sector starts out small and has higher per capita income and possibly a relatively high degree of inequality within the sector.

Economic development involves in part a shift of persons from agriculture to industry. The persons who move experience a rise in per capita income, and this change raises the economy's overall degree of inequality. That is, the dominant effect initially is the expansion of the small group of relatively rich persons in the industrial-urban sectors. Thus, at early stages of development, the relation between the level of per capita product and the extent of inequality is positive.

As the size of the agricultural sector diminishes, the dominant effect of continued mobility on inequality is the opportunity of more poor agricultural workers to join the relatively rich industrial sector. In addition, many workers who started on the bottom rungs of the industrial sector tend to move up in relation to the richer workers within this sector. The decreasing size of the agricultural labor force tends, in addition, to drive up relative wages in that sector. These forces combine to reduce indexes of overall inequality. Hence, at later stages of development, the relation between the level of per capita product and the extent of inequality is negative.

The full relationship between an indicator of inequality, such as a Gini coefficient, and the level of per capita product is described by an inverted U, which is the curve named after Kuznets. Inequality first rises and later falls as the economy becomes more developed.

More recent models that feature a Kuznets curve generalize beyond the shift of persons and resources from agriculture to industry. The counterpart of the movement from rural agriculture to urban industry may be a shift from a financially unsophisticated position to one that involves inclusion with the modern financial system (see Greenwood and Jovanovic 1990).

In another approach the poor sector may use an old technology, whereas the rich sector may use more recent and advanced techniques (see Helpman 1997 and Aghion and Howitt 1997). Mobility from old to new requires a process of familiarization and reeducation. In this context many technological innovations—such as the factory system, electrical power, computers, and the Internet—initially tend to raise inequality. The dominant factor here is the low number of persons who initially share in the relatively high incomes of the technologically advanced sector. As more people move into this favored sector, inequality tends to rise along with expanding per capita product. But subsequently, as more people take advantage of the superior techniques, inequality tends to fall. This equalization occurs because relatively few people remain behind eventually and because the newcomers to the more advanced sector tend to catch up to those who started ahead. The relative wage rate of those staying in the backward sector may or may not rise as the supply of factors to that sector diminishes.

In these theories inequality would depend on how long ago a new technological innovation was introduced into the economy. Since the level of per capita GDP would not be closely related to this technological history, the conventional Kuznets curve would not fit well. The curve would fit only to the extent that a high level of per capita GDP signaled a country's relatively recent introduction of advanced technologies or modern production techniques.

On an empirical level the Kuznets curve was accepted through the 1970s as a strong empirical regularity (see especially Ahluwalia 1976a, b). Papanek and Kyn (1986) find that the Kuznets relation is statistically significant but explains little of the variations in inequality across countries or over time. Subsequent work suggested that the relation had weakened over time (see Anand and Kanbur 1993). Li, Squire, and Zou (1998) argue that the Kuznets curve works better for a cross-section of countries at a point in time than for the evolution of inequality over time within countries.

7

My new results on the Kuznets curve and other determinants of inequality are discussed in a later section. I find that the Kuznets curve shows up as a clear empirical regularity across countries and over time and that the relationship has not weakened over time. I also find, however, that this curve explains relatively little of the variations in inequality across countries or over time.

Framework for the Empirical Analysis of Growth and Investment

The empirical framework is the one based on conditional convergence, which I have used in several places, starting in Barro 1991 and updated in Barro 1997. I include here only a brief description of the structure.

The framework, derived from an extended version of the neoclassical growth model, can be summarized by a simple equation:

$$Dy = F(y, y^*), \tag{1-1}$$

where Dy is the growth rate of per capita output, y is the current level of per capita output, and y^* is the long-run or target level of per capita output. In the neoclassical model the diminishing returns to the accumulation of capital imply that an economy's growth rate, Dy, is inversely related to its level of development, as represented by y.[7] In the present framework this property applies in a conditional sense for a given value of y^*.

For a given value of y, the growth rate, Dy, rises with y^*. The value y^* depends in turn on government policies and institutions and on the character of the national population. For example, better enforcement of property rights and fewer market distortions tend to raise y^* and hence increase Dy for a given y. Similarly, if people are willing to work harder, save more, and have fewer children, then y^* increases, and Dy rises accordingly for given y.

In this model a permanent improvement in some government policy initially raises the growth rate, Dy, and then raises the level of per capita output, y, gradually over time. As output rises, the workings of diminishing returns eventually restore the growth rate, Dy, to a value consistent with the long-run rate of technological progress (which is determined outside the model in the standard neoclassical framework). Hence, in the long run, the impact of improved policy is on the level of per capita output, not its growth rate. But since the transitions to the long run tend empirically to be lengthy, the growth effects from shifts in government policies persist for a long time.

The findings on economic growth reported in Barro 1997 provide estimates for the effects on economic growth and investment from a number of variables that measure government policies and other elements. That study applied to roughly 100 countries observed from 1960 to 1990. That sample has now been updated to 1995 and has been modified in other respects.

The framework includes countries at vastly different levels of economic development; places are excluded only because of missing data. The attractive feature of this broad sample is the great variation in the government policies and other variables to be evaluated. It is impossible to use the experience of one or a few countries to get an accurate empirical assessment of the long-term growth implications from factors such as legal institutions, size of government, monetary and fiscal policies, degree of income inequality, and so on.

One drawback of this kind of diverse sample concerns the difficulty in measuring variables in a consistent and accurate way across countries and over time. In particular, less-developed countries tend to have substantial measurement error in national accounts and other data. The hope is that the strong signal from the diversity of the experience dominates the noise.

The other empirical issue, which is likely to be more important than measurement error, is the sorting out of directions of causation. The objective is to isolate the effects of government policies and other variables on long-term growth. But in practice much of the government and private-sector behavior—including monetary and fiscal policies, political stability, and rates of investment and fertility—are reactions to economic events. In most cases in the following discussion, the labeling of directions of causation depends on timing evidence, whereby earlier values of explanatory variables are thought to influence subsequent economic performance. However, such an approach to determining causation is not always valid.

The empirical work considers average growth rates and average ratios of investment to GDP over three decades: 1965–1975, 1975–1985, and 1985–1995.[8] In one respect this long-term context is forced by the data, because many of the determining variables considered, such as school attainment and fertility, are measured at best over five-year intervals. Higher-frequency observations would be mainly guesswork. In any event the low-frequency context accords with the underlying theories of growth, which do not attempt to explain short-run business fluctuations. In these theories the short-run response—for example, of the rate of economic growth to a change in a public institution—is not as clearly specified as the medium- and long-run response. Therefore, the application of the theories to annual or other high-frequency observations would compound the measurement error in the data by emphasizing errors related to the timing of relationships.

Table 1–1 shows baseline-panel regression estimates for the determination of the growth rate of real per capita GDP. Table 1–2 shows corresponding estimates for the ratio of investment to GDP.[9] The estimation is by three-stage least squares. Instruments are mainly lagged values of the regressors (see the notes to table 1–1).

The effects of the starting level of real per capita GDP show up in the estimated coefficients on the level and square of the log of per capita GDP. The other regressors include an array of policy variables—the ratio of government consumption to GDP, a subjective index of the maintenance of the rule of law, a subjective index for democracy (electoral rights), and the rate of inflation. Also included are a measure of school attainment at the start of each period, the total fertility rate, the ratio of investment to GDP (in the growth regressions), and the growth rate of the terms of trade (export prices relative to import prices). The data—some constructed in collaboration with Jong-Wha Lee—are available from the World Bank and NBER websites.[10]

The results contained in tables 1–1 and 1–2 are intended mainly to provide a context to isolate the effects of income inequality on growth and investment. Briefly, the estimated effects on the growth rate of real per capita GDP from the explanatory variables shown in the first column of table 1–1 are as follows.

TABLE 1–1
PANEL REGRESSIONS FOR GROWTH RATE

	Estimated Coefficient	
Independent Variable	In full sample	In Gini sample
log(per capita GDP)	0.124 (0.027)	0.103 (0.030)
log(per capita GDP) squared	−0.0095 (0.0018)	−0.0082 (0.0019)
Government consumption/GDP	−0.149 (0.023)	−0.153 (0.027)
Rule-of-law index	0.0172 (0.0053)	0.0102 (0.0065)
Democracy index	0.054 (0.029)	0.043 (0.033)
Democracy index squared	−0.048 (0.026)	−0.038 (0.028)
Inflation rate	−0.037 (0.010)	−0.014 (0.009)
Years of schooling	0.0072 (0.0017)	0.0066 (0.0017)
log(total fertility rate)	−0.0251 (0.0047)	−0.0306 (0.0054)
Investment/GDP	0.059 (0.022)	0.062 (0.021)
Growth rate of terms of trade	0.165 (0.028)	0.124 (0.035)
Numbers of observations	79, 87, 84	39, 56, 51
R^2	0.67, 0.48, 0.42	0.73, 0.62, 0.60

NOTE: Dependent variables: The dependent variable is the growth rate of real per capita GDP over 1965–1975, 1975–1985, or 1985–1995. The first column has the full sample of observations with available data. The second panel is restricted to the observations for which the Gini coefficient, used in later regressions, is available.

Independent variables: Individual constants (not shown) are included in each panel for each period. The log of real per capita GDP and the average years of male secondary and higher schooling are measured at the beginning of each period. The ratios of government consumption (exclusive of spending on education and defense) and investment (private plus public) to GDP, the democracy index, the inflation rate, the total fertility rate, and the growth rate of the terms of trade (export over import prices) are period averages. The rule-of-law index is the earliest value available (for 1982 or 1985) in the first two equations and the period average for the third equation.

Estimation is by three-stage least squares. Instruments are the actual values of the schooling and terms-of-trade variables, lagged values of the other variables aside from inflation, and dummy variables for prior colonial status (which have substantial explanatory power for inflation). The earliest value available for the rule-of-law index (for 1982 or 1985) is included as an instrument for the first two equations, and the 1985 value is included for the third equation. Asymptotically valid standard errors are shown in parentheses. The R^2 values apply to each period separately.

TABLE 1–2
PANEL REGRESSIONS FOR INVESTMENT RATIO

Independent Variable	Estimated Coefficient	
	In full sample	In Gini sample
log(per capita GDP)	0.188 (0.083)	0.121 (0.111)
log(per capita GDP) squared	−0.0110 (0.0053)	−0.0077 (0.0070)
Government consumption/GDP	−0.271 (0.072)	−0.353 (0.104)
Rule-of-law index	0.064 (0.020)	0.070 (0.025)
Democracy index	0.072 (0.078)	0.047 (0.123)
Democracy index squared	−0.086 (0.068)	−0.057 (0.103)
Inflation rate	−0.058 (0.027)	−0.022 (0.028)
Years of schooling	−0.0013 (0.0058)	0.0045 (0.0065)
log(total fertility rate)	−0.0531 (0.0140)	−0.0592 (0.0187)
Growth rate of terms of trade	0.052 (0.067)	0.129 (0.114)
Numbers of observations	79, 87, 85	39, 56, 51
R^2	0.52, 0.60, 0.65	0.35, 0.64, 0.69

NOTE: The dependent variable is the ratio of real investment (private plus public) to real GDP. The measure is the average of the annual observations on the ratio over 1965–1975, 1975–1985, or 1985–1989. See the notes to table 1–1 for other information.

The relations with the level and square of the log of per capita GDP imply a nonlinear, conditional convergence relation. The implied effect of log(GDP) on growth is negative for all but the poorest countries (with per capita GDP less than $670 in 1985 U.S. dollars). For richer places, growth declines at an increasing rate with rises in the level of per capita GDP. For the richest countries, the implied convergence rate is 5–6 percent per year.

For a given value of log(GDP), growth is negatively related to the ratio of government consumption to GDP, where this consumption is measured net of outlays on public education and national defense. Growth is positively related to a subjective index of the extent of maintenance of the rule of law. Growth is only weakly related to the extent of democracy, measured by a subjective indicator of electoral rights. (This variable appears linearly and as a square in the equations.) Growth is inversely related to the average rate of inflation, which is an indicator of macroeconomic stability. (Though not shown in table 1–1, growth is insignificantly related to the ratio of public debt to GDP at the start of each period.)

Growth is positively related to the stock of human capital at the start of each period, as measured by the average years of attainment at the secondary and higher levels of adult males. (Growth turns out to be insignificantly related to secondary and higher attainment of females and to primary attainment of males and females.) Growth is inversely related to the fertility rate (the number of prospective live births per woman over her lifetime).

Growth is positively related to the ratio of investment to GDP. For most variables, the use of instruments does not much affect the estimated coefficient. However, for the investment ratio, the use of lagged values as instruments—as in the table—reduces the estimated coefficient by about one-half relative to the value obtained if the contemporaneous ratio is included with the instruments. This result suggests that the reverse effect from growth to investment is also important. Finally, growth is positively related to the contemporaneous growth rate of the terms of trade.

The main results for the determination of the investment ratio, shown in column 1 of table 1–2, are as follows. The relation with the log of per capita GDP is hump-shaped. The implied relation is positive for values of per capita GDP up to $5,100 (1985 U.S. dollars) and then becomes negative.

Investment is negatively related to the ratio of government consumption to GDP, positively related to the rule-of-law indicator, insignificantly related to the democracy index, and negatively related to the inflation rate. The results imply that several policy variables that directly affect economic growth (for a given ratio of investment to GDP) tend to affect the investment ratio in the same direction. This effect of policy variables on investment reinforces the direct effects on economic growth. Investment is insignificantly related to the level of the schooling variable, negatively related to the fertility rate, and insignificantly related to the growth rate of the terms of trade.

Measures of Income Inequality

Data on income inequality come from the extensive compilation for a large panel of countries in Deininger and Squire 1996 (henceforth denoted as D-S). The data provided consist of Gini

13

coefficients and quintile shares. The compilation indicates whether inequality is computed for income gross or net of taxes or for expenditures. Also, whether the income concept applies to individuals or households is indicated. These features of the data are considered in the subsequent analysis.

The numbers for a particular country apply to a specified survey year. To use these data in regressions for the growth rate or the investment ratio, I classed each observation on the inequality measure as 1960, 1970, 1980, or 1990, depending on which of these ten-year values was closest to the survey date.

Deininger and Squire denote a subset of their data as high quality. The grounds for exclusion from the high-quality set include the survey's being of less than national coverage; the basing of information on estimates derived from national accounts, rather than from a direct survey of incomes; limitations of the sample to the income-earning population; and derivation of results from nonrepresentative tax records. Data are also excluded from the high-quality set if there is no clear reference to the primary source.

A serious problem with the inequality data is the availability of far fewer observations than for the full sample considered in tables 1–1 and 1–2. As an attempt to expand the sample size— even at the expense of some reduction in the accuracy of measurement—I added to the D-S high-quality set a number of observations that appeared to be based on representative, national coverage. D-S excluded these observations primarily because of the failure to identify a primary source clearly.[11] In the end, considering also the data availability for the variables included in tables 1–1 and 1–2, I end up with eighty-four countries with at least one observation on the Gini coefficient (of which twenty are in sub-Saharan Africa). Sixty-eight countries offer two or more observations (nine of these are in sub-Saharan Africa). Table 1–3 provides descriptive statistics on the Gini values.

Much of the analysis uses the Gini coefficient as the empirical measure of income inequality. One familiar interpretation of this coefficient comes from the Lorenz curve, which graphs cumulated income shares versus cumulated population shares, when the population is ordered from low to high per capita incomes. In this context the Gini coefficient can be computed as

TABLE 1–3
STATISTICS FOR GINI COEFFICIENTS

	Gini 1960	Gini 1970	Gini 1980	Gini 1990
Number of observations	49	61	68	76
Mean	0.432	0.416	0.394	0.409
Maximum	0.640	0.619	0.632	0.623
Minimum	0.253	0.228	0.210	0.227
Standard deviation	0.100	0.094	0.092	0.101
Correlation with				
Gini 1960	1.00	0.81	0.85	0.72
Gini 1970	0.81	1.00	0.93	0.87
Gini 1980	0.85	0.93	1.00	0.86
Gini 1990	0.72	0.87	0.86	1.00

NOTE: The table shows descriptive statistics for the Gini coefficients. The years shown are the closest ten-year value to the actual date of the survey on income distribution. Two observations have been omitted (Hungary in 1960 and the Bahamas in 1970) because the corresponding data on GDP were unavailable.

twice the area between the 45-degree line that extends northeastward from the origin and the Lorenz curve. Theil (1967, 121 ff.) shows that the Gini coefficient corresponds to a weighted average of all absolute differences between per capita incomes (expressed relative to economywide per capita income) where the weights are the products of the corresponding population shares.

If the underlying data are quintile shares and we pretend that all persons in each quintile have the same incomes, then the Gini coefficient can be expressed in two equivalent ways in relation to the quintile shares:

$$\text{Gini coefficient} = 0.8*(-1 + 2Q5 + 1.5Q4 + Q3 + 0.5Q2)$$
$$= 0.8*(1 - 2Q1 - 1.5Q2 - Q3 - 0.5Q4), \quad (1\text{–}2)$$

where Qi is the share of income accruing to the ith quintile, with group 1 the poorest and group 5 the richest. The first form says that the Gini coefficient gives positive weights to each of the quintile shares from 2 to 5, where the largest weight (2) applies to the fifth quintile and the smallest weight (0.5) attaches to the second quintile. The second form says that the Gini coefficient can be viewed alternatively as giving negative weights to the quintile shares from 1 to 4, where the largest negative weight (2) applies to the first quintile and the smallest weight (0.5) attaches to the fourth quintile.

The Gini coefficient turns out to be highly correlated with the upper quintile share, $Q5$, and not as highly correlated with the other quintile shares. The correlations of the Gini coefficients with $Q5$ are 0.89 for 1960, 0.92 for 1970, 0.95 for 1980, and 0.98 for 1990. In contrast the correlations of the Gini coefficients with $Q1$ are smaller in magnitude: -0.76 in 1960, -0.85 in 1970, -0.83 in 1980, and -0.91 in 1990. Because of these patterns, the results that use Gini coefficients turn out to be similar to those that use $Q5$ but not so similar to those that use $Q1$ or other quintile measures. One reason that the correlation between the Gini coefficients and the $Q5$ values is so high is that the $Q5$ variables have much larger standard deviations than the other quintile shares.

Effects of Inequality on Growth and Investment

The second columns of tables 1–1 and 1–2 show how the baseline regressions are affected by the restriction of the samples to those for which data on the Gini coefficient are available. This restriction reduces the overall sample size for the growth-rate panel from 250 to 146 (and from 251 to 146 for the investment-ratio panel). This diminution in sample size does not affect the general nature of the coefficient estimates. The main effect is that the inflation rate is less important in the truncated sample.

Table 1–4 shows the estimated coefficients on the Gini coefficient when this variable is added to the panel systems from tables 1–1 and 1–2. In these results the raw data on the Gini coefficient are entered directly. A reasonable alternative is to adjust these Gini values for differences in the method of measurement, especially whether the data are for individuals or households and whether the inequality applies to income gross or net of taxes or to expenditures rather than incomes. Some of these features do matter significantly for the measurement of inequality, as discussed in the next section. However, the adjustment of the inequality measures for these elements turns out to have little consequence for the estimated effects of inequality on growth and investment. Therefore, the results reported here consider only the unadjusted measures of inequality.

For the growth rate, the estimated coefficient on the Gini coefficient in table 1–4 is essentially zero. Figure 1–1 shows the implied partial relation between the growth rate and the Gini coefficient.[12] This pattern looks consistent with a roughly zero relationship and does not suggest any obvious nonlinearities. Thus, overall, with the other explanatory variables considered in table 1–1 held constant, differences in Gini coefficients for income inequality have no significant relation with subsequent economic growth. One possible interpretation is that the various theoretical effects of inequality on growth, as summarized before, are nearly fully offsetting.

It is possible to modify the present system to reproduce the finding from many studies that inequality is negatively related to economic growth. If the fertility-rate variable, one of the variables that are correlated with inequality, is omitted from the system, then the estimated coefficient on the Gini variable becomes significantly negative. Table 1–4 shows that the estimated coefficient in this case is –0.037 (0.017). In this case a one-standard-deviation reduction in the Gini coefficient (by 0.1; see table 1–3) would be estimated to raise the growth rate on impact by 0.4 percent per year. Perotti (1996) reports effects of similar magnitude. However, it seems that this effect may represent merely a proxying for the correlated fertility rate.

More interesting results emerge when the effect of the Gini coefficient on economic growth is allowed to depend on the level of economic development, measured by real per capita GDP. The Gini coefficient is now entered into the growth system linearly and also as a product with the log of per capita GDP. In this case the estimated coefficients are jointly significant at usual critical levels (p-value of 0.059) and also individually significant: -0.33 (0.14) on the linear term and 0.043 (0.018) on the interaction term.

This estimated relation implies that the effect of inequality on growth is negative for values of per capita GDP less than $2,070 (1985 U.S. dollars) and then becomes positive.[13] (The median value of GDP was $1,258 in 1960, $1,816 in 1970, and $2,758 in 1980.) Quantitatively the estimated marginal impact of the Gini coefficient on growth ranges from a low of -0.09 for the poorest country in 1960 (a value that enters into the growth

17

TABLE 1-4
Effects of Gini Coefficients on Growth Rates and Investment Ratios

	Gini	Gini* log(GDP)	Gini, Low GDP	Gini, High GDP	Wald Tests (p-values)
Growth rate regressions					
	0.000 (0.018)				
	−0.331 (0.141)	0.043 (0.018)			0.059
			−0.033 (0.021)	0.054 (0.025)	0.011, 0.003[a]
Fertility variable omitted					
	−0.037 (0.017)				
	−0.367 (0.156)	0.043 (0.020)			0.012
			−0.036 (0.018)	−0.036 (0.034)	0.085, 0.99[a]

Investment ratio regressions

0.060		−0.062		
(0.070)		(0.062)		0.39
0.54				
(0.47)				

Fertility variable omitted

−0.027		−0.068		
(0.066)		(0.062)		0.51
0.50				
(0.48)				

NOTE: Gini coefficients were added to the systems shown in tables 1–1 and 1–2. The Gini value around 1960 appears in the equations for growth from 1965 to 1975 and for investment from 1965 to 1975; the Gini value around 1970 appears in the equations for 1975 to 1985 and 1975 to 1984; and the Gini value around 1980 appears in the equations for 1985 to 1995 and 1985 to 1989. The variable Gini log(GDP) is the product of the Gini coefficient and the log of per capita GDP. The system with Gini* (low GDP) and Gini* (high GDP) allows for two separate coefficients on the Gini variable. The first coefficient applies when log(GDP) is below the break point for a negative effect of the Gini coefficient on growth, as implied by the system that includes Gini and Gini* log(GDP). The second coefficient applies for higher values of log(GDP). Separate intercepts are also included for the two ranges of log(GDP). The variables that include the Gini coefficients are included in the lists of instrumental variables. The Wald tests are for the hypothesis that both coefficients equal zero. See the notes to table 1–1 for additional information.
a. These values are for the hypothesis that the two coefficients are equal (but not necessarily equal to zero).

19

FIGURE 1–1
GROWTH RATE COMPARED WITH GINI COEFFICIENT

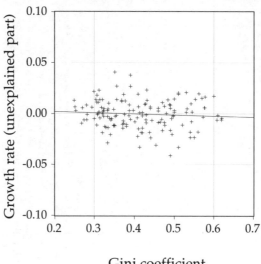

Gini coefficient

equation for 1965–1975) to 0.12 for the richest country in 1980 (which appears in the equation for 1985–1995). Since the standard deviation of the Gini coefficients in each period is about 0.1, the estimates imply that a one-standard-deviation increase in the Gini value would affect the typical country's growth rate on impact by a magnitude of around 0.5 percent per year (negatively for poor countries and positively for rich ones).

From a theoretical standpoint the effects may result because rising per capita income reduces the constraints of imperfect loan markets on investment. The positive effect of the Gini coefficient in the upper-income range may arise because the growth-promoting aspects of inequality dominate when credit-market problems are less severe.

Figure 1–2 shows the implied partial relation between economic growth and the Gini coefficient—in this case the explanatory variables held constant include the interaction term between the Gini coefficient and log(GDP). This partial relation is negative and corresponds to the significantly negative estimated coefficient on the linear term for the Gini variable in the panel system. Figure 1–3 shows the implied partial relation with

FIGURE 1–2
GROWTH RATE COMPARED WITH GINI COEFFICIENT
(taking account of Gini-log[GDP] interaction)

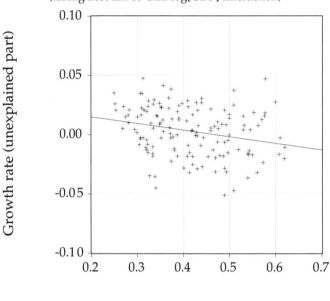

Gini coefficient

the Gini-log(GDP) interaction term (when the Gini coefficient and the other explanatory variables are held constant). The positive partial relation corresponds to the significantly positive estimated coefficient on the interaction term in the panel system.

The role of credit markets can be assessed more directly by using the ratio of a broad monetary aggregate, M2, to GDP, as an indicator of the state of financial development. However, if the Gini coefficients are interacted with the M2 ratio rather than per capita GDP, the estimated effects of the Gini variables on economic growth are individually and jointly insignificant.[14] This result could emerge because the M2 ratio is a poor measure—worse than per capita GDP—of the imperfection of credit markets.

As a check on the results, the growth system was reestimated with the Gini coefficient allowed to have two separate coefficients. One coefficient applies for values of per capita GDP less than $2,070 (the break point estimated above) and the other

FIGURE 1–3
GROWTH RATE COMPARED WITH GINI LOG(GDP) INTERACTION
(taking account of Gini coefficient)

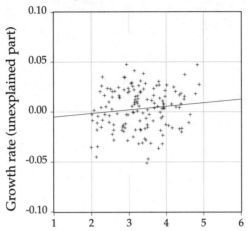

Interaction between Gini and log (GDP)

for values of per capita GDP greater than $2,070. The results, shown in table 1–4, are that the estimated coefficient of the Gini coefficient is -0.033 (0.021) in the low range of GDP and 0.054 (0.025) in the high range.[15] These estimated values are jointly significantly different from zero (p-value = 0.011) and also significantly different from each other (p-value = 0.003). Thus this piecewise-linear form tells a similar story to that found in the representation that includes the interaction between the Gini and log(GDP).

The bottom part of table 1–4 shows how the Gini coefficient relates to the investment ratio. The basic finding, when the other explanatory variables shown in table 1–2 are held constant, is that the investment ratio does not depend significantly on inequality, as measured by the Gini coefficient. This conclusion holds for the linear specification and also for the one that includes an interaction between the Gini value and log(GDP). (Results are also insignificant if separate coefficients on the Gini variable are estimated for low and high values of per capita GDP.) Thus there is no evidence that the aggregate saving rate, which would tend to influence the investment ratio, depends on the degree of income inequality.[16]

Table 1–5 shows the results for economic growth when the inequality measure is based on quintile-shares data rather than Gini coefficients. The highest-quintile share generates results that are similar to those for the Gini coefficient.[17] The estimated effect on growth is insignificant in the linear form. However, the effects are significant when an interaction with log(GDP) is included or when two separate coefficients on the highest-quintile-share variable are estimated, depending on the value of GDP. With the interaction variable included, the implied effect of more inequality (a greater share for the rich) on growth is negative when per capita GDP is less than $1,473 and positive otherwise. The similarity in results with those from the Gini co-efficient arises because, as noted, the highest-quintile share is particularly highly correlated with the Gini values.

Table 1–5 also shows results for economic growth when other quintile-share measures are used to measure inequality— the share of the middle three quintiles and the share of the lowest fifth of the population. In these cases the significant effects on economic growth arise only when separate coefficients are estimated on the shares variables, depending on the level of GDP.[18] The effects on growth are positive in the low range of GDP (with greater shares of the middle or lowest quintiles signifying less inequality) and negative in the high range.

Determinants of Inequality

The determinants of inequality are assessed first by considering a panel of Gini coefficients observed around 1960, 1970, 1980, and 1990. Figure 1–4 shows a scatter of these values against roughly contemporaneous values of the log of per capita GDP. A Kuznets curve would show up as an inverted-U relationship between the Gini value and log(GDP). This relationship is not obvious from the scatter plot, although one can discern such a curve after staring at the diagram for some time. In any event the relation between the Gini coefficient and a quadratic in log(GDP) does turn out to be statistically significant, as shown in the first column of table 1–6. This column reports the results

TABLE 1-5
EFFECTS OF QUINTILE-BASED INEQUALITY MEASURES ON GROWTH RATES

	Quintile Measure	Quintile Measure* log(GDP)	Quintile Measure, Low GDP	Quintile Measure, High GDP	Wald Tests (p-values)
Highest-quintile share					
	0.019 (0.020)	0.061 (0.019)			0.005
	−0.45 (0.15)		−0.056 (0.031)	0.058 (0.022)	0.002, 0.001[a]
Middle-three-quintiles share					
	−0.020 (0.025)	−0.001 (0.021)			0.66
	−0.017 (0.163)		0.058 (0.039)	−0.057 (0.027)	0.020, 0.010[a]

Lowest-quintile share

−0.044				
(0.060)				
0.16	−0.025	0.37	−0.155	0.71
(0.51)	(0.063)	(0.12)	(0.061)	
				0.000,
				0.000[a]

NOTE: The quintiles data on income distribution were used to form the share of the highest fifth, the share of the middle three quintiles, and the share of the lowest fifth. The quintile values around 1960 appear in the equations for growth from 1965 to 1975; the values around 1970 appear in the equations for 1975 to 1985; and the values around 1980 appear in the equations for 1985 to 1995. The interaction variable is the product of the quintile measure and the log of per capita GDP. The system with quintile share (low GDP) and quintile share (high GDP) allows for two separate coefficients on the quintile-share variable. The first coefficient applies when log(GDP) is below the break point for a change in sign of the effect of the highest-quintile-share variable on growth, as implied by the system that includes the highest quintile share and the interaction of this share with log(GDP). The second coefficient applies for higher values of log(GDP). Separate intercepts are also included for the two ranges of log(GDP). The variables that include the quintile-share variables are included in the lists of instrumental variables. The Wald tests are for the hypothesis that both coefficients equal zero. See the notes to table 1–1 for additional information.

a. These values are for the hypothesis that the two coefficients are equal (but not necessarily equal to zero).

FIGURE 1–4
SCATTER OF GINI AGAINST LOG(GDP)

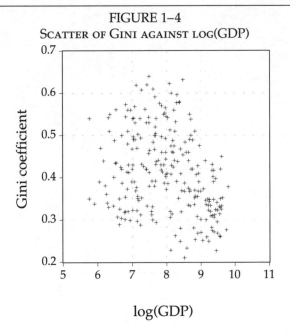

log(GDP)

from a panel estimation, using the seemingly-unrelated technique. In this first case log(GDP) and its square are the only regressors aside from a single constant term.

The estimated relation implies that the Gini value rises with GDP for values of GDP less than $1,636 (1985 U.S. dollars) and declines thereafter. The fit of the relationship is not good, as figure 1–4 clearly shows. The R-squared values for the four periods range from 0.12 to 0.22. Thus, in line with the findings of Papanek and Kyn 1986, the level of economic development would not explain most variation in inequality across countries and over time.

The second column of table 1–6 adds to the panel estimation a number of control variables, including some corrections for the manner in which the underlying distributional data are constructed. The first dummy variable equals 1 if the Gini coefficient is based on income net of taxes or on expenditures. The variable equals 0 if the data refer to income gross of taxes. The estimated coefficient of this variable is significantly negative—the Gini value is lower by roughly 0.05 if the data refer to income net of taxes or expenditures rather than income gross of taxes.[19]

This result is reasonable because taxes tend to be equalizing and because expenditures would typically be less volatile than income. (There is no significant difference between the Gini values for income net of taxes versus those for expenditures.)

The second dummy variable equals 1 if the data relate to individuals and 0 if the data relate to households. The estimated coefficient of this variable is negative but not statistically significant. It was unclear ex ante what sign to anticipate for this variable.

The panel system also includes the average years of school attainment for adults aged fifteen and older at three levels: primary, secondary, and higher. Primary schooling is negatively and significantly related to inequality, secondary schooling is negatively (but not significantly) related to inequality, and higher education is positively and significantly related to inequality.[20]

The dummy variables for sub-Saharan Africa and Latin America are each positive, statistically significant, and large in magnitude. Since per capita GDP and schooling are already held constant, these effects are surprising. Some aspects of these areas that matter for inequality—not captured by per capita GDP and schooling—must be omitted from the system. Preliminary results indicate that the influence of the continent dummies is substantially weakened when one holds constant variables that relate to colonial heritage and religious affiliation.

I also considered measures of the heterogeneity of the population with respect to ethnicity and language and to religious affiliation. The first variable, referred to as ethnolinguistic fractionalization, has been used in a number of previous studies.[21] This measure can be interpreted as (one minus) the probability of meeting someone of the same ethnolinguistic group in a random encounter. The second variable is a Herfindahl index of the fraction of the population affiliated with nine main religious groups.[22] This variable can be interpreted as the probability of meeting someone of the same religion in a chance encounter. My expectation was that more heterogeneity of ethnicity, language, and religion would be associated with greater income inequality. Moreover, unlike the schooling measures, the heterogeneity measures can be viewed as largely exogenous at least in a short- or medium-run context.

27

TABLE 1-6
DETERMINANTS OF INEQUALITY

Variable	No Fixed Effects				Fixed Effects
log(GDP)	0.407	0.407	0.437	0.415	0.132
	(0.090)	(0.081)	(0.078)	(0.084)	(0.013)
log(GDP) squared	−0.0275	−0.0251	−0.0264	−0.0254	−0.0083
	(0.0056)	(0.0051)	(0.0049)	(0.0053)	(0.0014)
Dummy of net income or spending	—	−0.0493	−0.0480	−0.0496	−0.0542
		(0.0094)	(0.0087)	(0.0094)	(0.0108)
Dummy of individual vs. household data	—	−0.0134	−0.0143	−0.0119	−0.0026
		(0.0086)	(0.0080)	(0.0087)	(0.0078)
Primary schooling	—	−0.0147	−0.0152	−0.0161	−0.0025
		(0.0037)	(0.0036)	(0.0037)	(0.0091)
Secondary schooling	—	−0.0108	−0.0061	−0.0109	−0.0173
		(0.0070)	(0.0070)	(0.0070)	(0.0099)
Higher schooling	—	0.081	0.072	0.082	0.102
		(0.034)	(0.032)	(0.034)	(0.030)
Dummy of Africa	—	0.113	0.135	0.113	—
		(0.015)	(0.016)	(0.015)	

Dummy of Latin America	—	0.094 (0.012)	0.089 (0.012)	0.092 (0.012)	—
Rule-of-law index	—	—	−0.040 (0.019)	—	—
Democracy index	—	—	—	−0.003 (0.015)	—
Number of observations	49, 61, 68, 76	40, 59, 61, 70	40, 57, 56, 67	35, 59, 61, 70	36, 56, 57, 59
R^2	0.12, 0.15 0.18, 0.22	0.52, 0.59 0.67, 0.67	0.50, 0.58 0.78, 0.72	0.56, 0.59 0.67, 0.67	—

NOTE: The dependent variables are the Gini coefficients observed around 1960, 1970, 1980, and 1990. See table 1–3 for statistics on these variables. Estimation is by the seemingly unrelated (SUR) technique. The first four columns include a single constant term, which does not vary over time or across countries. The last column includes a separate time-invariant intercept for each country (and includes only countries with two or more observations on the Gini coefficient). GDP is real per capita GDP for 1960, 1970, 1980, and 1990. The first dummy variable equals one if the Gini coefficient is based on income net of taxes or on expenditures. It equals zero if the Gini is based on income gross of taxes. The second dummy equals one if the income-distribution data refer to individuals and zero if the data refer to households. The schooling variables are the average years of attainment of the adult population aged fifteen and older for 1960, 1970, 1980, and 1990. The third and fourth dummy variables equal one if the country is in sub-Saharan Africa or Latin America, respectively, and zero otherwise. The rule-of-law and democracy indexes are described in the notes to table 1–1. The numbers of observations and the R-squared values refer to each of the four periods, 1960, 1970, 1980, and 1990.

FIGURE 1–5
GINI COEFFICIENT COMPARED WITH LOG(GDP)

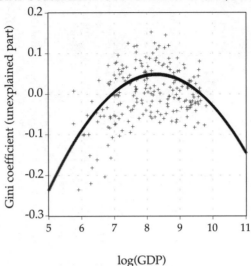

log(GDP)

Surprisingly the two measures of population heterogeneity had roughly zero explanatory power for the Gini coefficients. These results are especially disappointing because the heterogeneity measures would otherwise have been good instruments to use for inequality in the growth regressions. In any event the heterogeneity variables were excluded from the regression systems shown in table 1–6.

The addition of the control variables in column 2 of table 1–6 substantially improves the fits for the Gini coefficients—the R-squared values for the four periods now range from 0.52 to 0.67. However, this improvement in fit does not have a dramatic effect on the point estimates and statistical significance for the estimated coefficients of log(GDP) and its square. That is, a similar Kuznets curve still applies.

Figure 1–5 provides a graphical representation of this curve. The vertical axis shows the Gini coefficient after filtering out the estimated effects (from column 2 of table 1–6) of the control variables other than log(GDP) and its square. These filtered values have been normalized to make the mean equal 0. The horizontal axis plots the log of per capita GDP. The peak in the curve occurs at a value for GDP of $3,320 (1985 U.S. dollars).

I have tested whether the Kuznets curve is stable, that is, whether the coefficients on log(GDP) and its square shift over time. The main result is that these coefficients are reasonably stable. If the system allows for different sets of coefficients on these variables for each period, then the estimated coefficients on the linear terms are 0.40 (0.09) in 1960, 0.38 (0.09) in 1970, 0.40 (0.09) in 1980, and 0.41 (0.09) in 1990. The corresponding estimated coefficients on the squared terms are −0.025 (0.006), −0.023 (0.006), -0.024 (0.006), and −0.025 (0.005). (In this system the coefficients of the other explanatory variables are constrained to be the same for each period.) Given the close correspondence for the separately estimated coefficients of log(GDP) and its square, it is surprising that a Wald test rejects the hypothesis of equal coefficients over time with a p-value of 0.013.

For the schooling variables, the estimated coefficients for the different periods are as follows: primary schooling: -0.008 (0.005), -0.013 (0.005), -0.017 (0.011), and −0.010 (0.005); secondary schooling: -0.026 (0.023), -0.017 (0.011), -0.002 (0.010), and −0.010 (0.010); higher schooling: 0.051 (0.127), 0.043 (0.072), 0.047 (0.053), and 0.055 (0.045). There is little indication of systematic variation over time, and a Wald test for all three sets of coefficients jointly is not significant (p-value of 0.17).

These results conflict with the idea that increases in income inequality in the 1980s and 1990s in the United States and other advanced countries reflected new kinds of technological developments that were particularly complementary with high skills. Under this view the positive effect of higher education on the Gini coefficient should be larger in the 1980s and 1990s than in the 1960s and 1970s. The empirical results show instead that the estimated coefficients in the later periods are similar to those in the earlier periods.

The dummy variables for sub-Saharan Africa and Latin America show instability over time. The estimated coefficients for Africa are 0.073 (0.032), 0.053 (0.023), 0.097 (0.023), and 0.152 (0.017) and for Latin America, 0.097 (0.023), 0.070 (0.016), 0.068 (0.015), and 0.121 (0.016). In this case a Wald test for both sets of coefficients jointly rejects stability over time (p-value = 0.0001). This instability is probably a sign that the continent dummies are not fundamental determinants of inequality, but are rather proxies for other variables.

31

As mentioned, the underlying data set expands beyond the Gini values designated as high quality by Deininger and Squire 1996. If a dummy variable for the high-quality designation is included in the panel system, then its estimated coefficient is essentially 0. The squared residuals from the panel system are, however, systematically related to the quality designation. The estimated coefficient in a least-squares regression of the squared residual on a dummy variable for quality (1 if high quality, 0 otherwise) is −0.0025 (0.0008). However, part of the tendency of low-quality observations to have greater residual variance relates to the tendency of these observations to come from low-income countries (which likely have poorer-quality data in general). If the log of per capita GDP is also included in the system for the squared residuals, then the estimated coefficient on the high-quality dummy becomes −0.0018 (0.0008), whereas that on log(GDP) is −0.0012 (0.0003). Adjustments of the weighting scheme in the estimation to take account of this type of heteroscedasticity have little effect on the results.

Column 3 of table 1–6 adds another control variable: the indicator for maintenance of the rule of law. The estimated coefficient is negative and marginally significant, -0.040 (0.019). Thus there is an indication that better enforcement of laws goes along with more equality of incomes.

Column 4 includes the index of democracy (electoral rights). The estimated coefficient of this variable differs insignificantly from 0. If the square of this variable is also entered, then this additional variable is statistically insignificant (as are the linear and squared terms jointly). The magnitude of the estimated coefficients on log(GDP) and its square fall only slightly from the values shown in column 2 of table 1–6. Thus the estimated Kuznets curve, expressed in terms of the log of per capita GDP, does not involve a proxying of GDP for democracy.

The results described thus far are from a random-effects specification. That is, the panel estimation allows the error terms to be correlated over time for a given country. Column 5 shows the results of a fixed-effects estimation, where an individual constant is entered for each country. This estimation is still carried out as a panel for levels of the Gini coefficients, not as first differences. Countries are now included in the sample only if they have at least two observations on the Gini coefficient for 1960, 1970, 1980, or 1990. (The observations do not have to be adjacent in time.) This estimation drops the variables—the dummies for sub-Saharan Africa and Latin America—that do not vary over time.

The estimated Kuznets-curve coefficients—0.132 (0.013) on log(GDP) and −0.0083 (0.0014) on the square—are still individually and jointly significantly different from 0.[23] However, the sizes of these coefficients are about one-third of those for the cases that exclude country fixed effects. With the country fixed effects present, the GDP variables pick up only time-series variations within countries. Moreover this specification allows only for contemporaneous relations between the Gini values and GDP. Therefore the estimates would pick up a relatively short-run link between inequality and GDP. With the country effects not present, the estimates also reflect cross-sectional variations, and the coefficients on the GDP variables pick up longer-run aspects of the relationships with the Gini values. Further refinement of the dynamics of the relation between inequality and its determinants may achieve more uniformity between the panel and fixed-effects results.

It is also possible to estimate Kuznets-curve relationships for the quintile-based measures of inequality. If the upper-quintile share is the dependent variable and the controls considered in column 2 of table 1–6 are held constant, then the estimated coefficients turn out to be 0.353 (0.086) on log(GDP) and −0.0216 (0.0054) on the square. Thus the share of the rich tends to rise initially with per capita GDP and subsequently decline (after per capita GDP reaches $3,500).

For the share of the middle three quintiles, the corresponding coefficient estimates are −0.291 (0.070) on log(GDP) and 0.0181 (0.0044) on the square. Hence the middle share falls initially with per capita GDP and subsequently rises (after per capita GDP reaches $3,100). For the share of the lowest quintile, the coefficients are −0.080 (0.024) on log(GDP) and 0.0047 (0.0015) on the square. Therefore this share also falls at first with per capita GDP and subsequently increases (when per capita GDP passes $5,600).

Conclusions

Evidence from a broad panel of countries shows little overall relation between income inequality and rates of growth and investment. For growth, there is an indication that inequality retards growth in poor countries but encourages growth in richer places. Growth tends to fall with greater inequality when per capita GDP is below around $2,000 (1985 U.S. dollars) and to rise with inequality when per capita GDP exceeds $2,000.

The results mean that income-equalizing policies might be justified on growth-promotion grounds in poor countries. For richer countries, active income redistribution appears to involve a tradeoff between the benefits of greater equality and a reduction in overall economic growth.

The Kuznets curve—whereby inequality first increases and later decreases in the process of economic development—emerges as a clear empirical regularity. However, this relation does not explain the bulk of variations in inequality across countries or over time. The estimated relationship may reflect not just the influence of the level of per capita GDP but also the dynamic effect whereby the adoption of each new major technology has a Kuznets-type dynamic effect on the distribution of income.

Notes

1. Recent surveys of these theories include Benabou 1996 and Aghion, Caroli, and Garcia-Penalosa 1999.

2. For models of the economic effects of inequality with imperfect credit markets, see Galor and Zeira 1993 and Piketty 1997, among others.

3. For these kinds of political economy analyses, see Perotti 1996, Bertola 1993, Alesina and Rodrik 1994, Persson and Tabellini 1994, and Benabou 1996, among others.

4. For discussions, see Benabou 1996 and Rodriguez 1998.

5. For analyses in this area, see Hibbs 1973, Venieris and Gupta 1986, Gupta 1990, Alesina and Perotti 1996, and Benhabib and Rustichini 1996.

6. However, these results refer to fixed-effects estimates, which have relatively few observations and are particularly sensitive to measurement error.

7. The starting level of per capita output, y, can be viewed more generally as referring to the starting levels of physical and human capital and other durable inputs to the production process. In some theories the growth rate, Dy, falls with a higher starting level of overall capital per person but rises with the initial ratio of human to physical capital.

8. For the investment ratio, the periods are 1965–1974, 1975–1984, and 1985–1989.

9. The GDP figures in 1985 prices are the purchasing-power-parity–adjusted chain-weighted values from the Summers-Heston data set, version 5.6. These data are available on the Internet from the National Bureau of Economic Research. See Summers and Heston 1991 for a general description of their data. The figures provided through 1992 have been updated to 1995 with World Bank data. Real investment (private plus public) is also from the Summers-Heston data set.

10. See http://www.economics.Harvard.edu/faculty/barro/barro.html.

11. The forty-eight observations added were for Benin 1960, Chad 1960, Congo 1960, Gabon 1960 and 1970, Ivory Coast 1960, Kenya 1960 and 1980, Liberia 1970, Madagascar 1960, Malawi 1970 and 1980, Morocco 1960, Niger 1960, Nigeria 1960 and 1980, Senegal 1960 and 1970, Sierra Leone 1980, Tanzania 1960 (and 1970 for quintile data only), Togo 1960, Uganda 1970, Zambia 1960 and 1970, Barbados 1970, El Salvador 1970, Argentina 1960 and 1970, Bolivia 1970, Colombia 1960, Ecuador 1970, Peru 1960, Suriname 1960, Uruguay 1970, Venezuela 1960, Burma 1960, Iraq 1960, Israel 1960, Austria 1990, Denmark 1960, Finland 1960, Germany 1990, Greece 1960, Netherlands 1960, Sweden 1960, Switzerland 1980, and Fiji 1970.

12. The variable plotted on the vertical axis is the growth rate (for any of the three time periods) net of the estimated effect of all explanatory variables aside from the Gini coefficient. The value plotted was also normalized to make its mean value zero. The line drawn through the points is a least-squares fit (and therefore does not correspond precisely to the estimated coefficient of the Gini coefficient in table 1–4).

13. There is some indication that the coefficients on the Gini variables—and hence the breakpoints for the GDP values—shift over time. If the coefficients are allowed to differ by period, the results for the Gini term are -0.33 (0.15) for the first period, -0.33 (0.15) for the second, and -0.38 (0.14) for the third, and the corresponding estimates for the interaction term are 0.047 (0.020), 0.039 (0.019), and 0.043 (0.018). These values imply breakpoints for GDP of $1,097, $5,219, and $6,568, respectively. A Wald test for stability of the two coefficients over time has a p-value of 0.088.

14. The effects of the Gini variables on economic growth are also individually and jointly insignificant if the Gini values are interacted with the democracy index, rather than per capita GDP. This specification was suggested by models in which the extent of democracy influences the sensitivity of income transfers to the degree of inequality.

15. This specification also includes different intercepts for the low and high ranges of GDP.

16. In this case the Gini variables are insignificant even when the fertility-rate variable is excluded.

17. The sample size is somewhat smaller here because the quintile-share data are less abundant than the Gini values. The numbers of observations when the quintiles data are used are thirty-three for the first period, forty for the second, and forty-three for the third.

18. The breakpoint used, $1,473, is the one implied by the system with the interaction term between the highest quintile share and log(GDP).

19. I have also estimated the system with the gross-of-tax observations separated from the net-of-tax ones for the coefficients of all explanatory variables. The hypothesis that all these coefficients, except for the intercepts, are jointly the same for the two sets of observations is accepted with a p-value of 0.33.

20. If one adds the ratio to GDP of public outlays on schooling, then this variable is significantly positive. The estimated coefficients on the school-attainment values do not change greatly. One possibility is that the school-spending variable picks up a reverse effect from inequality to income redistribution (brought about through expenditures on education).

21. See, for example, Mauro 1995.

22. The underlying data are from Barrett 1982. The groupings are Catholic, Protestant, Muslim, Buddhist, Hindu, Jewish, miscellaneous eastern religions, nonreligious, and other religions. See Barro 1997 for further discussion.

23. These estimates are virtually the same—0.133 (0.012) on log(GDP) and −0.0090 (0.0013) on the square—if all other regressors aside from the country fixed effects are dropped from the system.

References

Aghion, P., E. Caroli, and C. Garcia-Penalosa. 1999. "Inequality and Economic Growth: The Perspective of the New Growth Theories." *Journal of Economic Literature* 37 (4): 1615–60.

Aghion, P., and P. Howitt. 1997. *Endogenous Economic Growth*. Cambridge: MIT Press.

Ahluwalia, M. 1976a. "Income Distribution and Development." *American Economic Review* 66 (5): 128–35.

———. 1976b. "Inequality, Poverty and Development." *Journal of Development Economics* 3: 307–42.

Alesina A., and R. Perotti. 1996. "Income Distribution, Political Instability and Investment." *European Economic Review* 81 (5): 1170–89.

Alesina, A., and D. Rodrik. 1994. "Distribution Politics and Economic Growth." *Quarterly Journal of Economics* 109: 465–90.

Anand S., and S. M. Kanbur. 1993. "The Kuznets Process and the Inequality-Development Relationship." *Journal of Development Economics* 40: 25–72.

Barrett, D. B., ed. 1982. *World Christian Encyclopedia*. Oxford: Oxford University Press.

Barro, R. J. 1991. "Economic Growth in a Cross Section of Countries." *Quarterly Journal of Economics* 106: 407–44.

———. 1997. *Determinants of Economic Growth: A Cross-Country Empirical Study*. Cambridge: MIT Press.

Benabou, R. 1996. *Inequality and Growth*. NBER Macroeconomics Annual, 11–73.

Benhabib, J., and A. Rustichini. 1996. "Social Conflict and Growth." *Journal of Economic Growth* 1 (1): 129–46.

Bertola, G. 1993. "Factor Shares and Savings in Endogenous Growth." *American Economic Review* 83: 1184–98.

Deininger, K., and L. Squire. 1996. "New Data Set Measuring Income Inequality." *World Bank Economic Review* 10 (September): 565–91.

Forbes, K. 1997. "A Reassessment of the Relationship between Inequality and Growth." Unpublished. MIT.

Galor, Oded, and Joseph Zeira. 1993. "Income Distribution and Macroeconomics." *Review of Economic Studies* 60 (1) (January): 35–52.

Greenwood, J., and B. Jovanovic. 1990. "Financial Development, Growth and the Distribution of Income." *Journal of Political Economy* 98 (5): 1076–1107.

Gupta, D. 1990. *The Economics of Political Violence*. New York: Praeger.

Helpman, E. 1997. *General Purpose Technologies and Economic Growth*. Cambridge: MIT Press.

Hibbs, D. 1973. *Mass Political Violence: A Cross-Sectional Analysis*. New York: Wiley.

Kuznets, S. 1955. "Economic Growth and Income Inequality." *American Economic Review* 45: 1–28.

Li, H., L. Squire, and H. Zou. 1998. "Explaining International and Intertemporal Variations in Income Inequality." *Economic Journal* 108: 26–43.

Li, H., and H. Zou. 1998. "Income Inequality Is Not Harmful for Growth: Theory and Evidence." *Review of Development Economics* 2: 318–34.

Mauro, P. 1995. "Corruption, Country Risk, and Growth." *Quarterly Journal of Economics* 110: 681–712.

Papanek, G., and O. Kyn. 1986. "The Effect on Income Distribution of Development, the Growth Rate and Economic Strategy." *Journal of Development Economics* 23 (1): 55–65.

Perotti, R. 1996. "Growth, Income Distribution, and Democracy: What the Data Say." *Journal of Economic Growth* 1: 149–87.

Persson, T., and G. Tabellini. 1994. "Is Inequality Harmful for Growth? Theory and Evidence." *American Economic Review* 84: 600–21.

Piketty, T. 1997. "The Dynamics of the Wealth Distribution and Interest Rates with Credit Rationing." *Review of Economic Studies* 64.

Robinson, S. 1976. "A Note on the U-hypothesis Relating Income Inequality and Economic Development." *American Economic Review* 66 (3): 473–40.

Rodriguez, F. 1998. "Inequality, Redistribution and Rent-Seeking." Unpublished. University of Maryland.

Summers, R., and A. Heston. 1991. "The Penn World Table (Mark 5):

An Expanded Set of International Comparisons, 1950–1988." *Quarterly Journal of Economics* 106: 327–69.

Theil, H. 1967. *Economics and Information Theory*. Amsterdam: North-Holland.

Venieris Y., and D. Gupta. 1986. "Income Distribution and Sociopolitical Instability as Determinants of Savings: A Cross Sectional Model." *Journal of Political Economy* 94: 873–83.

Commentary

Alan S. Blinder

Robert Barro's chapter is a fair-minded, thorough, and unabashedly empirical examination of how income inequality *is correlated with* the level and growth rate of GDP per capita. Creating a hard job for a discussant, it neither makes poorly supported claims nor jumps to unwarranted conclusions.

What Causes What? Notice that the verb in the first sentence is "is correlated with," not "affects." It is abundantly clear, as Barro realizes, that a country's degree of inequality and its level or growth rate of per capita income are *endogenous variables*, affected by many factors. Any claim that one variable *causes* the other must be heavily qualified and buttressed either by theory or by some other source of empirical evidence bearing on the question of causation. Barro appeals to the concept of *Granger causality*, that is, precedence in time, the idea that causes must precede effects. For example, the Gini ratio in 1980 is taken to be a determinant of income growth between 1985 and 1995. Income growth in 1985–1995 does not affect the 1980 Gini ratio.

This causal ordering is not unreasonable, but it is far from foolproof. For example, structural (and relatively unchanging) characteristics of countries may affect *both* inequality *and* growth and thus produce a correlation that implies no causation in either direction. Barro recognizes this problem, of course, and is appropriately modest in his claims, as he notes that "this approach to determining causation is not always valid." To see that some third factors may be driving the correlation between inequality and GDP, we need only look at the right-hand column of table 1–6. There Barro adds country dummies (fixed effects) to the statistical model explaining income inequality and finds that the estimated Kuznets curve changes dramatically.

TABLE 1–1C
INCOME DISTRIBUTION
(in percent)

Income Share of	Distribution A	Distribution B
Lowest fifth	3.6	0.6
Second fifth	8.9	11.9
Middle fifth	15.0	15.0
Fourth fifth	23.2	26.2
Highest fifth	49.4	46.4
Approximate Gini	.423	.423

I will return to the idea that the correlation between inequality and growth (or between inequality and GDP) may stem from other factors. But first I want to mention two technical points.

Two Technical Points. First, cross-country data on Gini ratios clearly contain an unusually large amount of measurement error. As Barro notes, there are substantial cross-country differences in the income concept, in population coverage and, I assume, in the method of calculating the Gini ratio. So any regression that uses the Gini ratio on the right-hand side must be afflicted by a large dose of classical measurement error, which biases the coefficients toward zero.

The second technical point is that the Gini ratio may not be a sensible measure of inequality. When two Lorenz curves cross as surely happens often in Barro's panel data, there is no real answer to the seemingly straightforward question, Which income distribution is more unequal? Nonetheless the Gini ratio always gives an answer. Here is a simple example to illustrate the point.

Consider two income distributions with quintile shares as shown in table 1–1C. Distribution A is the actual income distribution among U.S. households in 1997 with the Gini ratio calculated with the same approximation formula that Barro uses. Distribution B was created by shifting 3 percent of total income from the poorest quintile to the second quintile in a clearly *disequalizing* change and by shifting another 3 percent of total income from the top quintile to the fourth quintile in a clearly *equalizing* change. Which distribution has more inequality? That answer is unclear. It all depends on the relative importance attached to inequality at the bottom compared with inequality at the top. My own value judgments lead me to conclude that the change from A to B is disequalizing, but another observer might call the change equalizing. And the Gini ratio stubbornly insists that inequality has not changed at all. (Slight perturbations in the numbers could have made the Gini ratio rise or fall.)

Theory. Barro offers a good summary of various theories of how inequality might affect either the level or the growth rate of GDP per capita. I do not comment on this because he reaches the indubitably correct conclusion: theory is of little help. Some theories predict that greater inequality will increase growth, while others imply just the opposite. As so often the case, a priori theorizing undisciplined by empirical evidence can lead to any conclusion.

Regarding theories of how the level of per capita GDP might impact the Gini ratio, Barro seems partial to the Kuznets model (or some of its modern reincarnations), which posits that economic development first raises and then reduces inequality. But all this theory elides the bigger question: Which variable causes which? As I have suggested, both inequality and growth must be caused by some other exogenous factors or shocks. It is not meaningful to say that inequality causes growth or that growth causes inequality. As a contemporary example, consider the much-discussed phenomenon of skill-biased technological change. Many economists believe that such technology shocks underlie the trend toward rising wage inequality in the United States since the late 1970s. Have these technological developments also raised the growth rate of per capita GDP? "New economy" advocates say yes.

Barro's Main Findings. With theory providing such scant help, Barro sensibly concentrates on reading the messages in the data. What does he find?

Looking first at inequality (measured by the Gini ratio, henceforth G) as a potential determinant of economic growth (henceforth dy, where y is the log of per capita GDP), Barro finds a zero *linear* relationship. There does, however, appear to be a significant *nonlinear* relationship. The estimated derivative,

$$d(dy)/dG = -.331 + .043\, y,$$

varies with y. At low-income levels it is negative and indicates that more inequality hurts growth. But at high-income levels greater inequality seems to raise the growth rate. With a different functional form, however, Barro finds that the relationship disappears. The inference appears a bit less fragile, at least qualitatively, when assessing how the level of GDP affects inequality. Barro detects a fairly consistent Kuznets curve relationship: inequality first rises with y and then falls. However, as he notes, the correlation does not explain much of the variance of G. In addition, as mentioned, the *quantitative* dimensions of the estimated Kuznets curve change dramatically when fixed effects are allowed into the regression.

The Big Unanswered Question. Although Barro declined—perhaps wisely—to relate inequality to tax policy, I will take a stab at it. Government tax-transfer policies are clearly one of the prominent "other factors" that might account for any observed relationship between G and dy (or y). Unfortunately, but unsurprisingly, it is easy to think of examples in which equalizing policies have either a positive or a negative impact on growth.

First consider instituting a punitively progressive income tax of the sort once used in both the United States and the United Kingdom, with top marginal tax rates in excess of 90 percent. The Gini ratio would almost certainly fall, and either GDP or its growth rate would probably decline as well. (However, the U.S. economy grew very nicely in the early postwar period, when the top marginal tax rate was 90 percent.) A "policy shock" such as that should therefore induce a *positive* covariance between G and dy (or y).

Consider next redistributive policies that in poor countries ward off malnutrition or in rich countries enable low-income households to make high-return investments in human capital. Such policy actions would likely reduce the Gini ratio while raising GDP or its growth rate and would thereby induce a *negative* covariance between G and y (or dy). Now think about combining a variety of such policy shocks in a panel study of many countries at different stages of development and imagine that these shocks are the only third factor driving the correlation between growth and inequality. (I am plainly not being realistic here.) You might well find, as Barro did, that there is no linear relationship between G and dy. But if the shocks just used as examples are representative, you might also find a nonlinear relationship like the one Barro found: equalizing policies speed up growth in poor countries but slow it in rich ones.

Is this behind the empirical correlations that Barro discovers? I do not claim to know, and neither does Barro. But it is certainly a good question.

2

Tax Policy and Horizontal Equity

Alan J. Auerbach and Kevin A. Hassett

> Nothing is so firmly believed as what we least know.
> —Montaigne

Philosophers often consider separately questions of redistribution across income classes and questions of equal treatment of equals. There is a lively and often heated literature in both areas. Public policy debates, which necessarily occur at a different level, focus almost exclusively on the former question. Indeed battle lines in the tax debate are often drawn around issues of vertical equity. Flatter taxes may improve economic efficiency but usually at a cost of forgone redistribution. Seldom do heated debates surround the impact of a particular proposal on horizontal equity. The notion that equals should be treated equally is generally accepted by all sides.

Following the work of Atkinson (1970) and others, our ability to define and measure vertical inequality has advanced significantly in recent years. To some extent this advancement has helped to stir controversy since the impact of reform on the income distribution is, in a static sense at least, relatively easy to measure with generally accepted techniques. However, a workable, sensible measure of horizontal equity has been surprisingly elusive. From Musgrave (1959) on, there is general agreement

We thank Nancy Nicosia for her careful research assistance, Andy Mitrusi for his provision of simulations based on the NBER TAXSIM model, and the Burch Center for Tax Policy and Public Finance and AEI for research support. We also thank Jim Heckman, Louis Kaplow, John Roemer, and participants in workshops at AEI, the Institute for Fiscal Studies, New York University Law School, and the Georgetown Law Center for comments on earlier drafts.

that horizontal equity is important—but little agreement on quite what it is.

That something so intuitively appealing could be elusive in practice likely surprises many. But the problems are quite easy to grasp. These can be divided into three categories. First, there is the question of whether horizontal equity represents an independent concept in the context of a general aversion to inequality. If society is generally averse to inequality in the distribution of income, it has long been argued that horizontal equity will typically be implied by this aversion (see, for example, the discussion in Atkinson 1980). Thus measures of horizontal equity may simply represent components of overall measures of social welfare, and it is not clear why they merit independent inspection or concern. Second, and related to the first point, if one does impose independent criteria to assess horizontal equity that go beyond a general aversion to inequality, it is necessary to justify these criteria, which are likely to conflict with the general aversion to inequality. The most common such additional criterion imposes an aversion to changes in individuals' relative standing in the income distribution and leads to measures of horizontal equity based on rank reversals (for example, Feldstein 1976, Rosen 1978, Plotnick 1981, and King 1983). This approach has been criticized on the ground that it gives undue weight to the status quo income distribution (Kaplow 1989).

Third, even if one does establish a case for an independent evaluation of horizontal equity, it is necessary to define what is meant by *equals* and by requiring that the tax system *treat equals equally*. Because deviations from equal treatment are inevitable, we must also specify how these deviations are to be evaluated. Even if one uses a simple observable measure such as pretax income to classify individuals, it remains unclear where to draw the line in grouping individuals as equals. If our definition is not relevant for a comparison of two individuals whose incomes differ by a penny, then it is of limited importance—and one for which a tiny change in income can induce large changes in measured horizontal equity.

In this chapter we review the theoretical developments of the past two decades and discuss a solution to the horizontal equity problem recently suggested by Auerbach and Hassett

(2001). After reviewing in more detail the problems discussed above, we show that *horizontal equity* can represent a distinct and meaningful component of a general evaluation of inequality if global and local differences in the tax burden are accorded different weights in an evaluation of social welfare. That is, if society cares more (or less) about inequalities that arise from treating people who are close in the income distribution differently than it does about inequality across the entire income distribution, then by implication any evaluation of the equity of a particular tax system should have horizontal and vertical components. After laying out this argument, we discuss the application of this new measure to two tax-return data sets and evaluate the degree to which the horizontal equity of the U.S. personal income tax has changed over time and how horizontal equity would be altered by one version of a recent proposal to do away with the so-called marriage penalty.

An Approach to Horizontal Equity

There are a variety of standard approaches to measuring inequality in the distribution of income, with measures of horizontal and vertical equity in the literature that correspond to these alternative approaches. As our focus here is on distributional issues, we ignore behavioral considerations and assume that each individual's income and tax payments are exogenous.[1] A common tool in economics is the Lorenz curve. It is used to show the cumulative distribution of income in a society (see figure 2–1). A point on the curve reveals the cumulative percentage of income held by a given percentage of the population. The line labeled *A* (the 45-degree line) represents perfect equality, and line *B* represents a distribution of income that exhibits substantial inequality. On line *A* 50 percent of the income is held by 50 percent of the population, and so on. However, on line *B* the top 25 percent of the population holds approximately 75 percent of society's income.

For many years economists used Lorenz curves and a summary statistic based on the Lorenz curve known as the Gini coefficient to measure inequality. Its algebraic representation is

FIGURE 2–1
LORENZ CURVE

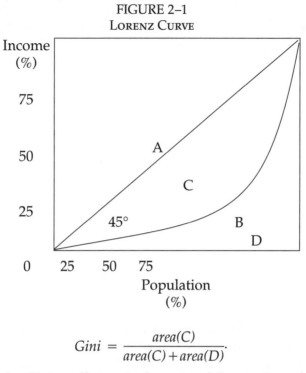

$$Gini = \frac{area(C)}{area(C) + area(D)}.$$

That is, the Gini coefficient is the ratio of the portion of a triangle's area to the triangle's entire area and takes on a value between 0 and 1. Perfect equality yields a Gini of 0 while extreme inequality (with one person holding all of society's income) would score a Gini of 1.

The Gini coefficient is a useful device for deriving conclusions about the relative inequality of two income distributions, but it works only if the two Lorenz curves being compared do not overlap. When two Lorenz curves do overlap, the result is ambiguous. Figure 2–2 illustrates this point. Since the area between lines *B* and *A* and the area between lines *C* and *A* are the same, the Gini coefficient will be the same for both distributions even though the two curves have dramatically different treatments of rich and poor.

Atkinson (1970) used data from many countries to show that Lorenz curves cross more often than not in the data; he concluded that the Gini coefficient was of little practical use in the study of inequality. He then demonstrated the possibility of de-

FIGURE 2–2
CROSSING LORENZ CURVES

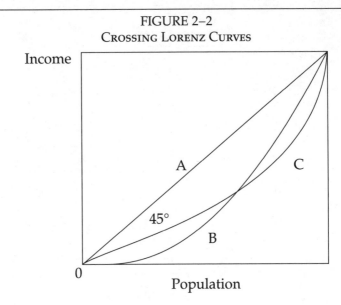

riving a meaningful measure of inequality that would be applicable in cases where Lorenz curves cross, given a willingness to begin with a social welfare function that applied a specific weight to inequality at different points in the income distribution. Atkinson's measure, derived from just such a social welfare function, measures inequality conditional on a social welfare parameter. This method might seem to be a drawback, but the many applications of his measure present estimates across a wide variety of parameter values and allow readers to evaluate how much inequality aversion in the social welfare function is needed to reverse a ranking of two distributions.

In his study of vertical equity Atkinson demonstrated that a measure based on a social welfare function with explicit preferences toward inequality could significantly extend the reach of inequality inquiry. The case of horizontal equity has similar problems; in particular it is difficult to choose among the various methods without access to an underlying objective function. Thus in Auerbach and Hassett 2001 we started with a general specification of preferences over individual after-tax incomes, with parameters that varied with the degree of aversion to inequality that in turn implied a metric consistent with the specification of preferences. We will sketch (without proof) the approach taken there.

The concept of horizontal equity is based on the concept of classes of individuals whom we would wish to label *equals*. Let us begin with the simplifying assumption of a finite number of income levels, say M, with N_i individuals at each level. More generally we might imagine these groups of equals as being defined by some characteristic, such as family structure, age, or region of residence. Following Atkinson 1970, we start with a flexible function that is based on individual after-tax incomes and that imposes an aversion to inequality, say, $\gamma \geq 0$, among different levels of after-tax income:

$$w = \left[\sum_{i=1}^{M} \sum_{j=1}^{N_i} (y_i - T_{ij})^{1-\gamma} \right]^{\frac{1}{1-\gamma}} \tag{2--1}$$

where y_i is the before-tax income of individuals in group i and T_{ij} is the tax payment by the jth individual in group i. The greater is γ, the more averse to inequality the social welfare function will be. At one extreme, for $\gamma = 0$, the welfare function in 2–1 is simply the sum of individual incomes—there is no aversion to inequality. At the other extreme, for $\gamma = \infty$, society adopts the Rawlsian perspective that places weight only on the person with the lowest income.

Expression 2–1 has two important properties. First, it respects the Pareto principle in that it is increasing in each person's after-tax income. Second, for $\gamma > 0$, it is increasing with respect to any experiment that shifts income from an individual with higher after-tax income to one with lower after-tax income. Thus it simultaneously incorporates notions of vertical equity (a wish to redistribute from the rich to the poor) and of horizontal equity (a wish to keep after-tax income equal for those with the same before-tax income). Clearly it requires some modification if it is to give rise to an independent notion of horizontal equity.

The function in 2–1 constrains differences among individuals within any class i to induce the same loss of social welfare as differences among individuals in different income classes. But if horizontal equity is to have any independent content, it seems both necessary and appropriate for attitudes to differ about these two types of inequality. Large differences among similar

49

individuals might be viewed as intrinsically arbitrary (regardless of whether they resulted from intentionally "abusive" government behavior) and therefore more costly to the social fabric, or they might simply be viewed as more costly because individuals compare themselves with those with similar characteristics. This logic suggests that we replace equation 2–1 with

$$w = \left[\sum_{i=1}^{M} N_i \left(\frac{1}{N_i} \sum_{j=1}^{N_i} (y_i - T_{ij})^{1-\gamma} \right)^{\frac{1-\rho}{1-\gamma}} \right]^{\frac{1}{1-\rho}}$$ (2–2)

where γ now represents the inequality aversion within classes and ρ the inequality aversion across classes. If $\rho = \gamma$, this reduces to expression 2–1. A similar functional form has been used in the literature to distinguish between preferences with respect to consumption over time and, at a given time, over states of nature. Just as we might wish to allow individuals to be more (or less) averse to variations in consumption over states of nature than to variations in consumption over time, we might wish to allow welfare to be more (or less) averse to the variations in after-tax income within a certain group than to variations among individuals in different groups.[2]

While the function in equation 2–2 still respects the Pareto principle, it does violate another characteristic sometimes imposed on social welfare measures:[3] a comparison of any two outcomes should depend only on the well-being of individuals who are not indifferent to the outcomes. For example, imagine that there are two income classes, with two individuals in each income class, and that $\gamma > 0$ and $\rho = 0$ (there is no aversion to inequality across classes). That is, the function w may be written

$$w = \left((y_1 - T_{11})^{1-\gamma} + (y_1 - T_{12})^{1-\gamma} \right)^{\frac{1}{1-\gamma}}$$
$$+ \left((y_2 - T_{21})^{1-\gamma} + (y_2 - T_{22})^{1-\gamma} \right)^{\frac{1}{1-\gamma}}$$ (2–3)

Further assume for simplicity that $y_1 = y_2$ and that there are two outcomes, A and B, between which the tax liabilities of individuals 12 and 22 do not change; let these fixed liabilities be $\overline{T}_{12}$ and $\overline{T}_{22}$, respectively. Suppose that under outcome A, $T_{11} = x > 0$ and

$T_{21} = 0$, while under outcome B, $T_{21} = x$ and $T_{11} = 0$. Consider two possible situations. In one, $\overline{T}_{12} = x$ and $\overline{T}_{22} = 0$; in the other, $\overline{T}_{22} = x$ and $\overline{T}_{12} = 0$. Then, in the first situation, A eliminates horizontal inequity and will be preferred to B, while in the second case, B eliminates horizontal inequity and will be preferred to A. That is, the relative weight given to individuals 11 and 21 will depend on the relative status of individuals 12 and 22. This dependence should not be surprising: comparisons across and within groups are presumed to differ in their relative importance.

Having provided scope for the independent evaluation of local differences, we must now consider the issue of how to delineate groups of individuals, in this case, income classes. One might wish to posit that individuals belong to a small number of quite distinct groups of equals. But whether our measure of similarity is income or an alternative such as age or location, the distribution much more closely resembles a continuum, with tiny gaps between contiguous groups and few individuals with exactly the same characteristics. Thus, if we define the preference parameter γ as applying only to individuals with precisely the same income, it will have essentially no impact. Indeed, such a restriction seems inappropriate if our intent is to define reference groups of similar individuals. But if we define a group of equals to include those with somewhat different incomes, the question remains how large that group should be and where to place its boundaries. It would seem that any group boundary would impose an arbitrary discontinuity, with a small change in income inducing a large change in a person's membership in a particular reference group. Indeed this discontinuity has been a problem with past approaches based on discrete groupings of income classes. However, the problem can be avoided; such unique income-class definitions are unnecessary to compare each individual with others with similar income.

As an alternative, we may define an appropriate reference group for each income level, with such reference groups overlapping, rather than assigning each individual to only one income class. We define these reference groups in terms of a density, or scaling, function, $f_i(\cdot)$, that applies at income level i, defined over group distance, as measured by the difference between y_i and the income of another group, say y_k. With this we generalize equation 2–2 so that γ applies within reference groups:

$$w = \left\{ \sum_{i=1}^{M} \left(\sum_{k=1}^{M} f_i(y_k - y_i) \, N_k \right) \left(\frac{1}{\sum_{k=1}^{M} f_i(y_k - y_i) N_k} \cdot \right. \right.$$

$$\left. \left. \sum_{k=1}^{M} f_i(y_k - y_i) \sum_{j=1}^{N_k} (Y_k - T_{kj})^{1-\gamma} \right)^{\frac{1-\rho}{1-\gamma}} \right\}^{\frac{1}{1-\rho}} . \qquad (2\text{–}4)$$

When $\rho = \gamma$, this reduces to expression 2–1 if the scaling functions are defined so that $\sum_{i=1}^{M} f_i(y_k - y_i) = 1$. The summation here is over i, rather than k. That is, the sum of weights applied to each household, not to each reference group, must sum to 1. To implement this, we define the shape of $f_i(\cdot)$ for each i but let the sum $\sum_{k=1}^{M} f_i(y_k - y_i) = z_i$, where z_i is unknown, and then solve for the vector z so that $\sum_{i=1}^{M} f_i(y_k - y_i) = 1 \; \forall k$.

In our applications below, we define income classes so that N_k is constant over k and assume that $f_i(\cdot)$ is normally distributed and peaks at $k = i$. The smaller the standard deviation of the normal distribution, the tighter the income range used to define a reference group for those in income class i. Clearly the shape of $f_i(\cdot)$ is not predetermined. Like the inequality aversion parameters ρ and γ, it depends on political and ethical considerations. However, the spirit of the calculation would seem to rule out distributions that end abruptly, for these would be subject to the critique leveled against other measures that small changes in income could lead to large changes in measured horizontal equity.

There is a certain analogy here between the specification of the function $f_i(\cdot)$ to estimate horizontal equity in the neighborhood of income level y_i and the choice of a kernel in the nonparametric estimation of the value of a function at a particular point in the function's domain. In that literature (for example, Yatchew 1998), there is a trade-off between the extra information gained from expanding the width of the kernel and the bias associated with using information from observations that are increasingly dissimilar to the observation of interest. Here we use observations other than those exactly at y_i because we believe that they provide information about conditions at y_i. For example, a tax system that yields wildly different burdens for individuals with incomes slightly different from y_i tells us something about horizontal equity at y_i, where there may be few observations with exactly that level of income. Conversely, as the distance from y_i grows, the similarity of individuals to those at y_i falls. The "correct" kernel width should depend on how much noise there is in y_i as an indicator of true income class.

In Auerbach and Hassett 2001, we showed that the social welfare expression 2–4 can be rewritten:

$$w = \left[\sum_i \left(\sum_k f_i (y_k - y_i) N_k \right) \tilde{y}_i^{1-\rho} (1 - \tilde{t}_i)^{1-\rho} H_i^{1-\rho} \right]^{\frac{1}{1-\rho}} \quad (2\text{–}5)$$

where $\tilde{y}_i$ and $\tilde{t}_i$ are weighted averages of income and tax rates in group i and the term H_i is defined by

$$H_i = \left[\sum_k b_{ki} \cdot \frac{1}{N_k} \sum_j \left(\frac{1 - t_{kj}}{1 - \tilde{t}_i} \right)^{1-\gamma} \right]^{\frac{1}{1-\gamma}} \quad (2\text{–}6)$$

where $t_{kj} = T_{kj} / y_k$ is the average tax rate for the jth member of group i and the terms b_{ki} are weights that sum to 1 over k. H_i is an index of horizontal equity and satisfies the intuitive requirement that it achieves its maximum (normalized to 1) when the average tax rates of all those in the reference group are equal.[4] This index depends on the "local" inequality aversion parameter γ but not on the "global" inequality parameter ρ. The weights assigned to different individuals in the reference group, b_{ki}, depend on the definition of comparison groups.

We can use equation 2–5 to decompose changes in social welfare over time into those due to changes in the level and distribution of income, changes in the burden and the progressivity of the tax system, and changes in the degree of horizontal equity. This decomposition holds even in the event that $\gamma = \rho$, although the motivation for the exercise, notably the specification of a reference group through the definition of $f(\cdot)$, clearly hinges on the fact that this equality need not hold.

An issue that has often arisen in the literature is how we should weight local measures of horizontal equity into a single, overall index. There may be no obvious answer for measures that start with some assumed metric for measuring deviations. Here, though, because our metric is defined by an underlying welfare function, decomposition procedure just followed dictates the answer. The overall index does depend on ρ. Intuitively we will care more about horizontal equity at lower income levels, the larger is the value of ρ, because we care more in general about what happens to lower-income individuals.

Discussion

Before a presentation of empirical applications of the measure just derived, it will be useful to review some of its attributes, in light of the difficulties mentioned in the introduction.

First of all, the measure is derived from a well-behaved social welfare function, so it will not lead to any anomalies inherent in alternative approaches that do not, for example, respect the Pareto principle in a world of certainty. Although we claim no particular knowledge of the function's specific parameter values, the approach provides a framework with logical foundations that can serve as a useful tool for evaluating alternative policy options. It allows those performing the evaluation to specify their own preferred parameter values within a single framework, rather than having the values be implicit in the choice of one measure over another.

As discussed, the particular functional form used here does allow the well-being of reference-group members to be relevant to comparisons of alternative outcomes, even if these members themselves are indifferent between such outcomes. Also, because the function is concave in the assumed linear individual utilities, its use in evaluating uncertain outcomes would not satisfy the Pareto criterion as characterized in terms of ex ante individual expected utilities.[5] We view neither of these attributes as particularly problematic. As discussed, the whole notion of horizontal equity suggests the relevance of reference groups; that such groups should matter should hardly be seen as an anomaly. The extension of the Pareto principle to apply to ex ante expected utilities requires not only that individual preferences satisfy the von Neumann-Morgenstern axioms but also that social welfare cannot be averse to ex post inequalities in the distribution of income, a requirement that strikes us as unnecessarily restrictive. How to think about equity in general and horizontal equity in particular becomes more complicated in the presence of uncertainty and is not a subject pursued further here.

Second, the measure is scaled in the same units as other factors that determine social welfare so we can make meaningful comparisons between a change in horizontal equity and, say, an increase in overall taxes or a decrease in the dispersion of income. Third, because the measure of horizontal equity is derived through a decomposition of the social welfare function (see 2–5), there is no problem in potential double counting of variations that affect both horizontal and vertical equity. A change in any individual's tax burden will affect the social welfare function through many channels, some through different indexes H_i and some through average tax rates $\bar{t}_i$, but these effects will each be distinctly measured. Finally, the measure allows great flexibility in the definition of *equals* so that slight variations in income need not trigger discontinuous changes in reference-group membership.

This new measure also suggests a response to a problem raised in the literature by Stiglitz (1982), who observed that in a more complicated model of the economy, the "utility possibilities frontier" facing the social welfare planner might not be convex.[6] In such a situation, as depicted by Atkinson (1980) and repeated in figure 2–3, the government might improve social welfare by providing two otherwise identical individuals with different tax burdens and utility levels, as depicted at points A and B. Based on this result, one can argue that horizontal equity need not be subsumed by a general maximization of social welfare and that if horizontal equity is desirable in its own right, it might be appropriately included as a separate argument of the social welfare function. In a sense our approach does precisely that. By allowing social welfare to be more averse to horizontal inequity than to vertical inequity, it can permit outcomes that push "equals" closer together. Indeed, for sufficiently HE-averse preferences—the extreme being the Leontief preferences

55

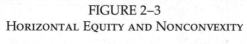

FIGURE 2–3
Horizontal Equity and Nonconvexity

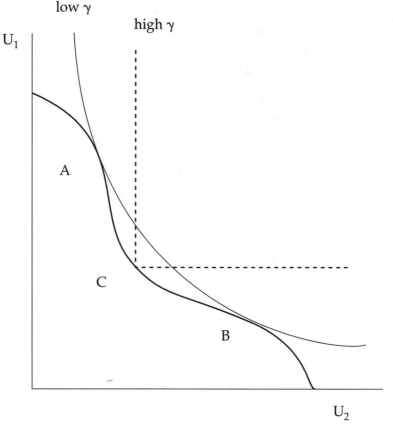

depicted by the dashed social indifference curve in Figure 2–3—no horizontal inequity would result, for then point C would be most preferred. However, our approach has the advantage that this outcome is generated in the context of social welfare maximization and does not require the inclusion of an ad hoc, distinct measure of horizontal equity subject to the various problems touched on above.

Figures 2–4 and 2–5 illustrate the ability of our social welfare function to accommodate sharply different preferences toward horizontal and vertical inequality. They illustrate a simple economy with three individuals. Mr. 1 is poor, with roughly

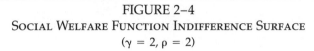

FIGURE 2–4
SOCIAL WELFARE FUNCTION INDIFFERENCE SURFACE
($\gamma = 2, \rho = 2$)

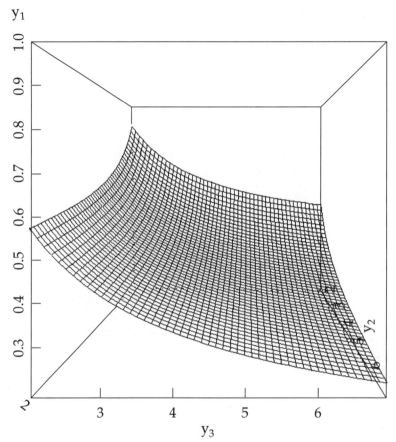

half the income of Mr. 2 and Mr. 3, who are a single comparison class for the purposes of horizontal equity. The origin, which is the set of incomes {0.2, 2, 2}, is in the back left-hand corner. In the first example, equation 2–2, $\rho = \gamma = 2$: the aversion to horizontal inequality is not particularly strong.[7] Since Mr. 1 is poorer than the others, we need to give Mr. 2 and Mr. 3 much more income than we take away from Mr. 1 to maintain indifference. But the indifference surface is relatively flat in the Mr. 2–Mr. 3 plane: inequality between Mr. 2 and Mr. 3 is not heavily penalized.

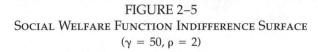

FIGURE 2–5
SOCIAL WELFARE FUNCTION INDIFFERENCE SURFACE
($\gamma = 50, \rho = 2$)

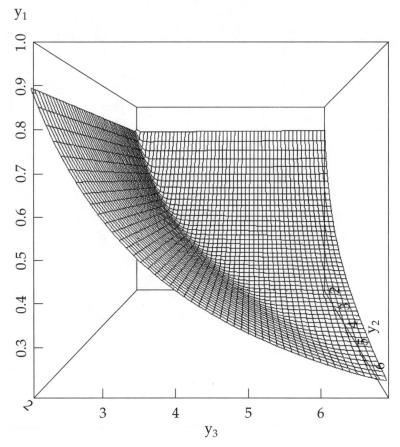

Figure 2–3 increases the parameter γ to 50 and makes preferences toward horizontal inequality between Mr. 2 and Mr. 3 almost Leontief. As income is taken away from Mr. 1, the total
income that must be devoted to Mr. 2 and Mr. 3 to maintain
indifference is much lower when they receive the same income.

Applications

To illustrate our measure of horizontal equity, we use two data
sets. Each is a public-use sample of individual income tax re-

turns. The first, the Michigan tax panel, has the advantage of following the same group of taxpayers over time but has two disadvantages. It has a relatively small number of households (about 5,000) and a terminal year of 1990, before many of the recent changes in the income tax code took place. Our second data set, the annual tax file of the National Bureau of Economic Research, does not provide the advantages of a panel but has several other advantages. First, it is available for 1994—after the 1993 tax increase. Moreover, it has roughly 96,000 households, with the added benefit of significant oversampling of high-income households. Finally, in conjunction with the NBER TAX-SIM model, this data set can be used to simulate the effects of a change in tax law on household tax liabilities. (The TAXSIM model allows the calculation of individual tax rates.)

We first examine the results from the Michigan panel. For this data set we define each household to be its own income class. That is, we set $N_i = 1$ $\forall i$. Initially we consider each household without regard to its filing status or the number of individuals in the household. That is, for each household, we consider only adjusted gross income (AGI) and federal income tax.

Figure 2–6 presents graphs of H_i for the panel, with both income and tax liability averaged over the panel's twelve-year period. Our sample of 5,022 consists of all observations with complete income and tax data for the full period, less 216 households that appeared to have anomalous tax or income patterns, based on gross filters.[8] For this and most other figures that follow, we plot H_i against household income percentile. To calculate a household's percentile in the income distribution, we first sort households in ascending order of average income by giving each household its twelve-year average sample weight and then dividing by the sum of average sample weights. Thus the household with income greater than other households' and with 35 percent of the sample weight will be located at the thirty-fifth percentile of the income distribution. Because the values of H_i trend downward at the apex of the distribution, we truncate the graphs at the ninety-eighth percentile to make more subtle variations at other incomes distinguishable.

The figure presents nine different graphs of H_i, based on all possible combinations of three different assumptions about the

FIGURE 2–6
INDEX OF HORIZONTAL EQUITY, 12-YEAR AVERAGE, 1979–1990
(γ = .5, 2, 5; scaling = .10, log scaling = .10, .25)

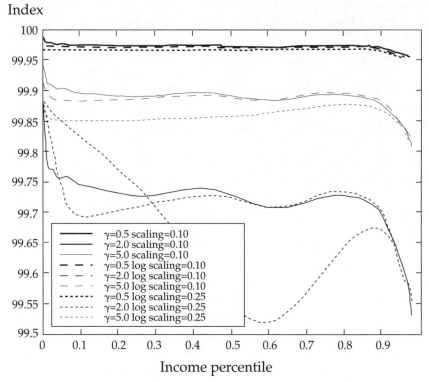

"local" inequality aversion parameter, γ, and three different shapes of the function $f_i(\cdot)$. For γ, we consider values of .5, 2, and 5, meant to reflect wide variation in preferences, from mild to strong aversion to inequality. For $f_i(\cdot)$ we use the normal distribution and let this distribution vary with respect to the degree of reference group dispersion—the distribution's standard deviation—and the extent to which this dispersion changes with income.[9] We consider three patterns. One specification sets the standard deviation equal to $.10y_i$. The second specification, which we refer to as log scaling, sets the standard deviation equal to $x \ln(y_i)$ with x scaled so that the distribution is the same at median income, y^m, that is, $x = .10y^m/\ln(y^m)$. These two specifications of $f_i(\cdot)$ differ in the extent to which the relevant distance for membership in an income level's reference group grows with income. The first approach assumes that the distance grows in proportion to income so that an individual with an income of $100,000 would be as relevant for reference when y_i = $200,000 as an individual with an income of $10,000 would be for y_i = $20,000. The log-scaling approach slows this widening of the income dispersion of the reference group, implying that the relative weight given to someone with $10,000 of income in the second case would correspond to the weight given to someone with $182,000 of income in the first case, rather than $100,000. Our third specification for $f_i(\cdot)$ also uses log scaling, but with a larger value of x, .25 rather than .10.

Figure 2–6 provides a number of interesting results. First, our measure of horizontal equity generally falls with γ—the greater the aversion to local inequality, the lower the index of horizontal equity. This is hardly surprising—we would expect to be willing to pay more to avoid dispersion, the higher our aversion to it. We can scale the values of H_i in terms of an equivalent increase in the average tax rate, $\tilde{t}_i$. From equation 2–5, the increase in the tax rate, say Δ_i, that has the same impact on social welfare as the deviation of H_i from 1 is

$$\Delta_i = (1 - H_i)(1 - \tilde{t}_i). \qquad (2\text{–}7)$$

Thus, for values of H_i near .9985-.9990, the range for γ = 2, and $\tilde{t}_i$ around .15, Δ_i equals roughly .001, or .1 percentage point. That is, the existing horizontal equity, as measured, costs society as much as an across-the-board increase of .1 percentage point in the average income tax rate.

One might be interested in how H_i varies with income rather than location in the income distribution. Figure 2–7 repeats one of the nine graphs of H_i from figure 2–4, for γ = 2 and log scaling of .10, against two alternative series on the horizontal axis: income percentile (bottom axis), as in figure 2–6, and real income (1990 dollars) (top axis). Because of the skewness of the income distribution, the second curve is compressed to the left, relative to the first.

A central issue that always arises in attempting to define horizontal equity—and one that our new approach must confront as well—is which adjustments are "correct," that is, mov-

FIGURE 2–7
Index of Horizontal Equity, by Alternative Income Classes
(γ = 2; log scaling = .10)

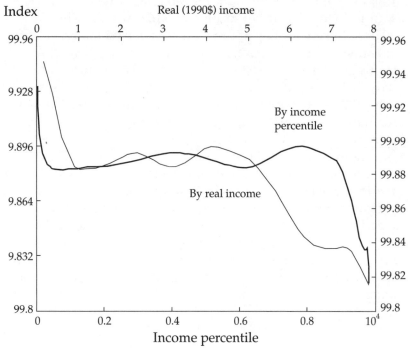

ing the tax burden closer to equitable, and which adjustments represent deviations from an equitable outcome. One could always do away with any measured horizontal inequity simply by assuming that any differences in burden between apparent equals are due to the actual differences in some respect that the tax system recognizes.

For example, if a certain expense, say, for medical care, should not be counted as income, then allowing a deduction for it should improve our measure of horizontal equity if we also measure income by subtracting this expense. Conversely, if we ignore such "appropriate" adjustments to income in our computation, then we may see a deviation in an average tax rate where none really exists. Thus the accuracy of our measure of horizontal equity depends on whether we have made the right adjustments to income. We do not wish to pursue this issue fully here,

FIGURE 2–8

INDEX OF HORIZONTAL EQUITY, ALTERNATIVE EQUIVALENCE SCALES

(γ = .5, 2, 5; log scaling = .10)

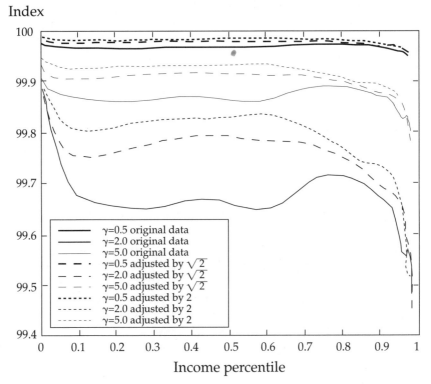

Index

but one important potential adjustment that relates to our consideration of the marriage penalty relates to household size, in particular, the number of adults in a household.

Presumably the view that such an adjustment is needed underlies the fact that married couples who file jointly receive a larger standard deduction and wider tax brackets than single filers. Indeed the notion of a marriage tax seems predicated on the view that the tax system does not adjust enough for joint filers. But this outlook leaves the question of how much we should adjust the income level of a joint-filing household to compare it with that of a single filer. Figure 2–8 considers three alternatives.[10] For the reference-group function, $f_i(\cdot)$, based on the .10 log-scaling assumption, and all three values of γ from figure 2–1, we measure each household's income (and taxes) at its original value, its original value divided by $\sqrt{2}$, and its original value divided by 2. That is, we consider equivalence scales of 1, $\sqrt{2}$, and 2 in deciding how to describe the taxes and income per unit in the household. The logic of not dividing by 2 is that there are economies of scale in living arrangements so that the living standard for joint filers may be higher than that of single filers with half their combined income.[11]

A striking pattern in the figure is that as the adjustments by $\sqrt{2}$ and then 2 are made in succession, the H_i curves rise almost uniformly. This result suggests that horizontal inequity may not be as bad as the unadjusted curves suggest. But it also has another interpretation if we think that the full adjustment by 2 represents an excessive correction: one of the sources of horizontal inequity may be the overcorrection of tax brackets for joint filers. We return to this issue below when considering the impact of potential reforms.

Figure 2–9 presents H_i curves for each individual year in the Michigan tax panel, with the full sample of 5,022, for .10 log scaling and $\gamma = 2$. The evolution of the curves is quite interesting in light of the fact that the two most important tax changes occurred in 1981, with the passage of the Economic Recovery Tax Act, and in 1986, with the Tax Reform Act of 1986. The most striking pattern in the figure is the general shift upward over time, at least since 1981, which is for most of the income distribution the lowest curve in the figure. Indeed, for most income levels above the twenty-fifth percentile, the curves for years 1987–1990—the only four years in the sample after the individual income tax provisions of the 1986 act took effect—are the four highest in the figure. Only at lower income levels is the pattern different. There the years 1979 and 1980 rate highest. From this simple analysis one might tentatively conclude that the 1981 act worsened horizontal equity at most income levels, particularly at the low end, and that the 1986 act reversed the pattern, particularly at middle- and upper-income levels.

The Marriage Penalty

In figure 2–10 we turn to our second data set, the NBER 1994 sample. Because of the size of this data set—90,132[12]—it was

FIGURE 2–9
INDEX OF HORIZONTAL EQUITY, INDIVIDUAL YEARS, 1979–1990
(γ = 2; log scaling = .10)

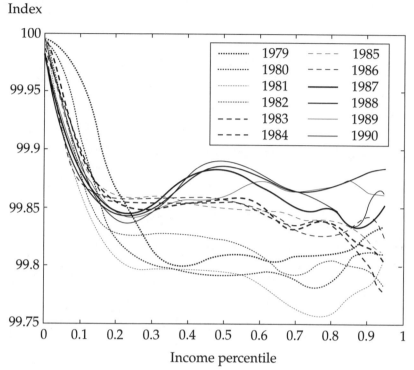

computationally infeasible to define each individual observation as an income group. Instead we defined each group i to include twenty individuals and produced a similar number of groups— 4,506—as in the previous exercise.[13] Figure 2–10 repeats the graphs of H_i, for .10 log scaling, γ = .5 and 2, and for joint filer adjustments of 1, $\sqrt{2}$, and 2. The general patterns are similar to those observed earlier, particularly that for 1990 in figure 2–7, with a general downward drift in H_i as income rises, followed by a slight rise around the seventieth percentile and then a resumption of the downward trend, accelerating near the top. One interesting difference is that the impact of the size adjustment to income for joint filers appears to raise H_i less than was the case for the 1979–1990 average. Taking a reverse engineering ap-

65

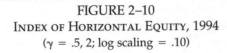

FIGURE 2–10
INDEX OF HORIZONTAL EQUITY, 1994
(γ = .5, 2; log scaling = .10)

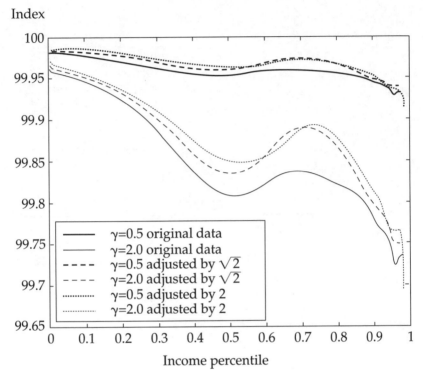

proach and asking what correct joint-filer size adjustment would be "implied by" the 1994 tax system if that system's tax adjustments were designed to minimize horizontal equity would imply a smaller such adjustment than the earlier tax system would.

How would these results differ if we attempted to solve the marriage penalty? As is well known, finding such a solution presents a problem much thornier than sometimes suggested in political debates. Even in comparing joint filers with two single filers in identical circumstances, the effect of marriage is often to reduce taxes rather than to raise them and to lead not to a marriage penalty but to a marriage bonus (CBO 1997). Even more problematic is the comparison of joint filers with individual single filers in different situations—the question posed above when considering the appropriate joint filer adjustment for measuring a family's income level. Still, many alternative solutions to the marriage penalty, generally structured to reduce the taxes of joint filers, have been proposed. We consider the impact of one such scheme, which would divide all income of joint filers equally between spouses, along with deductions and exemptions not directly tied to either taxpayer, and then would allow each spouse to file as a single taxpayer. This scheme is roughly equivalent to providing joint filers with tax brackets that are twice as large as those facing single filers. Clearly such a scheme would reduce the taxes of nearly all joint filers, because the current brackets are based on a lower ratio.[14] But whether this improves horizontal equity depends on whether joint filers now face burdens higher than those of single filers with whom they are being compared. The relevant comparison groups in turn depend on how we adjust for family size when computing income.

Figures 2–11 through 2–13 illustrate the effect of this change on our measure of horizontal equity. Each figure repeats two of the six graphs from figure 2–10 for $\gamma = .5$ and 2 and for one of the three joint-filer size adjustments and also presents two comparable graphs for the alternative tax system aimed at solving the marriage penalty. Figure 2–11 makes no joint-filer adjustment, figure 2–12 divides the income of joint filers by $\sqrt{2}$, and figure 2–13 divides income of joint filers by 2.

Not surprisingly, the results in figure 2–11 suggest that horizontal equity falls. If no family size adjustment were appropriate, then the current tax system already would be too generous to joint filers, and this system would exacerbate this bias. The pattern of this impact, occurring primarily in the upper-middle–income range, may be attributable in part to the fact that the current tax system becomes less favorable to joint filers as incomes rise. Thus, if we view size adjustments as inappropriate, we are closer to the correct treatment under current law and deviate more from this treatment under the proposal. However, this intuition fails to explain why no apparent worsening of horizontal equity occurs at lower income levels.

Figure 2–12 illustrates the impact of reform if the appro-

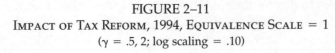

FIGURE 2–11
IMPACT OF TAX REFORM, 1994, EQUIVALENCE SCALE = 1
(γ = .5, 2; log scaling = .10)

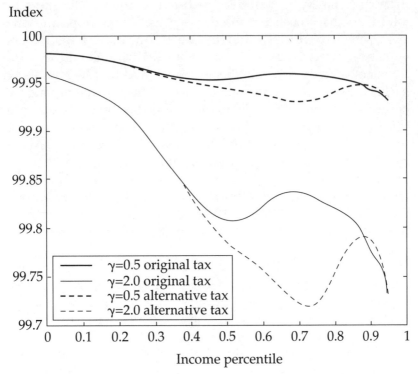

priate income adjustment is to divide joint income by $\sqrt{2}$. The pattern is similar to that in figure 2–11. As expected, the decline in measured horizontal equity is smaller in general because the appropriate treatment is now assumed to involve some family size adjustment. Again, though, the pattern observed for incomes below the median—in this case showing a small improvement in horizontal equity—is difficult to reconcile with the fact that the tax system is moving further away from the size adjustment assumed to be appropriate.

The adjustments in figure 2–13 are based on an equivalence scale of 2, essentially consistent with the policy being undertaken. If the only systematic variation in tax burdens between single filers and joint filers under current law were attributable

FIGURE 2–12
IMPACT OF TAX REFORM, 1994, EQUIVALENCE SCALE = $\sqrt{2}$
(γ = .5, 2; log scaling = .10)

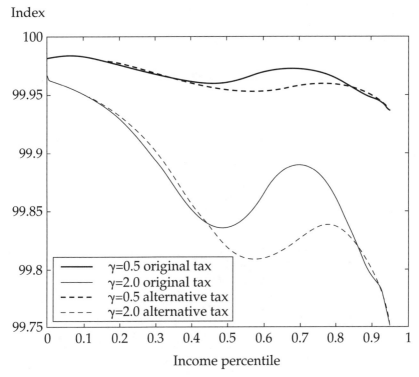

to differences in tax schedules, the new tax policy would eliminate all horizontal equity attributable to differences in filing
status. Yet measured horizontal equity does not rise uniformly
in the figure. Rather, it rises at lower income levels, as before,
and now also at higher income levels—but still falls at middle
income levels. This confirms what the other figures suggest: the
relative treatment of joint filers and single filers under the current code differs in ways not captured by the tax schedule itself,
with these differences varying over income distribution.

One systematic difference clearly omitted thus far is the
presence of dependents, for whom the tax code provides additional exemptions. This factor likely reduces the relative tax burdens of joint filers and might help explain why the reform

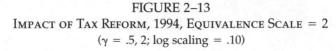

FIGURE 2–13
IMPACT OF TAX REFORM, 1994, EQUIVALENCE SCALE = 2
(γ = .5, 2; log scaling = .10)

Index

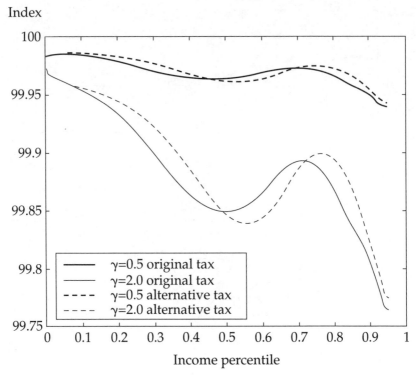

Income percentile

appears to worsen horizontal equity at some income levels, even in figure 2–13. But ignoring dependents also means that we are probably adjusting family size incorrectly and are therefore understating the extent to which joint filers, who are more likely to have dependents, are unfavorably treated under current law.

Figures 2–14 and 2–15 illustrate the impact of the tax reform, now adjusting family income by $\sqrt{N}$ and N, respectively, where N is the total number of individuals in the family's household. As one might expect, the latter figure now shows that the proposed reform raises horizontal equity at all income levels, for it is based on a size adjustment that implies that the current tax system treats joint filers with dependents far too severely. But

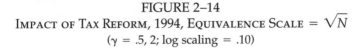

FIGURE 2–14
IMPACT OF TAX REFORM, 1994, EQUIVALENCE SCALE = $\sqrt{N}$
(γ = .5, 2; log scaling = .10)

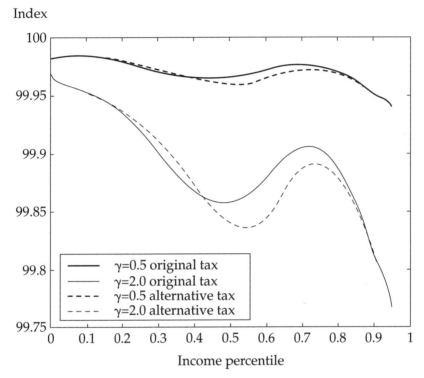

adjusting by $\sqrt{N}$ still leaves a large share of the income distribution over which the index falls. This result suggests that joint filers may be taking greater advantage of other provisions in the tax code that reduce tax payments (for example, mortgage interest deductions), making their current treatment more favorable than is implied by the simple rate schedules themselves.

Together, these figures confirm that the extent to which the marriage penalty should be "corrected" depends on how it is measured at present. But the figures also suggest that whatever the proper adjustment for the income of joint filers, the penalty may be least in need of correction at upper-middle–income levels.

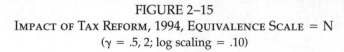

FIGURE 2–15
IMPACT OF TAX REFORM, 1994, EQUIVALENCE SCALE = N
(γ = .5, 2; log scaling = .10)

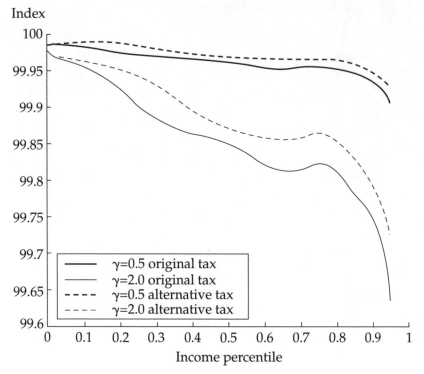

Conclusions

In this chapter we discussed a new measure of horizontal equity that allows for separate social preferences toward vertical and horizontal equity. To illustrate the application of our measure, we have explored the change in horizontal inequality of the U.S. federal income tax and have examined a recent proposal to undo the marriage penalty.

Notes

1. More generally one might use our approach with the measures of individual welfare that took account of issues of tax incidence and deadweight loss.

2. Although we make the analogy here to household decisions under uncertainty, our own analysis focuses exclusively on the evaluation of ex post income distributions.

3. See, for example, the discussion in Roemer 1996, chap. 4.

4. The precise definitions of the terms introduced in equations 2–5 and 2–6

are $\bar{y}_i = \left(\left(\sum_k f_i(y_k - y_i)N_k \right)^{-1} \sum_k f_i(y_k - y_i)N_k y_k^{1-\gamma} \right)^{\frac{1}{1-\gamma}}$; $\tilde{t}_i = \sum_k b_{ki} \left(\sum_j (t_{kj} / N_k) \right)$;

and $b_{ki} = \left(\sum_k f_i(y_k - y_i)N_k y_k^{1-\gamma} \right)^{-1} f_i(y_k - y_i)N_k y_k^{1-\gamma}$.

5. For example, since utility is linear in income, individuals would be willing to take on any risk in exchange for an arbitrarily small compensation, whereas society would not if it maximized expected social welfare.

6. With income and taxes exogenous in our model, the frontier is linear.

7. For simplicity, we are assuming here that the function $f(\cdot)$ is a spike so that Mr. 1 is not in the reference group for Mr. 2 and Mr. 3, and vice versa.

8. Most households eliminated had negative AGI or a tax rate greater than 100 percent in at least one panel year. A small additional number were eliminated because of a tax rate that deviated by more than twenty-five percentage points from the household's twelve-year average in any year. We omitted one additional household with a huge deviation in income to near 0 in one year.

9. Because the income distribution is bounded, the distributions actually used are truncated normals.

10. For this figure we eliminated all observations that experienced a change in filing status during the twelve-year period and moved from a sample of 5,022 to one of 3,389.

11. Below, when discussing the marriage penalty, we consider additional adjustments for family size. Determining the adjustment most appropriate for evaluating tax payments is a subject worthy of further discussion but beyond the scope of our current analysis.

12. This number is net of the elimination of 6,252 records with negative AGI or a tax rate over 100 percent.

13. For simplicity, to make the number of observations divisible by 20, we randomly dropped 12 observations.

14. The zero-bracket amount for a joint-filing couple, equal to the standard deduction plus two exemptions, is $11,650 for 1998, or roughly 1 2/3 times the single filer's zero-bracket amount of $6,950. The next two bracket floors, for the 28 percent and 31 percent rates, roughly preserve this ratio, at $42,350 and $102,300 for joint filers and $25,350 and $61,400 for single filers. However, the floors for the last two brackets (36 percent and 39.6 percent) for joint filers are 1.2 and 1.0 times those of single filers.

References

Atkinson, Anthony B. 1970. "On the Measurement of Inequality." *Journal of Economic Theory* 2: 244–63.

————. 1980. "Horizontal Equity and the Distribution of the Tax Burden." In *The Economics of Taxation*, edited by H. Aaron and M. Boskin, pages 3–18. Washington, D.C.: Brookings Institution.

Auerbach, Alan J., and Kevin A. Hassett. 2001. "A New Measure of Horizontal Equity." *American Economic Review.*

Congressional Budget Office. 1997. *For Better or for Worse: Marriage and the Federal Income Tax*, pages 1–56. Washington, D.C.: Government Printing Office.

Feldstein, Martin. 1976. "On the Theory of Tax Reform." *Journal of Public Economics* 6 (July/August): 77–104.

Kaplow, Louis. 1989. "Horizontal Equity: Measures in Search of a Principle." *National Tax Journal* 42: 139–54.

King, Mervyn. 1983. "An Index of Inequality: With Applications to Horizontal Equity and Social Mobility." *Econometrica* 51 (January): 99–115.

Musgrave, Richard A. 1959. *The Theory of Public Finance*. New York: McGraw-Hill.

Plotnick, Robert. 1981. "A Measure of Horizontal Inequity." *Review of Economics and Statistics* 63 (May): 283–88.

Roemer, John E. 1996. *Theories of Distributive Justice*. Cambridge: Harvard University Press.

Rosen, Harvey S. 1978. "An Approach to the Study of Income, Utility, and Horizontal Equity." *Quarterly Journal of Economics* 92 (May): 307–22.

Stiglitz, Joseph E. 1982. "Utilitarianism and Horizontal Equity: The Case of Random Taxation." *Journal of Public Economics* 18: 1–33.

Yatchew, Adonis. 1998. "Nonparametric Regression Techniques in Economics." *Journal of Economic Literature* 36 (June): 669–721.

Commentary

Louis Kaplow

Alan Auerbach and Kevin Hassett (1999, 2001) offer a new, sophisticated measure of horizontal equity that is designed to overcome the shortcomings of prior measures.[1] One cannot, however, assess their new index without first answering an essential, prior question: Why is it that we care about horizontal equity? After all, whether an index is a good one depends on its relationship to what it is supposed to measure. Like almost all of the previous literature that develops indexes of horizontal equity, however, Auerbach and Hassett do not really address this issue.

There is, in addition, a more serious problem with the tendency to take the importance of horizontal equity for granted. If the authors' approach to policy assessment is followed, society will be advised to adopt policies that sacrifice individuals' well-being on account of the policies' favorable effect on horizontal equity. But such a result is surely undesirable if, as it turns out, horizontal equity should not in itself be endowed with independent normative significance.

My argument here is that Auerbach and Hassett—indeed the whole literature that attempts to measure horizontal equity—has jumped the gun in a fundamental sense.[2] When one carefully examines the concept of horizontal equity and what its pursuit entails, one discovers no normative basis for its importance, and in fact it conflicts with the basic foundations of welfare economics. That is, horizontal equity stands in opposition to the advancement of human welfare. Indeed consistent pursuit

I thank Steven Shavell for comments, Susan Chen for research assistance, and the John M. Olin Center for Law, Economics, and Business at Harvard Law School for financial support.

of horizontal equity can conflict with the Pareto principle. To give weight to horizontal equity entails making policy judgments dependent on information (in the case of Auerbach and Hassett's index, pretax income levels) that has no bearing on any individual's actual well-being. And when one considers the factors that implicitly are given independent weight (such as individuals' genes and luck), they ultimately are arbitrary from almost any plausible moral perspective.

Why does the notion of horizontal equity have such intuitive appeal? The answer, in significant part, seems to be that the notion of horizontal equity—a concern for the equal treatment of equals—serves as a proxy device that enables us to identify factors that are potentially relevant to welfare. Notably, unequal treatment of equals may indicate mistakes in welfare maximization (for if individuals truly are equal, the optimal treatment for each will typically be the same), income inequality (which would already be captured by an ordinary social welfare function), imposition of risk, reasons for envy by those treated less well than their peers, or evidence of abuse of power (such as invidious discrimination or government officials' targeting of their enemies).

Clearly, contemplating the unequal treatment of equals brings to mind myriad instances in which something is amiss. Yet each of the problems just identified involves a reduction in welfare, as that notion is conventionally understood. Thus the role of horizontal equity in alerting us to these problems does not provide any basis for deeming horizontal equity to be an independent normative principle, to be pursued at the expense of individuals' well-being.

Finally, with regard to employing the notion of horizontal equity as a proxy device, the tax policy literature's use of horizontal equity is unfortunately not helpful. Some identified problems—especially invidious discrimination and abuse of power—have little or nothing to do with the defects of the tax code that are being studied, even though they have everything to do with why the concern for equal treatment is felt to be important. Moreover, the sort of index of horizontal equity developed by Auerbach and Hassett (and by others) does not relate directly, if at all, to any potential problems that may be caused by unequal treatment. That is, even though identifying instances of apparent unequal treatment of equals may aid the analyst in diagnosing various defects in the tax system, Auerbach and Hassett's aggregate measure, along with its focus on deviations from individuals' positions in the pretax distribution of income, provides little indication of whether any such defects exist or of how to go about remedying them.

The Moral Arbitrariness of Horizontal Equity

Because the implications of sophisticated indexes of horizontal equity like Auerbach and Hassett's are difficult to understand in complex settings, I begin by examining the most basic sort of example for assessing horizontal equity: there are only two income levels before tax and two after tax, and there are only two individuals at each initial income level (to allow for the possibility of the unequal treatment of equals). More precisely, the scenario is as follows.

Time 0. Nature creates four people: two of type H (for high income-earning ability) and two of type L (low ability). The two Hs are identical to each other in all morally relevant respects, and likewise for the two Ls. All individuals have the same utility functions, and all work the same amount of time.[3] The only difference is that, in the pretax world (or whatever other world serves as the benchmark), the two Hs earn more income than the two Ls. That is, the Hs have good "ability luck" and the Ls have bad "ability luck."

Time 1. A tax system is enacted to finance a public good. It is supposed to raise the same amount of revenue from each of the two Hs and from each of the two Ls.[4] It turns out, however, that due to human limitations, there is some bungling in the administration of the tax, so that not everyone in fact pays the proper amount of the tax. This bungling produces the following results:

• One H finishes exactly where an H should. This person will be designated HH.

• One H is mistakenly overtaxed and finishes exactly where the Ls are supposed to end up. Call this person HL. (Which H ends up in which position is determined by nature at time 1.)

77

- One of the Ls lands exactly where Ls should: LL.
- One of the Ls is mistakenly undertaxed, so much so that he ends up exactly where the Hs should: LH.[5] (Again, which L ends up in which position is determined by nature at time 1.)

Here there is unequal treatment both between the Hs and between the Ls. Individuals HH and LH have good "administrative luck" while HL and LL have bad administrative luck.

How Horizontal Equity Influences the Assessment of Social Welfare. Under a standard social welfare function, which is concerned only with where individuals end up, the extent of horizontal equity is no matter for concern. What matters is that we have two individuals who finish as Hs should end up and two who end up as Ls should end up. The actual utility profiles are precisely the same as they would be if tax administration were perfect. Because the welfare function weights all individuals equally, which individuals end up in which positions is of no consequence.

In contrast, by any measure of horizontal equity, including the Auerbach-Hassett measure, there is a gross violation of horizontal equity, so "welfare" is deemed to be lower on this account.[6] That is to say that there is some (strictly positive) amount of resources that society should be willing to sacrifice in order to eliminate the administrative error from the tax system. If this were done, as long as the cost was less than the implicit social reservation price, we would deem welfare to be higher. Alternatively, if society could simply choose between two systems, one with the above characteristics and one that resulted in HH, HH, LL, and LL (at the same admininstrative cost), society would be deemed to be strictly better off if it adopted the latter.

Implication. This example clearly demonstrates that the essence of horizontal equity lies in a willingness to sacrifice social welfare, that is, to reduce individuals' well-being, in order to ensure that some types of luck—here ability luck—have more influence than other types of luck—here administrative luck—on which individuals end up with higher welfare.[7] In this light, it is hard to imagine what plausible philosophical theory would warrant giving weight to horizontal equity. And any normative theory that might justify horizontal equity surely would conflict in the most basic way with the ethical foundations of welfare economics.

Variation. To illustrate this problem with horizontal equity further, reconsider the preceding illustration. There nature first determined (at time 0) individuals' ability luck; this sort of luck was morally significant (it was ability luck, after all, that determined where individuals were "supposed" to end up in the final income distribution); and nature only later (at time 1) determined who had administrative luck.

Now suppose that we change the assumptions slightly so that the order is reversed. That is, assume instead that nature first determines administrative luck, that this sort of luck is deemed to be morally significant, and that only later does nature (arbitrarily) determine who has ability luck.[8]

How does this recharacterization change our analysis? Under conventional welfare economics, of course, none of this is relevant. This is because, as noted, individuals are viewed anonymously; it does not matter who in particular ends up in each position, but only the levels of welfare that individuals are able to achieve. Accordingly, the order in which nature bestows traits is not of independent normative significance per se.

But under the welfare function as modified by Auerbach and Hassett (and others in the literature), everything reverses. The reason is simple. Horizontal equity requires the equal treatment of equals. Here, it is the administrative luck attribute that exists first and is thereby deemed to be the proper determinant of individuals' positions in the final income distribution. That is, the (previously) latter attribute now determines who are the "equals" who should be treated equally, not the former. As a result, what previously was viewed as an "error" in tax administration now must be understood as a correction to the now-viewed-as-inequitable pretax distribution of income. (In terms of the original notation, the change in assumptions means that the second letter, not the first, is morally privileged. In the pretax world, HL, who should be treated as an L, was treated as an H, and LH, who should be treated as an H, was treated as an L. The tax system's administrative scheme gives everyone a welfare level indicated by their second letter, making all equitable.) Incurring costs to eliminate this "error" not only would be wasteful but would actually reduce "welfare" even exclusive of these costs.

Comments. Simply changing assumptions about the order in which nature's luck is manifested (perhaps invisibly) in individuals or about which aspects of such luck (the timing of their origin or their first manifestation, for example) are deemed morally significant changes fundamentally what violates horizontal equity. Indeed the direction of the effect is reversed. But given the essential nature of horizontal equity, noted above, this result should not be surprising. After all, the horizontal equity view consists of a normative stance that some of nature's random moves (ability in the initial example) are to be endowed with normative significance whereas subsequent random moves (administrative luck)—or earlier random moves that are observed subsequently or are simply listed subsequently by the analyst—are to be treated as normatively irrelevant, mere noise that interferes with the proper moral order.[9]

Should any of these traits be endowed with moral significance? Which ones? And why? A basic feature of the tradition of welfare economics is that such traits have no intrinsic moral significance. Moreover, the philosophical basis for many views favorable to any redistribution of income—such as Harsanyi's (1953) derivation of utilitarianism and Rawls's (1971) argument for maximin, both of which appeal to an "original position"—are grounded in the moral conviction that such background traits (and, in particular, traits affecting income-earning ability, which are primarily responsible for the pretax distribution of income) are morally irrelevant.[10] That, after all, is why efforts at enhanced equality in the distribution of income are viewed positively rather than seen as an evil.[11]

To continue to pursue horizontal equity, therefore, it seems that two steps are necessary. First, a proponent must identify particular traits (genetic ones, for instance) and offer moral arguments indicating why they should have normative significance. Second, analysts would need to determine the actual distribution of the relevant traits in society and use this information in constructing a measure of horizontal equity. (That is, one cannot simply choose the pretax income distribution as in Auerbach and Hassett or the prereform income distribution, as in much prior literature on horizontal equity; instead one would need to know how close each individual was to everyone else with regard to the identified, morally relevant set of traits.)[12]

Why Horizontal Equity Is Indefensible: Conflict with the Pareto Principle

The literature on horizontal equity has never really made an explicit, affirmative attempt to justify the concept as an independent normative principle.[13] And as the foregoing discussion suggests, pursuing horizontal equity seems, as its core, to entail giving weight to morally arbitrary factors at the expense of social welfare. This latter point, it turns out, can be put more sharply: giving any weight to horizontal equity is ruled out if one adheres to two rather basic ideas, logical consistency and the Pareto principle.[14] Thus, although Auerbach and Hassett appeal directly to the utilitarian tradition and to economists' conventional social welfare function and offer a measure of horizontal equity that has a mathematical form suggestive of such roots, their index for horizontal equity—in fact any index of horizontal equity—fundamentally conflicts with the basic premises of the entire approach that they draw on for support.

First Demonstration of Pareto Conflict. One way to demonstrate that horizontal equity conflicts with the Pareto principle is to examine a case involving uncertainty, paralleling the approach of Harsanyi (1955, 1977), who used this method to show (roughly) that logical consistency plus the Pareto principle implied that an individualistic social welfare function had to be utilitarian. To do this, consider a simple example in which everyone is initially equal. The reader may interpret this example as involving any number of groups of individuals at different income levels, with everyone in each group identical to each other.

The tax regime at issue has the following characteristics: it raises the mean income (of each group) but also involves some variance. That is, the tax regime entails some randomization, so that some individuals (in each group) will end up with incomes

81

above the mean (for the group) and others will end up with incomes lower than the mean, and perhaps lower than their initial income level.

Such a tax regime involves some loss in horizontal equity. Let I be the per capita income-equivalent measure of the resulting inequity under whatever measure of horizontal equity is deemed to be appropriate. Now, suppose that individuals' risk aversion is such that the increase in the mean income minus the risk premium associated with the randomization is strictly positive but less than I.[15] What implications follow?

Under the Pareto principle, the tax regime would be deemed desirable, for everyone prefers that it be adopted.[16] Moreover, under any conventional social welfare function (which will give no weight to horizontal equity), this regime will be favored as well. But under the Auerbach and Hassett approach—or any other that gives horizontal equity positive weight—this regime would be deemed undesirable because the reduction in horizontal equity outweighs the gain in welfare. That is, a "welfare" function that gives weight to horizontal equity and is applied in a logically consistent manner to evaluate all possible tax regimes will in some instances favor regimes that are Pareto dominated.

Comments. That giving weight to horizontal equity may involve a conflict with the Pareto principle reinforces the point that the failure in the prior literature to give an affirmative justification for horizontal equity is not merely a gap waiting to be filled. Rather, the notion that horizontal equity should be given independent normative weight in assessing policy is fundamentally flawed.

It is worth elaborating on this result in two ways. First, consider the logical status of the example. If one believes that moral principles need to be logically consistent, then this fundamental failure of horizontal equity in the preceding sort of example is decisive. (The fact that, in a population of hundreds of millions of people, actual violations of the Pareto principle will not occur is of no moment.)

Nor should it matter that the demonstration involved introducing uncertainty. Again, if one's principles are to be consistent, they should not lead one astray in any potentially relevant context. Nor is it acceptable to adopt one set of principles (adhering to horizontal equity) when there is no uncertainty but to shift to an inconsistent set of principles (rejecting horizontal equity) when there is some threshold amount of uncertainty. In any event, introducing uncertainty is entirely realistic. Uncertainty is pervasive in tax administration and enforcement and in predicting the effects of tax reforms. Any system for evaluating tax policy must be able to address such cases.

Second, this example should be considered in the broader context of previous writing on welfare economics. As already noted, Harsanyi (1955) first proved almost a half-century ago that adherence to the Pareto principle combined with basic notions of rationality implies that an individualistic social welfare function is utilitarian.[17] In the light of this demonstration, it seems incumbent on those who advocate conflicting approaches to admit that they reject either the Pareto principle or one (or more) of the basic rationality postulates and to give some good reasons for their position. This point seems particularly apropos with respect to Auerbach and Hassett, who seek to draw support from the conventional welfare economic approach.[18]

Auerbach and Hassett briefly acknowledge the Pareto conflict in the current versions of their papers, but they question the extension of the principle to cases involving uncertainty, wherein reference is made to ex ante expected utilities.[19] In the present context, however, in which everyone is fully informed and has the same (correct) probability estimates, it is unclear why the ex ante perspective is not decisive. Why is it acceptable to make everyone worse off prospectively when it is unacceptable to do so in a world of certainty? Would Auerbach and Hassett, for example, favor widespread government restrictions on the ability of fully informed individuals to engage in risky activities—ranging from driving to hiking to entrepreneurship—that in fact raised those individuals' expected utilities? Although others have likewise questioned demonstrations that employ uncertainty, it is simply unclear why adding this realistic feature to the analysis should render the Pareto principle inoperative.

Second Demonstration of Pareto Conflict. As it turns out, however, it is possible to demonstrate that most horizontal equity indexes, including the Auerbach and Hassett proposal, violate the Pareto principle even in a world of certainty. Any welfare function that meets very minimal requirements (notably, continuity, which Auerbach and Hassett's welfare function does) and depends on information other than individuals' utilities (which Auerbach and Hassett's does) can be shown to violate the Pareto principle (Kaplow and Shavell 2001).[20]

A brief sketch of the argument is as follows. Initially, because the welfare function modified for horizontal equity depends on information other than individuals' utilities (in particular, it depends on income differences between individuals that are derived using income levels in a reference distribution of some sort), it is possible that there exist two regimes, X and X', such that individuals' utility profiles are the same in the two regimes but the social welfare evaluation differs.[21] Suppose, for example, that X is deemed to be strictly socially preferred to X'. Now, construct regime X" from regime X' by giving everyone a very small amount more of some good (in the Auerbach-Hassett construct, one can slightly raise everyone's income). By continuity, we can make this increase small enough so that X, which originally was strictly socially preferred to X', will continue to be strictly socially preferred to X". But, by construction, everyone in X" has greater utility than in X. Hence the welfare function modified for horizontal equity violates the Pareto principle.

Comment. On reflection, the foregoing result should not be surprising. If a proposed method of policy evaluation gives weight to something that is not itself a component of individuals' utilities, then it follows that one is willing to sacrifice individuals' well-being to at least some extent. (For example, an evaluator who follows Auerbach and Hassett's prescriptions would strictly prefer one regime over another because of differences in horizontal equity even in cases in which every individual is precisely as well off in both regimes. By continuity the evaluator would still strictly prefer the regime with better horizontal equity even when the other regime is somewhat better in terms of individuals' levels of well-being.) If one simply constructs cases in which this sacrifice in individuals' well-being happens to be shared, say, pro rata among all individuals, there will necessarily be a violation of the Pareto principle. It should be apparent, moreover, that this basic argument holds regardless of the presence of uncertainty, possible differences between ex ante expected utility and ex post realizations of utility, and the like.

Reconciling the Appeal of Horizontal Equity with Its Unacceptability as an Independent Normative Principle

Throughout this comment, I have argued that there has not been offered, and there cannot really exist any defensible justification for horizontal equity as an independent normative principle to be given weight in making social policy decisions at the expense of individuals' well-being. Yet one may wonder how this can be. After all, doesn't everyone agree that it is important to treat equals equally?

The explanation for this apparent paradox may lie in the fact that unequal treatment is often something we care about, but not necessarily in the contexts in which measures of horizontal equity are applied. Moreover, we do not care about unequal treatment for reasons independent of individuals' well-being; nor do we care about unequal treatment in ways that are identified by the indexes of horizontal equity that have been proposed in the literature.

With regard to the first point, unequal treatment at the hands of the government brings to mind such phenomena as racial discrimination, religious persecution, prosecution of political enemies, government officials who act as if they are above the law, and so forth. When one examines the actual sources of unequal treatment under the existing and various proposed tax systems, however, these generally are not what one finds.[22]

To elaborate on the latter two points, it is useful to consider the various ways in which unequal treatment may serve as a proxy indicator that helps to identify potential problems in the tax system. There are, as will be seen, many ways that unequal treatment indicates shortcomings, which further helps to explain why we are inclined to think that horizontal equity is important. In each instance, however, it is the case that violations of horizontal equity merely indicate losses in welfare (as conventionally understood) rather than some other phenomenon that is normatively significant in its own right. Moreover, summary measures of differences in individuals' positions in the pre- and post-tax distributions of income (and other indexes of horizontal equity in the literature) simply are often not very probative of the nature of various problems that may be indicated by the presence of unequal treatment. Following a discussion of these points, I will illustrate the arguments by examining some particular sources of unequal treatment in the tax system that are registered by Auerbach and Hassett's index.

Unequal Treatment as a Proxy for Conventional Welfare Losses. First, as a matter of ordinary welfare maximization, unequal treatment of equals will be undesirable.[23] If it maximizes welfare to treat individual 1 in manner X and not Y, then if individual 2 is in every relevant respect identical to individual 1, it usually will be optimal to treat individual 2 in manner X and not Y.[24] Hence, upon observing individuals 1 and 2 being treated differently, there is a prima facie reason to believe that a mistake is being made. Thus, if 1 should be allowed some business expense deduction to measure his true net income more accurately and 2 is in the identical situation, 2 typically should be allowed the deduction for the same reason.

Three observations about this case should be noted. (1) Whether individuals 1 and 2 are equal in relevant respects may have nothing to do with whether their pretax incomes are equal. (For example, whether two individuals' medical expense deductions should be equal may depend primarily on whether both individuals were equally sick.) (2) The argument for equal treatment of individuals involves a failure to maximize welfare, not the difference in treatment per se.[25] That is, treating individual 2 incorrectly would involve a mistake even if individual 1 (who is treated correctly) did not exist. (3) Unequal treatment may not result in "inequity" of any kind, such as when unequal treatment causes market responses, with the result that only inefficiency remains (as discussed below).

Second, unequal treatment of equals may raise inequality, conventionally measured. Typically, unequal treatment adds "noise" to the income distribution, raising the variance and thus, *ceteris paribus*, lowering welfare as conventionally measured. For example, if one observes that a reform does not change the average tax burden of each decile in the income distribution, one might be misled because, if the variance in each decile rises, there will be greater resulting inequality. (See Atkinson 1980.) Hence, it is useful to analyze disaggregated data (such as that employed by Auerbach and Hassett in their applications), but the end remains measuring social welfare. Thus, an unmodified welfare function, not one like Auerbach and Hassett's that places weight on horizontal equity, provides the correct basis for policy assessment.

Third, and related, provisions that add noise to the system may involve exposing individuals to risk, which tends to reduce welfare (again, as conventionally measured). And uncertainty does exist in the process of tax assessment and enforcement, even though it is not usually as extreme as in the illustration above.

Fourth, individuals might be upset by what they view to be arbitrary, unequal treatment. For example, when individuals learn that others are able to avoid their taxes, they may become envious. Of course, whether this is true is an empirical question, depending on individuals' actual tastes about such matters and whether they are aware of the unequal treatment. With regard to the latter, it is worth noting that the sort of horizontal equity violation that can be uncovered only by applying a sophisticated index of horizontal equity to detailed data sets is unlikely to be an important actual source of envy. (Indeed most individuals probably do not know their neighbors' taxes, nor whether those who benefit from various tax provisions do or do not have the same pretax income.) In any case, if individuals prefer to be treated equally, this taste would count in a proper measure of social welfare, just as any other taste would, because the taste would be reflected in individuals' utility functions.[26] There is no independent normative principle involved.

Furthermore, it is not obvious whether any envious preferences that may exist in this context are limited to or even focused on unequal treatment of individuals with equal (or similar) pretax incomes. Working-class individuals, for example, may be more upset by the unique access of the rich to myriad tax loopholes than by the tax avoidance of their own class. And we might

87

suppose that they would be more, not less, upset if they knew that every rich person took advantage of such loopholes rather than only some of them, the opposite of the horizontal equity problem (which would exist only if there were unequal treatment among the rich). It also seems plausible that the most likely sources of upset from unequal treatment would arise from particular provisions that were understood to involve improper discrimination (such as taxes that differed by race or religion).[27] In all, it does not seem that aggregate measures of horizontal equity of the Auerbach-Hassett type would be very good at identifying what actually makes taxpayers upset.

Additional possibilities exist. Consider, for example, the earlier discussion of concerns about the abuse of power. Also, in making political judgments, decisionmakers will wish to know who gains, who loses, and when individuals are treated unequally, as this will allow a better assessment of the legislative vote count, who may be depended upon to make campaign contributions, and how one's constituents are likely to react.[28]

In summary, a number of conclusions are apparent. First, there are many reasons why observed instances of unequal treatment may suggest relevant concerns. This helps to explain why we instinctively feel that horizontal equity is important. Second, we know that equal treatment is important in other contexts and, indeed, in the post–civil-rights–movement era in which we live, we have internalized the notion that equality is important in its own right. This further explains our automatic inclination to be concerned about unequal treatment. Third, and most importantly, none of this implies that horizontal equity is an independent normative principle. Rather, in each instance, we can identify rather precisely how concerns about unequal treatment dissolve into matters of social welfare, as conventionally measured. Fourth, the indexes for horizontal equity presented in the literature—including Auerbach and Hassett's new measure—seem largely unrelated to the identified bases for concern about unequal treatment.

Sources of Unequal Treatment Captured by Indexes of Horizontal Equity. One point of the preceding discussion was that most of the problems that may exist when there is unequal treatment of equals are not well diagnosed by an index of horizontal equity. I now consider some of what is captured by indexes of horizontal equity.

One major source of potential unequal treatment involves the tax treatment of different family configurations. In such instances, there is often genuine disagreement about who should be deemed equal to whom in the the first place. As Auerbach and Hassett make clear in their discussion, one first must resolve these disputes before one knows how to measure any loss in horizontal equity in the tax system. The index for horizontal equity proposed by Auerbach and Hassett cannot help to identify or resolve such problems.[29]

A similar situation exists with respect to many tax deductions, such as the deduction for medical expenses (also addressed by Auerbach and Hassett). Allowing this deduction will reduce the measure of horizontal equity if the pretax reference distribution is taken to be, say, adjusted gross income but will increase horizontal equity if the reference distribution is defined as pretax income minus medical expenses. As Auerbach and Hassett suggest, we will have identified real—rather than spurious—reductions in horizontal equity only when we have first identified a provision that we believe incorrectly measures the ideal tax base. But if this is the case, we will have already reached our policy conclusion. If it should turn out that we need some measure of the extent of an existing problem (perhaps how much we mismeasure the ability to pay by using an incorrect provision for medical expenses), the measure should be derived from the same principles that motivate our tax regime and guide us in identifying the ideal tax base, that is, the principles that tell us what is incorrect about the provision. There is no need for a generic measure with an aesthetically appealing functional form but no apparent connection to the principles at hand.[30] This concern seems applicable to many tax provisions.

Another important characteristic of indexes of horizontal equity is that much of the inequity that they do measure is spurious. One of the main instances in which an index like Auerbach and Hassett's will register reductions of horizontal equity is when pretax prices (including wages and rates of return on investments) are influenced by the tax system itself, which is often the case. (Remember that the Auerbach and Hassett index privileges the pretax distribution of income, which depends on pretax prices.)

Consider the familiar example of tax-free interest on municipal bonds. Two taxpayers have identical pretax incomes, all from bond interest. One has all taxable interest. The other has all tax-free interest. After taxes, the former has a lower income. An index like that proposed by Auerbach and Hassett will identify an inequity. The problem, as we all know, is that the two individuals were not equal pretax. Rather, the one with municipal bonds must have made a greater investment in order to earn the same interest, so his ending up with more after-tax income is correct.

Suppose instead that one compared two investors with the same wealth, one investing in municipal bonds and one in taxable bonds. Here, the Auerbach-Hassett measure would also show a violation of horizontal equity, because the individual with taxable bonds had greater pretax income but only equal after-tax income. (Recall that the Auerbach-Hassett measure does not confine itself to comparisons of precise pretax equals.) But this too is misleading: it is not really correct to say that the individual investing in municipal bonds "pays no taxes"; rather, the pretax return on the municipal bonds is depressed relative to the taxable rate of return. These two taxpayers are in reality treated equally.

This example is hardly atypical. Pretax rates of return on all investments—ranging from rental real estate to manufacturing equipment to timberland—tend to be influenced by the tax system. With regard to labor income, a variety of fringe benefits as well as nonpecuniary amenities and disadvantages of jobs will be reflected in pretax wages and thus confound the index for horizontal equity. The general (and familiar) point is, as Bittker (1979) observed, that inefficiencies tend to drive out inequities because the market takes the tax system into account.

Consider the implications of this phenomenon for a measure of horizontal equity based on pretax incomes. In general, one would expect that many identified losses in horizontal equity will involve no inequity at all.[31] Moreover, if one could measure true or comprehensive pretax income more accurately (as

Auerbach and Hassett's discussion implicitly suggests would be appropriate), one might then find even more instances of apparent losses in horizontal equity that involve no inequity at all, even accepting horizontal equity as a valid normative principle. For example, if we include the value of free travel available to airline employees in measuring their pretax income, they would appear to have a lower tax rate than others with the same pretax income, but this would ignore that compensating wage differentials already take any tax benefit into account.

Conclusion

Horizontal equity should not be measured—and new measures of social welfare should not be deployed—until we know what we are trying to measure and why. Auerbach and Hassett, like previous authors on the subject, develop indexes of horizontal equity without addressing these foundational questions. To adopt their approach is to ask society to sacrifice individuals' well-being, yet there is no indication of what we are getting in return. I have suggested that there is in fact no good argument for viewing horizontal equity as an independent evaluative principle and that pursuing horizontal equity is in conflict with the very core of welfare economics, the Pareto principle.

Despite these criticisms, most of us feel that equal treatment of equals is important. This concern is apt in other settings, and unequal treatment often indicates problems in the tax policy context. But these problems all involve reductions in social welfare, as conventionally understood, and do not signal the existence of some independent evaluative principle. Moreover, measures of horizontal equity, including the new one advanced by Auerbach and Hassett, do not seem related to the sorts of problems that may exist. Thus, there is no basis for continuing to develop increasingly refined measures of horizontal equity.

Notes

1. Similarly, Musgrave (1990) attempts to derive a horizontal equity index that is closely related to the conventional social welfare function. In Kaplow (1992), I criticized Musgrave's measure not only because it applied solely to precise equals but also because it was not grounded in—and was inconsistent

with—each of the normative principles (including social welfare maximization) that Musgrave identified in the first portion of his article.

2. Many arguments discussed here derive from ideas that were originally advanced in Kaplow (1989). Also Kaplow (1995) discusses in detail the point that the pursuit of horizontal equity clashes with the values underlying welfare economics and in particular with the Pareto principle.

3. To obtain this result, one can simply take labor as exogenous (as in Auerbach and Hassett), or instead suppose that individuals' utility functions are such that income and substitution effects are offsetting.

4. Whether it is a lump-sum tax, a tax proportional to income, or any other tax does not matter.

5. One can suppose that the tax owed by the Hs is sufficiently large (or that the difference between the incomes of the Hs and Ls is sufficiently small) that this is possible. Alternatively, one could allow for negative taxes (transfers) in the overall system.

6. For indexes that express a concern for rank reversals in the income distribution, there is also a violation of horizontal equity in this illustration.

7. Auerbach and Hassett's approach is to compare individuals to those with similar pretax incomes. Thus, the focus in the preceding illustration was on earnings ability, a primary determinant of one's relative position in the pretax income distribution. Most other writers have instead examined the effect of tax reforms rather than tax systems, with the benchmark being the after-tax income distribution that exists prior to the tax reform in question. Similarly, one could refer to any benchmark for the distribution of income (such as one determined by some caste system or by lot) or for the distribution of wealth, consumption, or whatever. The common point is that any approach to horizontal equity must privilege some distribution that will not exist once the system under examination is in place. In particular, the posited distribution will count—in some manner that depends on the particular measure—to an extent that depends on how much the actual resulting distribution of income (the only one under which individuals will actually live once a policy is chosen) deviates from the benchmark distribution.

8. This recharacterization can be described in many ways, depending on when nature determines the underlying characteristics, when we observe them, and so forth. Also, one could hold all of this constant and have different technologies. (For example, the original H type might be the administratively lucky type rather than the high-ability type, and the trait that previously led to administrative luck might instead lead to higher productivity.)

9. In many instances, we do not even know which traits came first, and we may suppose that they often arise simultaneously (as would be true of genetic traits).

10. Libertarian views, which are opposed to redistribution, are more consistent with favoring some such notion of horizontal equity, but they are also opposed to redistributive taxation in the first place. See Kaplow (1989).

11. In other words, the Auerbach-Hassett approach gives special normative weight to the pretax distribution of income whereas the very purpose of the

tax system, both as a whole and with respect to many particulars, is to alter that distribution. Thus, our tax system is explicitly redistributive, and many detailed provisions are designed to favor certain individuals over others. To privilege the pretax distribution is thus, in general, not merely unwarranted but literally backwards. (Much of the prior literature instead privileges the prereform distribution instead of the pretax distribution, but, of course, the purpose of a reform is precisely to make changes from what previously existed. See Kaplow (1989).)

12. To reinforce the point that these demands are inherent in the nature of horizontal equity, it is worth elaborating further on the concept. The notion that equals should be treated equally presupposes that some individuals are equals who must in turn be treated equally. That is, there are predefined groups, the members of each group are more or less equal to each other in some morally relevant sense, and this is all understood to exist before application of the relevant "treatment" (in the present context, the tax system, which determines individuals' actual levels of well-being).

Another defining feature of horizontal equity is that the relevant groups must to some extent be insular. In contrast, if one were to define a single relevant group, the entire population (deeming all humans to be equals), horizontal equity would vanish as an independent concept. After all, if we were concerned about the treatment of each individual with respect to all others, and each of these relationships were to be viewed equally, we would be left with a conventional social welfare function, which treats everyone equally and places weight on equality of income (whether on account of the declining marginal utility of income or because the welfare function is itself concave in utilities). (The ordinary concern for overall equality is sometimes referred to under the rubric of vertical equity, from which horizontal equity is sharply distinguished. In Kaplow (1989), however, I suggest that there may be some confusion about this because the standard examples used in the literature to motivate concern for horizontal equity often involve the sort of inequality that would already be registered by an ordinary welfare function, which gives weight to inequality per se.)

Thus, in considering the circumstances of individuals, the comparison with all others is *not* viewed equally under horizontal equity. Rather, how individuals are treated relative to those others deemed sufficiently comparable in some respects is asserted to be of different moral importance from how the individuals are treated relative to those not deemed comparable. (The measure proposed by Auerbach and Hassett allows for the reference groups to be defined continuously in the sense that everyone can be in everyone else's group, with those having more nearly equal pretax incomes being weighted more heavily. The point is not to challenge the precise weighting or whether the reference group has a definite boundary, but rather to question the basis of giving different normative weight to comparisons with different individuals in the first place.)

13. Musgrave (1990) is the only essay that comes close. As I explain in Kaplow (1992), however, he merely shows that horizontal equity is *consistent*

93

with various philosophical theories in a simple, first-best world. (This is related to the point, noted below, that when a particular treatment is optimal, under some criterion, for individual 1, and individual 2 is identical to 1, the same treatment will, in simple cases, likewise be optimal for 2.) Musgrave does not explain why any of the identified normative theories would call for giving independent weight to horizontal equity, to be pursued at the expense of what the theory deems important.

14. See Kaplow (1995) and Kaplow and Shavell (2001).

15. Taking a given measure of horizontal equity, one can construct such an example by choosing individuals' utility functions with sufficiently small risk aversion that their welfare rises as a result of implementing the tax (or tax reform) but with sufficiently large risk aversion that, when one subtracts I, the aggregate welfare function (which incorporates horizontal equity) falls. (Assuming that the measures are continuous, which Auerbach and Hassett emphasize as a prerequisite of any plausible measure of horizontal equity, this will generally be possible.)

16. One strategy to avoid the problem raised by the example in the text would be to apply the Auerbach-Hassett welfare function not to the ex post distribution of income but rather to the ex ante expected utilities. (That is, one would modify the Auerbach-Hassett approach by looking ex ante rather than ex post and substituting utility for income.) Taking this view to its logical conclusion, however, implies that one should consider expected utility behind a "veil of ignorance." As Vickrey (1945) suggests and Harsanyi (1953, 1977) proves, however, such an approach also implies a utilitarian welfare function, in which horizontal equity receives no weight. (Relatedly, there is a sort of time consistency problem with the ex ante approach when horizontal equity is given weight. Ex ante, as just observed, the posited tax is favored. Once it is implemented, however, and the uncertainty is resolved, it would be optimal— applying a welfare function of the horizontal-equity type—to repeal the tax, for the existing situation is evaluated as inferior to that which would exist without the tax.)

17. More precisely, his assumptions were (1) individuals follow the rationality postulates in choosing among alternatives (that is, he assumed what is required to derive an expected utility function for individual behavior), (2) the rationality postulates apply to social choices as well, and (3) the Pareto principle is respected. (Actually, these assumptions only imply that welfare must be a weighted sum of individuals' utility. If one assumes further that individuals should be weighted equally, then the welfare function must be utilitarian.) See Harsanyi (1955, 1977). This derivation of utilitarianism seems to be less well known than Harsanyi (1953), his earlier and much simpler demonstration that rational individuals behind a veil of ignorance would adopt a utilitarian decision rule. See also Vickrey (1945).

18. Economists do not often invoke this branch of the welfare economics literature, perhaps because of the general belief that in the modern academy utilitarianism (and welfarism and consequentialism more generally) are not in vogue. Although this is the case it is not (in my view) because of the merits of

the critical arguments. Critiques of Harsanyi (himself a philosopher who has regularly published impressive papers defending utilitarianism in philosophical journals) are limited. Responses to some of the original utilitarians' powerful arguments, such as Mill's (1863), often ignore their excellent analysis, which already answers many of the contemporary objections. In addition, modern utilitarians, such as Hare (1981), have offered elaborate rebuttals to many of the familiar points, which often consist of provocative examples rather than analytical claims. See generally Kaplow and Shavell (2002), which criticizes many of the arguments of philosophers and legal academics against welfarism (and more generally against consequentialism).

19. Specifically, Auerbach and Hassett refer to the "extension of the Pareto principle to apply to ex ante expected utilities." However, one might have thought that it is not really an extension of the Pareto principle to state that the principle is relevant to assessing government policies on health care, unemployment insurance, social security annuities, occupational health and safety, contract law, and all other matters in which some uncertainty may be involved. Also, they state that the Pareto principle when applied to settings involving uncertainty "requires . . . that social welfare cannot be averse to ex post inequalities in the distribution of income," which obviously is incorrect (most obviously because of declining marginal utility of income). Presumably, they are referring to demonstrations such as Harsanyi's (1955, 1977) that the Pareto principle, when combined with other assumptions, can be shown to have certain implications for the social welfare function. But this merely states that, if one is logically consistent and adheres to the Pareto principle, one cannot favor policies that trump individuals' unanimous preferences.

20. Auerbach and Hassett repeatedly emphasize the importance of continuity and the fact that their proposed evaluation function and their corresponding measure of horizontal equity are continuous. With regard to nonutility information, their assessment depends on a factor that is a function of individuals' pretax incomes (which, as noted above, are not incomes that anyone ever can consume and thus obviously are neither utility information nor variables that perfectly correlate with utilities).

21. For the Auerbach-Hassett method of assessment, one can suppose, for example, that everyone's after-tax income is the same in X and in X', but that there is a significant horizontal equity violation only in X' (because pretax incomes are more "scrambled" relative to after-tax incomes in that regime).

22. To be sure, corruption in tax administration that may give rise to unequal treatment is widespread in some economies. But this is not the sort of unequal treatment that the literature on horizontal equity, including Auerbach and Hassett, addresses.

23. There are exceptions, such as when there are nonconvexities, but our intuition about the general problem presumably reflects the typical case.

24. This point can usually be extended, by continuity, to individuals who are similar rather than identical, in parallel with Auerbach and Hassett's extension of the notion of horizontal equity from identical to similar individuals.

25. Thus, under a conventional welfare function, mismeasuring a taxpayer's

income (say, by overestimating the income of some poor people) will result in the imposition of a tax that will tend to reduce welfare relative to what would otherwise be optimal; no independent measure of horizontal equity is appropriate. See Kaplow (1996b).

26. At one point, Auerbach and Hassett make comments suggestive of individuals having tastes pertaining to unequal treatment, but their observation is used to motivate a welfare function that does not depend only on individuals' utilities rather than a modification to individuals' utility functions.

27. Another instance where some taxpayers may be upset involves the so-called marriage penalty (and other rules regarding how family units are treated differently). See the discussion below.

28. This final set of concerns is more relevant to the problem of predicting government behavior (political economy) than that of evaluating the effects of policy (welfare economics). In any case, the relevance of indexes of horizontal equity is dubious in this context. Natural groupings of individuals—such as farmers, retirees, and so on—may occur. But each group's lobbyist is presumably concerned about the treatment of his group compared with everyone else, not about the degree of equality of treatment within the various groups.

29. I would note further that the usual manner of talking about these sorts of problems is itself deficient in a manner similar to the problems with justifying horizontal equity as an independent normative principle. After all, what is meant by asserting that one or another definition of the family unit is "better"? Presumably, what should matter is not the resolution of semantic debates but rather the outcome of actual policies and, in particular, their effects on individuals' well-being. Thus, the question of what is the right way to conceive of the family unit for tax purposes is usefully restated as the question of which tax rules regarding families best promote social welfare. This is a problem that can be addressed directly, using the conventional welfare economic framework. See Kaplow (1996a).

30. Suppose, for example, that a tax deduction is undesirable because it implicitly subsidizes wasteful entertainment expenditures. The proper measure of the extent of the problem would be one that indicates the extent of inefficiency, not an index of horizontal equity.

31. This problem is one of the reasons that prior writers, such as Feldstein (1976), offered for using the prereform (status quo) after-tax distribution as a benchmark and focusing on the effects of tax changes.

References

Atkinson, Anthony B. 1980. "Horizontal Equity and the Distribution of the Tax Burden." In *The Economics of Taxation*, edited by Henry Aaron and Michael J. Boskin. Washington, D.C.: Brookings Institution.

Auerbach, Alan J., and Kevin A. Hassett. 1999. "A New Measure of Horizontal Equity." National Bureau of Economic Research Working Paper 7035. Washington, D.C.

———. 2001. "Tax Policy and Horizontal Equity." In *Inequality and Tax*

Policy, edited by Kevin A. Hassett and R. Glenn Hubbard. Washington, D.C.: AEI Press.

Bittker, Boris I. 1979. " Equity, Efficiency, and Income Tax Theory: Do Misallocations Drive Out Inequities?" *San Diego Law Review* 16: 735–48.

Feldstein, Martin. 1976. "On the Theory of Tax Reform." *Journal of Public Economics* 6: 77–104.

Hare, R. M. 1981. *Moral Thinking: Its Level, Method, and Point*. Oxford: Oxford University Press.

Harsanyi, John C. 1953. "Cardinal Utility in Welfare Economics and in the Theory of Risk-Taking." *Journal of Political Economy* 61: 434–35.

———. 1955. "Cardinal Welfare, Individualistic Ethics, and Interpersonal Comparisons of Utility." *Journal of Political Economy* 63: 309–21.

———. 1977. *Rational Behavior and Bargaining Equilibrium in Games and Social Situations*. Cambridge: Cambridge University Press.

Kaplow, Louis. 1989. "Horizontal Equity: Measures in Search of a Principle." *National Tax Journal* 42: 139–54.

———. 1992. "A Note on Horizontal Equity." *Florida Tax Review* 1: 191–96.

———. 1995. "A Fundamental Objection to Tax Equity Norms: A Call for Utilitarianism." *National Tax Journal* 48: 497–514.

———. 1996a. "Optimal Distribution and the Family." *Scandinavian Journal of Economics* 98: 75–92.

———. 1996b. "How Tax Complexity and Enforcement Affect the Equity and Efficiency of the Income Tax." *National Tax Journal* 49: 135–50.

Kaplow, Louis, and Steven Shavell. 2001. "Any Non-Welfarist Method of Policy Assessment Violates the Pareto Principle." *Journal of Political Economy* 109: 281–86.

———. 2002. *Fairness versus Welfare*. Cambridge: Harvard University Press.

Mill, J. S. 1863. *Utilitarianism*. London: Parker, Son and Bourn.

Musgrave, Richard A. 1990. "Horizontal Equity, Once More." *National Tax Journal* 43: 113–22.

Rawls, John. 1971. *A Theory of Justice*. Cambridge: Harvard University Press.

Vickrey, William. 1945. "Measuring Marginal Utility by Reactions to Risk." *Econometrica* 13: 319–33.

3
Entrepreneurial Saving Decisions and Wealth Inequality

R. Glenn Hubbard

The concentration of household wealth in the United States has received considerable attention in public policy discussions (see, for example, Wolff 1995). This concentration is significant; the top 1 percent of U.S. households in 1989 owned about 36 percent of household wealth (based on data from the Federal Reserve Survey of Consumer Finances). Many dynamic models of household decisions used for policy analysis are not well suited to the study of household wealth inequality. Indeed intragenerational inequality in the distribution of wealth is often explicitly ignored by assuming that high–lifetime-income households save the same proportion of lifetime income as low–lifetime-income households (see, for example, Auerbach and Kotlikoff 1987 for tax incidence). This assumption is convenient because it allows a heterogeneous distribution of households to be defined effectively as a single "representative" household.

While recent models of household saving decisions emphasizing insurance- and capital-market imperfections can explain much heterogeneity in saving among U.S. households (see, for example, Hubbard, Skinner, and Zeldes 1994, 1995; Aiyagari 1994; Huggett 1996), those models do not adequately explain the behavior of the wealthiest households, which hold a dispropor-

This essay was prepared for the American Enterprise Institute Conference on Perspectives on Inequality, Washington, D.C. The discussion draws significantly on my research program with Bill Gentry on entrepreneurship and saving. I am grateful to Eric Engstrom for careful research assistance and to the American Enterprise Institute for financial support.

tionately large share of household assets. One interpretation of this poor performance is that wealthy households may be solving dynamic problems different from those of other households (for example, labor supply and retirement saving).

A key difference between wealthy and nonwealthy households is the importance of business ownership, or entrepreneurial activity, for the former. Entrepreneurs hold a disproportionate share of household wealth, and entrepreneurship is associated with high levels of wealth relative to nonentrepreneurs.

Entrepreneurial investment decisions likely differ substantially from the portfolio decisions of nonentrepreneurs. Starting and remaining in business require upfront investments (in, say, fixed or working capital) to realize potentially high returns from ideas, skill, or market power. Although such expected returns may far exceed those obtained from financial assets (returns typically used to study household saving decisions), entrepreneurs must often finance investments with personal assets or income. The potentially high returns available to entrepreneurs—coupled with constraints on external financing—could in principle lead to relatively high saving rates for entrepreneurs and a concentration of assets in the hands of a group of continuing entrepreneurs.[1]

Much research on costly external financing for closely held businesses suggests that selection into entrepreneurship (and increases in the scale or scope of the entrepreneurial firm) may depend on household wealth (see, for example, Evans and Jovanovic 1989; Holtz-Eakin, Joulfaian, and Rosen 1994a, b; Gentry and Hubbard 2000a, b). That is, with costly external financing, ownership of an active business requires internal financing and therefore wealthier participants. If this were the only link between capital-market imperfections and entrepreneurship, no connection between entrepreneurship and wealth inequality per se would be needed.

The accumulation of more wealth relative to income by entrepreneurs than by nonentrepreneurs would enhance a connection between entrepreneurial activity and wealth inequality. That is, higher saving rates by entrepreneurial households because of costly external financing and because of the illiquidity of business assets can lead to a greater wealth inequality.

Following the approach of Gentry and Hubbard (2000a), I evaluate these connections in four steps: formulating an economic definition of *entrepreneur*, illuminating the link between entrepreneurial activity and saving decisions, analyzing the wealth and portfolio allocation of entrepreneurs relative to nonentrepreneurs, and investigating differences in the saving of entrepreneurs and nonentrepreneurs. The emphasis on entrepreneurial decisions leads to three conclusions. First, realistic capital-market imperfections facing entrepreneurs can lead to both a link between wealth and entrepreneurial selection and a link between ongoing entrepreneurial investment opportunities and entrepreneurial saving. Second, business entrants and continuing entrepreneurs have more wealth than other households. Third, continuing entrepreneurs accumulate more wealth than nonentrepreneurs, and entrepreneurship is a factor in upward mobility in the distribution of wealth. Taken together, these findings suggest a connection between entrepreneurship and household wealth inequality in the presence of capital-market imperfections.

Who Is an Entrepreneur?

The rich may be different from the rest of us for many reasons;[2] the links to active business ownership described by economists (see, for example, Schumpeter 1942) or by businesspeople are quite broad and complicate empirical work. Moreover, one's choice of a definition of *entrepreneurship* is linked to the choice of data for testing the links between business ownership and decisions about household saving.

Given a focus on the interdependence of saving and investment decisions of business owners, Gentry and I (2000a) follow a concept of an *entrepreneur* as someone who combines upfront business investments with entrepreneurial skill to obtain the opportunity to earn economic profits. Specifically we define an *entrepreneurial household* as one owning one or more active businesses with a market value of at least $5,000. To study connections among saving, portfolio allocation, and business ownership and investment, we use the cross-section of households in the 1989 Federal Reserve Board Survey of Consumer

Finances and the panel of households spanning the 1983 Survey of Consumer Finances and the 1989 Survey of Consumer Finances.[3] Because the SCF attempts to describe the wealth characteristics of the population, it oversamples higher-income households. The 1989 SCF contains data on 3,143 households. The 1983–1989 panel component of the SCF includes a subsample of the households in the 1983 and 1989 cross-sectional surveys. The data include population weights that allow the calculation of estimates of population statistics.

Costly External Financing and the Saving and Wealth of Entrepreneurs

Many models of asymmetric information and incentive problems in financing and investment decisions focus on the decisions of entrepreneurs. Most empirical studies of "costly external financing," however, have concentrated on the investment decisions of large publicly traded corporations, for which longitudinal data on income-statement and balance-sheet items are available (see, for example, the review of studies in Hubbard 1998). Those studies emphasize that shifts in internal funds can affect investment to the extent that information and incentive problems in capital markets raise the cost of external financing relative to internal financing, holding constant true underlying investment opportunities. In addition, the anticipation of binding financing constraints can lead firms to accumulate assets to finance future investment (see, for example, Calomiris, Himmelberg, and Wachtel 1995; Fazzari, Hubbard, and Petersen 2000).

To illustrate the connection between entrepreneurship and saving, suppose that entrepreneurs have two sources of income: earnings from entrepreneurial activity and returns on capital invested outside the business. Denoting entrepreneurial earnings by y, let

$$y = \theta k^\alpha \epsilon, \qquad (3\text{–}1)$$

where θ indexes the ability for entrepreneurship; k is the amount of fixed capital invested in the business; α is a constant in the unit interval; and ϵ is an independently and identically distributed productivity shock (with a mean of unity and a variance of σ_ϵ^2). Higher levels of entrepreneurial ability imply greater average and marginal earnings for any given level of capital (as in Lucas 1978 and Jovanovic 1982). Net income for an entrepreneur equals the sum of entrepreneurial earnings and investment income where investment income equals the return on assets, a, less entrepreneurial investment, k. In this static example entrepreneurial investment income equals $R(a-k)$ where R is the gross rate of return. Total net income for an entrepreneur then equals $y + R(a-k)$. Absent any capital-market imperfection, the desired capital stock for entrepreneur I is given by $k_i = (\theta_i \alpha / R_i)^{1/(1-\alpha)}$.

In the presence of a simple borrowing constraint, the capital stock may be less than this first-best level. If one assumes that an entrepreneur may borrow a multiple λ of assets ($\lambda \geq 0$), then $0 \leq k \leq (1 + \lambda) a$. For any given ability θ, low–net-worth individuals are more likely to have their business capital stock constrained by the requirement that $k \leq (1 + \lambda) a$.[4]

To emphasize the interdependence of entrepreneurial saving and investment decisions, one can represent the idea of costly external financing by an upward-sloping supply schedule for uncollateralized external financing. When $k > a$, we represent the cost of funds as given by $\overline{R} + \phi \left(\dfrac{k-a}{k} \right)$ where $\phi \geq 0$ is the premium in the cost of external financing; $\theta_k' \, \phi > 0$ (higher collateral relative to capital reduces the costs of external financing). If the entrepreneur's assets are at least as large as his capital investment, $\phi = 0$, and the cost of funds is given simply by $\overline{R}$. Under this representation of costly external financing, the entrepreneur chooses the capital stock to

$$\max \theta k^{\alpha-1} - \overline{R}(k-a) - \phi k. \tag{3-2}$$

The equilibrium capital stock for an unconstrained firm remains $k^* = (\alpha \theta / \overline{R})^{(1/(1-\alpha))}$. When $a < k$, the capital stock solves

$$a \theta k^{\alpha-1} = \overline{R} + \phi + \theta_k' \left(\frac{a}{k} \right),$$

so that

$$k = \left[\alpha\theta \bigg/ \left(\left(\overline{R} + \theta + \theta_k' \right) \left(\frac{a}{k} \right) \right) \right]^{\frac{1}{1-\alpha}} < k^* \qquad (3\text{--}3)$$

as long as $a < k$, ϕ and θ_k are positive, and the constrained capital stock is less than the desired capital stock. In addition, while $\partial k / \partial a = 0$ when $a \geq k^*$, $\delta k / \delta a > 0$ when $a < k^*$ (because increases in collateralizable resources a reduce ϕ).

For an individual entrepreneur, the link between net worth and investment affects the saving decision. Letting π represent expected entrepreneurial income (that is, $\pi = \phi k^\alpha - \overline{R}(k - a) - \phi k$), one can analyze the effect of a change in the entrepreneur's assets (a) on entrepreneurial income. When there is no uncollateralized financing (that is, when $a \geq k^*$), $\partial k / \partial a = 0$, and $\partial \pi / \partial a = \overline{R}$. An increase in entrepreneurial saving produces a return $\overline{R}$. When the entrepreneur faces costly external financing, however, $\partial k / \partial a > 0$, and entrepreneurs experience a higher return on saving in business assets than they could earn on financial assets. The magnitude of that additional return depends on the extent of costly external financing (magnitude of $\partial k / \partial a$, ϕ, and θ_k') and on entrepreneurial ability ϕ. In the presence of costly external financing, entrepreneurs face a greater incentive to save than nonentrepreneurs.[5] This enhanced substitution effect arises not just because of high expected entrepreneurial returns, but because of the joint effect of those high returns on entrepreneurial saving and investment decisions.

Costly external financing also implies that net worth constraints affect selection into entrepreneurship. In the spirit of Lucas (1978), Jovanovic (1982), and Evans and Jovanovic (1989), consider the individual's decision about whether to work for someone else (for wage income) or for himself (as an entrepreneur). The individual would enter entrepreneurship if expected entrepreneurial earnings (defined above) exceed expected wage income, w, where

$$w_{it} = w(x_{it}, e_i) + \eta_{it}, \qquad (3\text{--}4)$$

where x and e denote experience and education, respectively, and where η is an independently and identically distributed disturbance term with a mean of zero and a variance of σ_η^2. In perfect capital markets, assets of potential entrants are not relevant to the selection problem.

Costly external financing distorts the entry decision for low–net-worth potential entrepreneurs. Holding ability constant, entrepreneurial earnings depend on capital invested, k. When external financing is costly relative to internal financing, $\partial k / \partial a > 0$ and $\partial \, prob \, (entry) / \partial a > 0$. Hence one selection problem to analyze is whether initial assets influence the probability of becoming an entrepreneur by the next period, after controlling for household characteristics and work experience, given that a household is not entrepreneurial in one period.

Available empirical evidence corroborates the link between wealth and entrepreneurial financing. Using data from the 1989 Federal Reserve Board Survey of Consumer Finances, Gentry and Hubbard (2000a) show that higher initial assets raise the probability of entry into entrepreneurship, except for the highest levels of initial assets. Such a pattern is consistent both with an explanation based on entrepreneurial ability (in which unobserved variation in entrepreneurial ability among households is correlated with initial assets) and with an explanation based on costly external financing. In Gentry and Hubbard 2000a, the overwhelming importance of the internal financing of businesses supports a role for costly external financing (as pointed out by the authors with reference to the much less diversified portfolios of business owners).

What about the decisions of continuing entrepreneurs? In perfect capital markets, nonbusiness asset holdings should not affect business investment decisions, controlling for investment opportunities. Using different data sets, Evans and Jovanovic (1989), Holtz-Eakin, Joulfaian, and Rosen (1994a, b), and Gentry and Hubbard (2000a) find that a household's nonbusiness assets affect the growth of its business income, inconsistent with perfect capital markets for entrepreneurs. Moreover, Holtz-Eakin, Joulfaian, and Rosen (1994a, b) and Gentry and Hubbard (2000a) find that the probability of continuing as an entrepreneur is positively related to nonbusiness asset holdings.

While such results suggest strongly that entrepreneurial wealth and investment decisions are not independent, the question of whether entrepreneurs save more remains. To the extent

TABLE 3–1

CONCENTRATION OF POPULATION, ASSETS, AND NET WORTH BY INCOME

| | Entrepreneurs' Percentage of | | |
	Population	Assets	Net worth
Overall	8.6	37.7	39.0
Income quintile			
Bottom	0.9	6.0	6.3
Second	4.9	17.8	18.3
Third	7.3	22.4	23.9
Fourth	11.2	28.1	30.9
80–90	13.4	25.2	26.5
90–95	16.9	30.0	29.4
95–99	26.7	43.9	44.7
99–100	56.3	68.6	68.0

SOURCE: Calculations by Gentry and Hubbard (2000a), based on data from the 1989 Survey of Consumer Finances.

that entrepreneurs expect higher returns on funds invested in active businesses than on financial assets, they have an incentive to invest their assets in their business and, if their achievable capital investment is less than the desired capital stock, increase their saving to finance business investment.

Are Entrepreneurs Wealthier?

Although only 8.6 percent of U.S. households match this description of entrepreneurs, this group holds 37.7 percent of household assets and 39 percent of net worth[6] (see table 3–1). Table 3–1 also points up the significant association between business ownership and wealth within income groups.[7] Higher income is associated with entrepreneurship; for example, more than half of the households in the top 1 percent of the income distribution are entrepreneurs. Wealth concentration nonetheless remains within income groups;[8] for example, the 13.4 percent of entrepreneurial households in the ninth income decile own 26.5 percent of that decile's net worth.

Though not shown in table 3–1, both the average net worth and the median net worth of entrepreneurs are substantially higher than the corresponding measures for nonentrepreneurs.

TABLE 3–2
WEALTH-INCOME RATIOS, BY AGE, BY INCOME, AND BY
ENTREPRENEURIAL STATUS

	Average W/Y			Median W/Y		
	All	Entre-preneurs	Nonentre-preneurs	All	Entre-preneurs	Nonentre-preneurs
Overall	4.6	8.1	3.6	1.8	6.0	1.5
By age						
Young	1.8	6.5	1.2	0.4	4.3	0.3
Middle	3.8	6.6	2.9	1.8	5.8	1.4
Old	7.6	11.0	6.5	4.4	11.2	4.1
By education						
Low	3.9	11.8	3.2	1.6	7.5	1.5
Middle	4.1	8.8	3.1	1.5	5.7	1.2
High	5.4	7.5	4.4	2.5	6.0	2.2
By income						
1st quintile	4.5	41.1*	4.2	0.4	14.7*	0.4
2nd quintile	4.3	15.4	3.7	1.5	10.1	1.3
3rd quintile	3.8	11.8	3.1	1.6	5.9	1.4
4th quintile	3.4	9.4	2.6	1.6	4.9	1.4
9th decile	3.7	7.3	3.1	2.4	5.0	2.1
90–95th percentile	4.8	8.3	4.1	2.9	7.6	2.5
95–99th percentile	6.3	10.2	4.8	3.7	5.9	3.3
99–100th percentile	6.1	6.7	5.3	4.5	4.7	4.4

SOURCE: Calculations by Gentry and Hubbard (2000a) based on data from the 1989 Survey of Consumer Finances.
NOTE: Asterisk denotes cells with fewer than 10 households. The average ratios are the ratio of average wealth to average income for each group.

Combined with the information presented in the table, the patterns suggest that differences in how households decide on investing in active business assets and other assets may provide saving through financial assets. Because wealthier households are more likely to be entrepreneurs, these modifications may shed additional light on the saving decisions of the well-to-do.

In contrast to the predictions of simple life-cycle models, wealth-income ratios are also higher for entrepreneurs than for nonentrepreneurs.[9] Table 3–2 (taken from Gentry and Hubbard 2000a), based on the 1989 SCF cross-section of households, presents average and median household wealth-income ratios by age, education, income, and entrepreneurial status. The table reports information for three age groups: the young (younger than thirty-five), the middle-aged (thirty-five to fifty-four), and the old (fifty-five and older). Three education groups (less than high school, high school graduate, and college graduate) and income-quintile breakdowns are also reported.

Overall, entrepreneurs have a median wealth-income ratio four times larger than that of nonentrepreneurs. Similar differences hold for all age, education, and income groups. Wealth-income ratios are consistently high for entrepreneurs of all income levels but rise with income for nonentrepreneurs. For the sample as a whole, wealth-income ratios generally rise with income, consistent with the results for various groups of households of Diamond and Hausman (1984), Hubbard (1986), and Dynan, Skinner, and Zeldes (2000). Combining the high wealth-income ratios of entrepreneurs with the positive correlation between entrepreneurship and income suggests that wealth-income ratios rise with income and may be related to entrepreneurial selection and investment decisions.

Cross-sectional differences tell only part of the story of the economic relationship between entrepreneurship and wealth accumulation. Entry and exit play a significant role in entrepreneurship. Cross-sectional comparisons cannot distinguish the possibility that wealth levels affect entrepreneurial selection from the possibility that entrepreneurship (or the desire to become an entrepreneur) increases saving.

Table 3–3 (taken from Gentry and Hubbard 2000a) compares the median and the average wealth-income ratios in 1982 and 1988 for continuing entrepreneurs, entrants, households that exit entrepreneurship, and nonentrepreneurial households. The tabulations support the association of entrepreneurship with greater wealth accumulation. Continuing entrepreneurs have the highest wealth-income ratio. The median wealth-income ratio for households that exit entrepreneurship falls between 1982 and 1988, but the 1988 value is still substantially larger than the wealth-income ratio of households that have never entered entrepreneurship.

To examine the effects of entrepreneurial transitions on

TABLE 3–3
WEALTH-INCOME RATIOS IN 1982 AND 1988,
BY ENTREPRENEURIAL STATUS

| | Wealth-Income Ratio in 1982 | | Wealth-Income Ratio in 1988 | |
	Average	Median	Average	Median
Stay in	9.01	6.11	11.40	7.91
Enter	3.87	2.50	7.26	3.95
Exit	8.40	6.45	6.43	3.98
Stay out	2.87	1.30	3.56	1.72

NOTE: Averages are the ratio of average wealth to average income for the group.
SOURCE: Calculations by Gentry and Hubbard (2000a) based on data from the 1983 and 1989 Surveys of Consumer Finances.

wealth more systematically, one can use the panel of households to decompose entrepreneurial decisions into entry (ENTRY = 1 if the household is entrepreneurial in 1988 but not in 1982, and zero otherwise), continuing (CONTINUE = 1 if the household is entrepreneurial in both 1982 and 1988), exiting (EXIT = 1 if the household is entrepreneurial in 1982 but not in 1988), and nonentrepreneurial. Such panel data permit a better measure of "permanent" household income by defining *income* as the average constant-dollar value of income in the two survey years.

Gentry and Hubbard (2000a) also provide evidence of the effects of entrepreneurship on wealth accumulation by examining the mobility of the four groups of households in terms of wealth-income ratios and wealth between 1982 and 1988. They find that households continuing as entrepreneurs or entering as entrepreneurs are more likely to move up in the overall wealth-income distribution and wealth distribution.

Do Entrepreneurs Save More?

Again, from the perspective of examining a relationship between entrepreneurship and wealth inequality, it is important to study whether entrepreneurs save more (as illustrated by the earlier analytical example). Using the panel data, one can define the *saving rate* as the change in net worth divided by the average income in the two years (divided by six, the number of years

TABLE 3–4
MEDIAN SAVING-INCOME RATIOS FOR 1983–1989, BY
ENTREPRENEURIAL BEHAVIOR

	Stay In	Enter	Exit	Stay Out	Overall
Overall S/Y	0.165	0.361	−0.483	0.042	0.045
Overall S	9,998	13,547	−20,976	4,671	1,245
Overall Y	61,666	42,001	46,455	24,727	27,619
Median S/Y, by age in 1986					
Young	0.219*	0.387	0.0679*	0.0617	0.072
Middle	0.153	0.358	−0.558	0.0600	0.062
Old	0.244	0.487	−0.431	0.0060	0.0035
Median S/Y, by income in 1982					
1st quintile	−0.622*	1.34*	−1.79*	0.0041	0.0034
2nd quintile	−0.167*	0.128*	−1.88*	0.0203	0.020
3rd quintile	0.352*	0.209	−0.429	0.0664	0.069
4th quintile	0.156	0.387	−0.692	0.103	0.102
9th decile	0.191	0.450	0.0692*	0.0938	0.126
10th decile	0.257	0.454	−0.475	0.113	0.113
Median S/Y, by wealth in 1982					
1st quintile	0.357*	0.423*	n/a*	0.0336	0.0341
2nd quintile	n/a*	0.344	n/a*	0.0609	0.0718
3rd quintile	0.257*	0.445*	−0.0294*	0.0347	0.0445
4th quintile	0.144	0.439	0.0679	0.0953	0.118
9th decile	0.165	−0.182	−0.510	−0.00033	−0.0086
10th decile	0.212	0.407	−0.815	−0.196	−0.330

NOTE: Income is measured as the average income (in 1988 dollars) using household income from 1982 and 1988. Saving is measured as the change in the real value of wealth over the six-year period divided by six. The asterisk denotes cells with fewer than 10 households.
SOURCE: Calculations by Gentry and Hubbard (2000a) based on data from the 1983–1989 Panel of the Surveys of Consumer Finances.

between the two surveys). Defined in this way, entrepreneurial entrants and continuing entrepreneurs have substantially higher saving rates than nonentrepreneurs (see table 3–4); the higher saving rates persist for most age, wealth, and income groups.

Table 3–5 presents median regression results for the wealth-income ratio with controls for entrepreneurship variables, age (A1, A2, and A3 correspond to the younger, middle-aged, and older groups mentioned earlier), demographic vari-

TABLE 3–5
ENTREPRENEURIAL DECISIONS AND SAVING-INCOME RATIOS

Variable	
Constant	− 0.080
	(0.043)
ENTRY	0.352
	(0.029)
EXIT	− 0.285
	(0.023)
CONTINUE	0.169
	(0.023)
MARRIED	0.0471
	(0.021)
GOT DIVORCED	− 0.105
	(0.032)
BECAME WIDOWED	− 0.051
	(0.031)
GOT MARRIED	0.006
	(0.031)
KIDS	0.00351
	(0.00683)
A2	0.0253
	(0.020)
A3	0.021
	(0.023)
UNEMPLOYED	− 0.00497
	(0.040)
OWN HOME	− 0.021
	(0.019)
EDUC	0.00521
	(0.00261)
DEFBEN	0.0522
	(0.0147)
INHERIT	0.157
	(0.0211)
INC21–40	− 0.0354
	(0.0270)
INC41–60	− 0.0191
	(0.0282)
INC61–80	0.0323
	(0.0303)

(Table continues)

TABLE 3–5 (continued)

Variable	
INC81–90	0.0236
	(0.0349)
INC91–95	0.0213
	(0.03998)
INC96–99	0.158
	(0.0364)
INC99 +	0.270
	(0.036)
Adj. R²	0.065

NOTE: Standard errors are in parentheses. Regressions use 4,434 observations, representing approximately 1,478 households. Standard errors are multiplied by the square root of 33 to adjust for the replications. Income in the saving-income ratio is measured as the average income (in 1988 dollars) using household income from 1982 and 1988. Saving is measured as the change in the real value of wealth over the six-year period divided by 6. Meridian regressions are unweighted.
SOURCE: Gentry and Hubbard (2000a); estimates using panel data from the 1983–1989 Surveys of Consumer Finances.

ables, and income (to address the extent to which links between entrepreneurship and wealth reflect a nonlinear relationship between income and wealth). Demographic variables include education (EDUC = number of years of schooling), marital status (MARRIED = 1 if the household head is married in 1982 and 0 otherwise; proxies for changes in marital status: GOT MARRIED, GOT DIVORCED, and BECAME WIDOWED), number of children (KIDS), employment status (UNEMPLOYED = 1 if the household head is unemployed in 1988 and 0 otherwise), home-ownership status, and pension status (DEFBEN = 1 if the household is covered by a defined-benefit pension plan). To capture a possible nonlinear income influence, table 3–5 adds variables, based on 1982 income, corresponding to whether the household is in the second income quintile (between the twenty-first and fortieth percentile, INC 21–40), the third income quintile (between the forty-first and sixtieth percentile, INC 41–60), the fourth income quintile (between the sixty-first and eightieth percentile, INC 61–80), the ninth income decile (between the eight-first and ninetieth percentile, INC 81–90), the ninety-first through ninety-fifth percentile (INC 91–95), the ninety-sixth through ninety-ninth percentile (INC 96–99), or the top 1 percent (INC 99 +). Because inheritances can raise household wealth, I include a dummy variable for whether the household received an inheritance between the two survey years (INHERIT).

As table 3–5 shows, continuing entrepreneurs and entrants have much higher saving rates than nonentrepreneurs, all else being equal. Saving rates are lower for households exiting entrepreneurship than for nonentrepreneurs. Entrepreneurial decisions are also associated with differences in household wealth-income ratios, all else being equal.

The reduced-form implication for saving confirms that entrepreneurs accumulate more wealth—and began their enterprises with more wealth—and suggests a link between entrepreneurship and the concentration of wealth. Still at least three questions remain. First, how much of this change in wealth actually took the form of a change in business wealth? Second, why would already well-to-do entrepreneurs save more? Third, to what extent is this change in wealth explained by active saving?

To answer the first question, both entering and continuing entrepreneurs hold undiversified portfolios. Finally, for both entering and continuing entrepreneurs, the majority of the change in wealth over our sample period is accounted for by changes in business wealth; that is, business saving accounts for much of the saving of entrepreneurs. For entrants as a whole, their increase in business value is 84.7 percent of their total increase in wealth. Among entrants whose real wealth increases by at least 25 percent over the six-year period, the change in business value accounts for 70.8 percent of the increase in real wealth and the median ratio of the change in business value to the change in wealth is 68.7 percent. Among continuing entrepreneurs, the aggregate change in business value over the period is 66.8 percent of the change in aggregate wealth. Because either business value or wealth could fall in value, again we condition on households that experience a greater than 25 percent increase in wealth (49.3 percent of the continuing entrepreneurs). For this sample, the change in business value accounts for 61.6 percent of the change in wealth, and the median ratio of the change in business value to the change in wealth is 43.0 percent. Again these statistics emphasize that entrepreneurs do not grow more diversified as their business grows older. Taken together, these patterns suggest a link between capital-market imperfections for entrepreneurial selection and investment and the saving decisions of entrepreneurs.

Second, how much of the increase in business wealth required investment by the entrepreneur? One possibility is that entrants acquire significant wealth from ideas or luck with little upfront investment. A related possibility is that continuing entrepreneurs become wealthier with little additional investment and perhaps do not diversify because of the illiquidity of business assets. While the SCF does not contain data on investment per se, these possibilities can be considered by examining ex post (that is, 1988) data on average Q for entrepreneurs, that is, the market value of the assets relative to replacement cost. To the extent that a business's value is near unity for an entrant, the change in business value reflects an upfront investment. Likewise, for a continuing entrepreneur, Q values that are not too much greater than unity suggest the presence of investment.

Average Q proxies for active business holdings can be constructed for households in the 1989 SCF. The survey asks detailed questions on up to three active businesses for each household; remaining active business assets are lumped together. To have data on both the market value and the book value of assets, one is limited to using only the separately listed businesses for each household. To calculate average Q, the sum of the households' market value of different active businesses is divided by its share of these firms' book value.

The median Q value for entrants of 1.01 suggests the significance of upfront investment; the interquartile range of 0.99 –2.5 suggests further the significance of upfront investment. The median Q value for continuing entrepreneurs is somewhat higher (1.47) than that for entrants as one might expect, but it is still suggestive of the importance of investment in generating business wealth. Finally, even among entrepreneurial households with annual saving rates over the 1982–1988 period (in excess of 25 percent), Q values indicate the importance of investment (that is, the median Q for entrants is 1.03 and the median Q for continuing entrepreneurs is 1.71). Hence one may reasonably conclude that changes in business value reflect substantial commitments of funds, that is, incremental active saving by the business owner.

Third, while one's intuition may suggest that wealthy households may not need to worry about costly external financing, models of costly external financing depend critically on the household's assets relative to its investment opportunities. A household with $1 million of wealth may easily undertake some projects (for example, a project that requires $20,000 of capital) but may face binding financing constraints for larger projects (for example, a project requiring $5 million of capital). Unfortunately investment opportunities are unobservable to outsiders. Nonetheless the SCF allows comparisons of the distribution of household net worth and the distribution of the size of equity stakes in entrepreneurial ventures. The distribution of net worth serves as a benchmark for household resources; the distribution of the size of existing equity positions proxies for the distribution of possible entrepreneurial investments. Conditional on qualifying as an entrepreneur, the median entrepreneurial equity stake has a market value of $107,000 (the median book value is $60,000) in the 1989 SCF. This venture value easily exceeds the median wealth of $46,960 in the overall sample of households. Indeed the household at the seventy-fifth percentile of the overall wealth distribution would need to invest 73 percent of its wealth ($146,370) in order to own this asset. Obviously most households would require substantial external financing to start businesses.

The more surprising comparison is the financing needs required by existing entrepreneurs who want to move up in the distribution of projects. To own the median equity stake with a value of $107,000, the entrepreneur with the median wealth of $318,940 in 1989 would need a portfolio share of 34 percent. However, for this same entrepreneur to own the project at the seventy-fifth percentile of the distribution of active business assets ($350,000) would require the entrepreneur to invest all his wealth plus borrow 10 percent of that amount.[10] This pattern continues at higher wealth levels. For the entrepreneur at the eightieth percentile of the wealth distribution ($922,800 of net worth) to own the venture at the ninetieth percentile of the distribution of active business assets requires an investment of one and one-half times the household's wealth ($1.38 million). Thus costly external financing may play a role for households that want to enter entrepreneurship and for entrepreneurs at all wealth levels that want to expand.

Conclusions and Directions for Future Research

Focusing on the interdependence of entrepreneurial saving and investment decisions, this chapter reaches three principal conclusions. First, entrepreneurs face different incentives for wealth accumulation from nonentrepreneurs in the presence of costly external financing of business projects. Second, entrepreneurs hold a disproportionately large share of household net worth. Third, although entrepreneurial selection is associated with higher levels of wealth, available evidence also suggests that entrepreneurs have higher saving rates. Hence entrepreneurial decisions are a significant factor in explaining the concentration of household wealth. These findings suggest three extensions for future research.

First, the link between entrepreneurship and wealth accumulation suggests the importance of adding business decisions to the dynamic models of household decisions. Recent adaptations of the life-cycle model stress the importance of uninsured idiosyncratic risk and imperfections of the lending market (see, for example, Hubbard, Skinner, and Zeldes 1994, 1995). The inclusion of margins for entrepreneurial entry, saving, and investment is likely to be useful for explaining wealth accumulation, given the observed concentration of household wealth and the empirical significance for total wealth of business owners' decisions on household wealth accumulation.

Quadrini (2000) has embarked on one research program in this area. He nests a formalization of entrepreneurial choice within an intertemporal general-equilibrium model of an economy of infinitely lived households. The production sector has both large firms and small firms, the latter being "financially constrained" (in the spirit of Fazzari, Hubbard, and Petersen 1988 and Gertler and Gilchrist 1994). Potential entrepreneurs face higher costs for external financing than for internal financing (their own saving). Calibrating the model with data from the

115

Panel Study of Income Dynamics (PSID), Quadrini does relatively well in matching the variation on wealth-income ratios by income class for entrepreneurs and nonentrepreneurs and the distribution of wealth and income for the model economy and the PSID data. Moreover he finds that eliminating the entrepreneurial selection and investment margins significantly reduces the model's ability to explain the observed concentration of wealth and income. The empirical findings presented here suggest that further research along these lines may be fruitful.

Second, a link between entrepreneurship and saving may imply a link between entrepreneurial transitions and old-age dissaving. The discussion thus far focuses on the preretirement saving decisions of entrepreneurs. Higher saving rates for higher-income households are principally a feature of entrepreneurs; not explicitly considered are the dissaving decisions of the very affluent (see, for example, the discussion in Carroll 2000). An emphasis on business ownership may, however, shed light on the "slow" dissaving of the elderly (relative to the conventional life-cycle predictions) observed by some researchers.[11]

Three potential channels could account for slow dissaving by business owners even in the absence of a bequest motive. The first is the possibility of continuing economic profits for older business owners. In this case the relevant "interest rate" in the life-cycle consumption decision is not the expected return on financial assets, but the higher expected returns on business assets; in effect the price of old-age consumption is higher for business owners than for workers. Second, just as information and incentive problems make it costly to obtain external financing, selling off portions of an active business is likely to prove difficult. Third, the capital gains tax acts in part as a transactions tax on exit from business ownership.

Studying variation in rates of dissaving between business owners and nonbusiness owners can shed light on alternative theories of greater relative preretirement saving by higher-income households. For example, if greater relative preretirement saving by higher-income households simply reflects a bequest motive, one would not necessarily expect different rates of dissaving in old age between affluent business owners and affluent workers.

Finally, ascertaining the significance of entrepreneurial decisions in explaining heterogeneity in household wealth accumulation informs analysis of the distributional consequences of tax reform. Consider a switch from a broad-based uniform-rate income tax to a broad-based uniform-rate consumption tax. Relative to the former, the latter eliminates the taxation of the risk-free return to capital (see, for example, Gentry and Hubbard 1997). To the extent that persistent heterogeneity in saving rates is reflected in corresponding variation in risk-free return to capital received by households, a consumption tax may be more regressive than an income tax. To the extent that the heterogeneity in saving rates is associated with capital income in the form of risk premiums or inframarginal returns (as in the case of entrepreneurial ventures), the distributional consequences of a consumption tax are less regressive (Gentry and Hubbard 1997).

Notes

1. The notion that entrepreneurial shares in saving significantly outweigh entrepreneurs' proportion in the population is not new (see, for example, Klein, Straus, and Vandome 1956; Friend and Kravis 1957; and Klein 1960). Friedman (1957) highlights a role for economic rents in entrepreneurial investment decisions and argues that business owners may obtain a higher rate of return from their business than from the capital market.

2. A number of non–life-cycle stories may help explain wealth accumulation by the affluent, including (1) differences in the importance of pensions and Social Security across income groups (see Hubbard, Skinner, and Zeldes 1994, 1995); (2) bequest motives (see Gokhale, Kotlikoff, Sefton, and Weale 1998); (3) precautionary saving (see Hubbard, Skinner, and Zeldes 1994, 1995); (4) differences in rates of time preference (see Lawrance 1991 and Dynan 1994); (5) differences in attitudes toward risk; (6) nonhomothetic preferences (see Attanasio and Browning 1995 and Atkeson and Ogaki 1996); and (7) differences in whether households derive direct utility from holding wealth (see Carroll 2000). Dynan, Skinner, and Zeldes (2000) present evidence suggesting that saving rates rise with income and review some reasons why saving rates may vary with income.

3. Other definitions and data sets are possible, of course; see the discussion and evaluation in Gentry and Hubbard 2000a. We did not use the 1992 and the 1995 Surveys of Consumer Finances because those surveys did not collect data on the book value of assets invested in active businesses. The later surveys also do not have a longitudinal component, which is important for measures of saving.

4. In general, an entrepreneur is unconstrained if $\theta \leq (1 + \lambda)^{1-\alpha} (R/\alpha)$. For constrained entrepreneurs, $\partial k/\partial a > 0$ as long as $k < (\theta a/R)^{1/(1 - \alpha)}$.

5. This effect presumes that costly external financing applies to debt financing as well (see, for example, Diamond 1991 and the empirical evidence in Petersen and Rajan 1994; Avery, Bostic, and Samolyk 1998; and Hubbard, Kuttner, and Palia forthcoming).

6. Gentry and Hubbard (2000a) use a broad definition of *net worth*. Assets include financial assets, the net market value of active and passive business holdings, the value of residential and investment real estate, vehicles, and other miscellaneous financial and nonfinancial assets. Assets include the value in quasi-liquid retirement accounts (for example, 401(k) plans) but not the value of defined-benefit pension plans or Social Security wealth. *Net worth* subtracts mortgage and other personal debt from the value of assets.

7. *Income* includes wages, salaries, business income, distributions from pension plans, interest and dividend income, gains on the sale of stock or other assets, rents and royalties, unemployment insurance, workers' compensation, gifts (including child support and alimony), and transfer payments.

8. The use of current income raises concerns, particularly for entrepreneurs. For example, entrepreneurs in the bottom quintile may have transitorily low income (as in the case of a startup firm) but have high permanent income. Later, when I examine saving decisions, I use an average income measure from the SCF panel to mitigate this problem.

9. The comparison is not exact. The simple life-cycle model predicts that the ratio of wealth to permanent income should be constant within an age cohort. While the life-cycle model comparison is based on permanent income, data restrictions limit consideration to annual income (or, later in the chapter, to average income). Because the variance of transitory income may vary across households, wealth-income ratios using annual income are a noisy proxy for wealth to permanent income.

10. The seventy-fifth percentile of the distribution of book values of equity stakes is $200,000, which would still require almost two-thirds of this household's net worth.

11. Empirical tests of dissaving in the life-cycle model have tested the hypothesis of a hump-shaped wealth-age profile, but results have by no means unambiguously validated the model (see, for example, Mirer 1979). Even after controlling for the effects of permanent income, Mayer (1972), King and Dicks-Mireaux (1982), Diamond and Hausman (1984), Hubbard (1986), and Bernheim (1987) found results only mildly supportive of the basic theory.

References

Aiyagari, S. Rao. 1994. "Uninsured Idiosyncratic Risk and Aggregate Saving." *Quarterly Journal of Economics* 109 (August): 659–84.

Atkeson, Andrew, and Masao Ogaki. 1996. "Wealth-Varying Intertemporal Elasticities of Substitution: Evidence from Panel and Aggregate Data." *Journal of Monetary Economics* 38: 507–34.

Attanasio, Orazio, and Martin Browning. 1995. "Consumption Over the Life Cycle and Over the Business Cycle." *American Economic Review* 85: 1118–37.

Auerbach, Alan J., and Laurence J. Kotlikoff. 1987. *Dynamic Fiscal Policy*. Cambridge: Cambridge University Press.

Avery, Robert B., Raphael W. Bostic, and Katherine A. Samolyk. 1998. "The Role of Personal Wealth in Small Business Finance." *Journal of Banking and Finance* 22: 1019–61.

Bernheim, B. Douglas. 1987. "Dissaving after Retirement: Testing the Pure Life Cycle Hypothesis." In *Issues in Pension Economics*, edited by Zvi Bodie, John B. Shoven, and David A. Wise. Chicago: University of Chicago Press.

Calomiris, Charles W., Charles P. Himmelberg, and Paul Wachtel. 1995. "Commercial Paper and Corporate Finance: A Microeconomic Perspective." *Carnegie-Rochester Conference Series on Public Policy* 41.

Carroll, Christopher D. 2000. "Why Do the Rich Save So Much?" In *Does Atlas Shrug? The Economic Consequences of Taxing the Rich*, edited by Joel R. Slemrod. Cambridge: Harvard University Press.

Diamond, Douglas W. 1991. "Monitoring and Reputation: The Choice between Bank Loans and Directly Placed Debt." *Journal of Political Economy* 99: 688–721.

Diamond, Peter A., and Jerry A. Hausman. 1984. "Individual Retirement and Savings Behavior." *Journal of Public Economics* 23 (February/March): 81–114.

Dynan, Karen E. 1994. "Relative Wage Changes and Estimates of the Rate of Time Preference." Mimeograph, Board of Governors of the Federal Reserve System, September.

Dynan, Karen E., Jonathan Skinner, and Stephen P. Zeldes. 2000. "Do the Rich Save More?" Mimeograph, Board of Governors of the Federal Reserve System.

Evans, David S., and Boyan Jovanovic. 1989. "An Estimated Model of Entrepreneurial Choice under Liquidity Constraints." *Journal of Political Economy* 97 (August): 808–27.

Fazzari, Steven M., R. Glenn Hubbard, and Bruce C. Petersen. 1988. "Financing Constraints and Corporate Investment." *Brookings Papers on Economic Activity* 1: 141–95.

———. 2000. "Investment–Cash Flow Sensitivities: A Comment on Kaplan and Zingales." *Quarterly Journal of Economics* 113 (May): 695–706.

Friedman, Milton. 1957. *A Theory of the Consumption Function*. Princeton: Princeton University Press.

Friend, Irwin, and Irving Kravis. 1957. "Entrepreneurial Income, Savings, and Investment." *American Economic Review* 47: 269–301.

Gentry, William M., and R. Glenn Hubbard. 1997. "Distributional Implications of Introducing a Broad-Based Consumption Tax." In *Tax Policy and the Economy*, vol. 11, edited by James M. Poterba. Cambridge: MIT Press.

———. 2000a. "Entrepreneurship and Household Saving." Working Paper 7894, National Bureau of Economic Research.

———. 2000b. "Tax Policy and Entry into Entrepreneurship." Mimeograph, Columbia University.

Gertler, Mark, and Simon Gilchrist. 1994. "Monetary Policy, Business Cycles, and the Behavior of Small Manufacturing Firms." *Quarterly Journal of Economics* 109 (May): 309–40.

Gokhale, Jagadeesh, Laurence J. Kotlikoff, James Sefton, and Martin Weale. 1998. "Simulating the Transmission of Wealth Inequality via Bequests." Mimeograph, Boston University, August.

Holtz-Eakin, Douglas, David Joulfaian, and Harvey S. Rosen. 1994a. "Sticking It Out: Entrepreneurial Survival and Liquidity Constraints." *Journal of Political Economy* 102 (February): 53–75.

———. 1994b. "Entrepreneurial Decisions and Liquidity Constraints." *RAND Journal of Economics* 23 (summer): 334–47.

Hubbard, R. Glenn. 1986. "Pension Wealth and Individual Saving: Some New Evidence." *Journal of Money, Credit, and Banking* 18 (May): 167–78.

———. 1998. "Capital-Market Imperfections and Investment." *Journal of Economic Literature* 36 (March): 157–86.

Hubbard, R. Glenn, Kenneth N. Kuttner, and Darius N. Palia. Forthcoming. "Are There Bank Effects in Borrowers' Costs of Funds? Evidence from a Matched Sample of Borrowers and Banks." *Journal of Business.*

Hubbard, R. Glenn, Jonathan Skinner, and Stephen P. Zeldes. 1994. "The Importance of Precautionary Motives for Explaining Individual and Aggregate Saving." *Carnegie-Rochester Conference Series on Public Policy* 40 (June): 59–126.

———. 1995. "Precautionary Saving and Social Insurance." *Journal of Political Economy* 105 (April): 360–99.

Huggett, Mark. 1996. "Wealth Distribution in Life-Cycle Economies." *Journal of Monetary Economics* 38 (December): 469–94.

Jovanovic, Boyan. 1982. "Selection and the Evolution of Industry." *Econometrica* 50 (May): 649–70.

King, Mervyn A., and Louis Dicks-Mireaux. 1982. "Asset Holdings and the Life Cycle." *Economic Journal* 92 (June): 247–67.

Klein, Lawrence R. 1960. "Entrepreneurial Saving." In *Consumption and Saving*, vol. 2, edited by Irwin Friend and Robert Jones. Philadelphia: University of Pennsylvania Press.

Klein, Lawrence R., K. H. Straus, and P. Vandome. 1956. "Saving and Finances of the Upper Income Groups." *Bulletin of the Oxford University Institute of Statistics* 18: 293–319.

Lawrance, Emily. 1991. "Poverty and the Rate of Time Preference: Evidence from Panel Data." *Journal of Political Economy* 99 (February): 54–77.

Lucas, Robert E., Jr. 1978. "On the Size Distribution of Business Firms." *Bell Journal of Economics* 9 (autumn): 508–23.

Mayer, Thomas. 1972. *Permanent Income, Wealth, and Consumption: A Critique of the Permanent Income Theory, the Life-Cycle Hypothesis, and Related Theories.* Berkeley: University of California Press.

Mirer, Thad W. 1979. "The Wealth-Age Relation among the Aged." *American Economic Review* 69 (June): 435–43.

Petersen, Mitchell, and Raghuram Rajan. 1994. "The Benefits of Lending Relationships: Evidence from Small Business Data." *Journal of Finance* 49 (March): 3–37.

Quadrini, Vincenzo. 2000. "Entrepreneurship, Saving, and Social Mobility." *Review of Economic Dynamics* 3 (January): 1–40.

Schumpeter, Joseph A. 1942. *Capitalism, Socialism, and Democracy.* New York: Harper and Row.

Wolff, Edward N. 1995. *Top Heavy: A Study of the Increasing Inequality of Wealth in America.* New York: Twentieth Century Fund.

Commentary

Roger H. Gordon

In this chapter Hubbard provides intriguing evidence that entrepreneurs save substantially more and end up with higher wealth for any given income level than the rest of us. Given that entrepreneurs own 37 percent of total assets, therefore, any study of aggregate savings behavior must take into account the more complicated saving incentives faced by entrepreneurs.

Hubbard proposes a particular explanation for the evidence that he reports showing a higher savings rate by entrepreneurs. Following Fazzari, Hubbard, and Petersen (1988), he hypothesizes that entrepreneurs face costly external financing, which makes it expensive to raise external funds to finance needed investment in their firms. As a result, the marginal rate of return that the entrepreneur can earn on new investment could well be high, and the only obvious alternative source of funds would be additional savings by the entrepreneur. The hypothesis is then that entrepreneurs save more to take advantage of this high rate of return. The reported differences in savings rates are substantial and suggest that saving is very responsive to the available rate of return.

The observed high saving rates for entrepreneurs then provide indirect support for the presence of credit constraints, at least among small firms. Such confirmation of the importance of credit constraints is important in itself. To begin with, credit constraints imply underinvestment in small firms and thus too slow an entry by too few potential entrepreneurs. Given credit constraints, the rich have an advantage in becoming entrepreneurs since entrepreneurs need to draw on their own wealth to finance a new business. Credit constraints also provide an explanation for cyclical fluctuations, as argued for example by Gertler and Gilchrist (1994). Such credit constraints could justify lower tax payments by small firms, particularly during business downturns.

In commenting on the chapter, I first examine this explanation for the reported high savings rate of entrepreneurs and argue that it is not quite as robust as it appears. I then compare this explanation with an alternative story, that the high observed value for entrepreneurs' wealth/income is due to underreporting of income arising from income shifting between the personal and the corporate tax bases. Finally, I compare the consistency of the forecasts from these alternative stories with the reported empirical evidence.

Proposed Explanation for the High Savings Rate

Hubbard argues that because entrepreneurs face a much higher marginal rate of return on their savings than the rest of us do, they choose to save more. Of course, if entrepreneurs could borrow freely at the market interest rate to finance any desired investment, then the rate of return that they could earn on their savings would simply be the market interest rate, the same rate of return earned by other individuals. Hubbard argues that due to problems in the credit market, entrepreneurs cannot raise outside funds so easily and as a result face more pressure to finance investments in their firm with their own savings. Plausibly their own saving is insufficient by itself to finance the efficient level of investment; that factor implies that entrepreneurs face a marginal rate of return on their savings above the market interest rate.

While this story is intuitively plausible, I need to point out some qualifications. Hubbard assumes that entrepreneurs face a cost of funds given by $R + \phi(d/k)$ where d is the amount of borrowed funds and k is the firm's capital stock. Keep in mind, however, that competition in the banking sector implies that the expected rate of return earned by the bank on this loan should equal the risk-free rate[1] regardless of the firm's debt/capital ratio—because firms with a higher debt/capital ratio are more likely to default, banks charge these firms a higher interest rate to compensate for the higher default rate. This situation implies

123

that the expected rate of return paid by a firm on its loan is also the risk-free rate regardless of the firm's debt/capital ratio.[2] If entrepreneurs are all homogeneous, the expected rate of return on extra savings by an entrepreneur would then equal the risk-free rate, which implies the same incentives to save as are faced by other individuals.[3]

What does this story leave out? One omission is real costs of bankruptcy. Extra savings lower the risk of bankruptcy and save these added costs. This condition raises the marginal return to savings. With real costs of bankruptcy, though, equity finance would be preferable. As long as venture capital funding is available in competitive markets, the expected rate of return to savings by the entrepreneur would again equal the risk-free rate.

Another key omission from this story is the fact that the bank does not know the quality of the entrepreneur, measured in the paper by θ_i. Not knowing θ_i, the bank has to offer all entrepreneurs the same credit schedule equal to $R + \phi(d/k)$. Competition again implies that the bank breaks even on average, given observable characteristics of a firm, and further implies that for any d/k, entrepreneurs as a group pay on average the risk-free rate on their loans. For any given d/k, high-productivity entrepreneurs pay a rate above the risk-free rate since they have a lower chance of defaulting, while low-productivity entrepreneurs pay less than the risk-free rate.

To determine the expected rate of return to savings for an entrepreneur, we need to know the fraction of high- versus low-productivity entrepreneurs among borrowers at each d/k. If the fraction is the same at all d/k, then the average return to savings for entrepreneurs as a group is still the risk-free rate. (High-productivity entrepreneurs will have a higher rate of return, and the converse for low-productivity entrepreneurs.)[4] In contrast, if low d/k borrowers are more likely to be high productivity, then borrowers with a higher d/k face on average a higher return to savings, since by reducing their d/k they are thereby grouped with a lower-cost set of borrowers. The converse is true if high-productivity borrowers tend to have higher d/k.

The presumption that the rate of return to savings for entrepreneurs is above the risk-free rate on average is then linked to the presumption that high-productivity entrepreneurs have lower debt/capital ratios than do low-productivity entrepreneurs. I do not find this presumption compelling, although it is possible. The optimal k in high-productivity firms is presumably larger than in low-productivity firms. Unless the high-productivity entrepreneurs are proportionately wealthier to begin with, they are likely to have a higher d/k.

The key omission from the above story is credit constraints. As Stiglitz and Weiss (1981) have argued, credit constraints are likely to be a common phenomenon. When the entrepreneur contributes additional funds to the firm as emphasized by Hoff (1994), this contribution can act as a credible signal that the entrepreneur is higher quality and can enable the firm to get more and cheaper credit. Securing such credit does generate a higher marginal rate of return to savings for high-quality entrepreneurs. The point here is simply that Hubbard's claims are more delicate than they may at first appear.

Even accepting the story that entrepreneurs face a higher marginal return to savings, the argument in the chapter also requires a high elasticity of savings with respect to the available rate of return. Past studies estimating the interest elasticity of savings do not provide much support for such a high elasticity. Besley and Meghir (1998) provide a survey of such evidence and find, if anything, that studies report a slightly negative rather than a positive interest elasticity of savings. Of course, the marginal rate of return on savings possibly available to a credit-constrained entrepreneur could be very high, beyond the range examined in these empirical studies. But past evidence does not support the high elasticity of savings with respect to the available rate of return that Hubbard's hypothesis requires.

Alternative Explanation for a High Savings Rate

The hypothesis that problems in the credit market generate a high return to savings for entrepreneurs is not the only available explanation for the high wealth/income and savings/income ratios reported for entrepreneurs, however. Let me develop briefly an alternative story, developed in more detail in Gordon (1998).

This alternative story focuses on the behavior of individuals facing a personal tax rate t that is above the corporate rate τ.

These individuals could save on taxes if they could somehow reclassify their earnings as corporate rather than personal income for tax purposes.[5] While employees in a large corporation can do this to some extent through qualified stock options, the amount of such compensation is limited by statute. If an individual becomes an entrepreneur, however, then he can leave as much income as desired within his firm rather than paying it out as wages or dividends. This retained income is then taxed that year at the corporate rate rather than the personal tax rate. Of course, some personal taxes may be due in the future when the accumulated earnings are ultimately received by the entrepreneur. If this money is obtained by selling shares, for example, then capital gains taxes will eventually be due. Deferral, the lower statutory rate on capital gains, and the write-up of basis at death all reduce the importance of these capital gains taxes. On net, therefore, individuals in high personal tax brackets will commonly save on taxes by setting up a corporation and leaving their earnings within the firm.

So far this story ignores the fact that entrepreneurial firms tend to be highly risky. Normally, new firms generate tax losses during their first few years, given the rapid write-off of the initial investments and the slower development of a sales clientele. During these initial years when the firm had tax losses, the entrepreneur would save on taxes by classifying this income as personal rather than corporate and so would initially organize the firm in noncorporate form.[6] When the firm (hopefully) became profitable, then the firm could be incorporated. As a result, losses would be reported as personal income while profits would take the form of accruing capital gains.

What are the implications of this story for how the observed savings/income and wealth/income ratios change when an individual chooses to be an entrepreneur rather than an employee? When an individual first becomes an entrepreneur, his reported income drops for several reasons. To begin with, new firms generally have losses. If the firm is noncorporate at that point as expected, then these losses reduce reported personal income. When the firm finally has enough profits to justify incorporating, then the entrepreneur has an incentive to leave earnings within the firm. Because these accruing capital gains are not included in taxable personal income, taxable personal income continues to be lower than the income for that individual as an employee.

This chapter partly avoids this possible understatement of personal income by including as personal income the entire amount of business income accruing to the individual, whether or not it is paid out. However, a large fraction of the true income of an entrepreneur in any period can take the form of capital gains, reflecting an increase in future profit rates as a result of the current innovations of the entrepreneur. Had the individual made these contributions as an employee, the reported wage payments should have included the entire present value of the returns to the individual's efforts that year—delayed payment would create a costly barrier to job mobility. In contrast, for an entrepreneur who owns the shares of the firm, this increase in future profits simply shows up as unreported capital gains in the price of the shares in the firm.

What are the implications of this hypothesis for the entrepreneur's savings and wealth? The problem the entrepreneur faces when retaining a sizable fraction of earnings within the firm to save on taxes is that he receives less current income. As a result, his consumption expenditures may need to fall until the income accruing within the firm is eventually paid out. This fall in consumption implies a rise in savings. Here the added incentive to save comes from tax incentives rather than from credit market problems. This fall in savings may be alleviated, however, if the entrepreneur can borrow with his firm as collateral to maintain current consumption.[7] If the value of the collateral is clear and the shares are liquid, then borrowing should be straightforward and imply little or no difference in savings incentives for entrepreneurs relative to other individuals.[8] The composition of wealth will change, however, since the entrepreneur will borrow to finance a high retention rate within the firm. Therefore, most of the entrepreneur's assets would be held within the firm.

The incentive to leave savings within the firm, where the income is subject to the lower corporate tax rate rather than the higher personal tax rate, suggests the possibility of overinvestment in the firm when the entrepreneur's wealth exceeds the efficient capital stock for the firm. Because firms cannot easily invest excess funds in financial assets given the risk of tax penalties, the extra retentions must be invested instead in productive capital.

The size of this tax incentive to become an entrepreneur depends on the difference between the corporate tax rate and the individual's personal tax rate. While individuals in high personal tax brackets save on taxes by becoming entrepreneurs, individuals in low tax brackets face a tax penalty for becoming entrepreneurs—given the variability in entrepreneurial income, losses would be deductible at a low personal tax rate[9] while profits would be taxable at much higher personal or corporate tax rates. Given the progressive personal rate structure, those with high taxable income are much more likely to become entrepreneurs, whether their taxable income is high because of high labor income or high asset holdings. Therefore, this story forecasts unambiguously that entrepreneurs will be drawn primarily from those in the highest tax brackets. When they become entrepreneurs, their reported income falls, though it will still likely remain high relative to that reported by nonentrepreneurs. It is less clear that being an entrepreneur leads to a higher savings rate, although the lock-in effect for accrued capital gains could well imply that they will have a slower dissaving rate when retired.

How do the policy implications of this story compare with those of the credit-rationing story? Credit rationing presumes that because constrained firms invest less than the efficient amount, policies that increase investment can well raise efficiency. Also, too few people become entrepreneurs, given the need to self-finance any investment in the firm. Under the proposed alternative story, those in high tax brackets face too strong an incentive to become entrepreneurs (ignoring information spillovers from entrepreneurs), while those in lower tax brackets face a tax penalty for becoming entrepreneurs. Each individual who does enter, however, could well end up overinvesting, given the strong incentive for entrepreneurs to leave their accumulated savings within the firm.

Comparison of the Alternative Stories

The differing forecasts from these two stories are summarized in table 3C–1. The forecasts from the two stories overlap in many

TABLE 3C–1
TESTABLE IMPLICATIONS OF ALTERNATIVE THEORIES

Entrepreneurship	Credit Constraints	Tax Incentives
Who?	High wealth	High tax rate
Effects on income	Positive	Negative for rich
Effects on savings	Positive	Positive?
Effects on wealth	Positive	Positive?
Portfolio composition	Mostly in firm	Mostly in firm
Observed profit rate	High	High
Capital intensity	Too low	Too high?
Number of entrants	Too few	Too many rich, too few poor

ways and thus limit the range of empirical tests that can differentiate between them. Where the forecasts coincide, they do seem consistent with the data reported by Hubbard. In particular, both stories forecast that entrepreneurs are drawn from those who have high income and high wealth, and both forecast that the wealth of entrepreneurs will be heavily concentrated within their firm.

The two stories do, however, have different explanations for the higher wealth/income ratios for entrepreneurs: one story forecasts that the wealth/income ratio is high because savings rates are higher for entrepreneurs and generate higher wealth, while the other story forecasts that these ratios are high because of lower reported income for entrepreneurs.

Unfortunately, the figures reported in the tables in chapter 3 do not provide any direct evidence that higher wealth or lower income is responsible for the higher wealth/income ratios of entrepreneurs. The evidence therefore has to be indirect. If entrepreneurs have a higher savings rate than nonentrepreneurs, their wealth/income should start at about the same level as for nonentrepreneurs when they first become self-employed, and then grow more quickly over time. Table 3–2 suggests, however, that the difference in the average wealth/income ratios for entrepreneurs and for nonentrepreneurs does not change much with age, a condition seemingly contrary to this forecast.

In addition, the dramatic fall of this ratio for those who exit entrepreneurship is much more consistent with a jump in reported income for these individuals rather than a sudden consumption boom. In particular, based on the figures in table 3–3, assuming income remained constant over time, wealth falls by 37 percent between 1982 and 1988 for those who exit entrepreneurship. Since on average these individuals would have had three years post self-employment, this drop suggests that they are consuming more than 12 percent of their accumulated assets each year—sharply inconsistent with a life-cycle model of savings.[10] In contrast the same change in the wealth/income ratio can arise if entrepreneurs understate their income by 37 percent relative to that of nonentrepreneurs—a situation that seems very plausible.[11] To my mind the large jump in the wealth/income ratio for those who enter self-employment during this period again seems more likely to represent a drop in income rather than a higher annual savings rate. In particular the reported change in median wealth/income for those who enter self-employment can arise from a 37 percent fall in reported income or a 48 percent annual savings rate while self-employed.[12]

In unreported tables, however, Hubbard reports that the income of those who become entrepreneurs tends to grow rather than fall compared with that of nonentrepreneurs. On the surface this evidence contradicts the forecast of a fall in reported income when an individual becomes an entrepreneur. One omitted complication, however, is the fact that the data include as new entrepreneurs only those whose new businesses survive until 1988—given the high failure rate for new businesses, a large fraction of entrants will not survive that long. The expected reported income for those whose businesses survived until 1988 could easily be higher than that for nonentrepreneurs even if the expected reported income for all new entrants were lower. These successful entrants could still be engaging in income shifting, however, which implies low reported income relative to the market value of their wealth.

The tax story suggests that the incentive to shift earnings into the firm should be greatest for those in the highest tax brackets. This forecast is consistent with the results in table 3–5, broken down by income quintiles. Here the reported savings/income ratios are normally higher for those in the highest income brackets. Since these high-income individuals should have better access to outside credit than lower-income individuals, the credit-rationing story if anything would forecast a stronger savings incentive on those with lower income.

Under either story, effects must be quite dramatic. According to the estimates in table 3–4, those who have been self-employed throughout the sample period have 4.5 times their annual income in assets beyond what would have been expected, given their other observable characteristics. If this figure represents an underreporting of income, then reported income must be roughly half of what it would otherwise have been.[13]

Since tax audits suggest that the self-employed underreport their earnings by roughly 40 percent, this figure requires only moderate further underreporting through income shifting. In contrast, if extra saving is responsible for this higher figure, if these entrepreneurs have been in business for, say, ten years on average, and if they earn a 10 percent rate of return on their added savings, then they would have needed to save an additional 26 percent of their income, relative to the amount saved by nonentrepreneurs, throughout this ten-year period.[14]

Based on the evidence reported in chapter 3, I find it more plausible that the reported figures arise from an underreporting of income by entrepreneurs rather than an increase in their savings rate. However, this evidence is largely indirect. Further study of entrepreneurial behavior will be needed to understand better what explains this behavior.

Notes

1. This assumes, for simplicity, that the risks faced by a new firm are independent of market risks more generally.

2. This statement assumes that me-first rules are enforced so that old lenders are repaid in full before any new lender receives anything. In practice, repayment patterns often deviate from me-first priority rules. Competition among new lenders still implies that they have an expected return equal to the risk-free rate, but deviations from me-first rules imply that old lenders can be made worse off because of the new loan. As a result, the net expected cost to the firm of a new loan is less than the risk-free rate.

3. Since loans provide some form of risk-sharing with outside investors, a risk-averse entrepreneur will in fact find the certainty-equivalent cost of the debt to be less than the risk-free rate. If extra savings must replace bank debt, then the incentive to save for entrepreneurs would be less than for other individuals.

4. Low-productivity entrepreneurs cannot simply shift their savings instead into financial assets, where the return is higher, since they would then identify themselves as low-productivity borrowers.

5. During the period of this study, the corporate tax rate on the first $50,000 of income varied between 15 percent and 18 percent, while on the next $25,000 of income it ranged from 25 percent to 30 percent. Most individuals would therefore face a tax incentive to set up at least a small corporation.

6. See Gordon and MacKie-Mason 1993 for further discussion.

7. This borrowing further reduces the amount of income subject to the high personal tax rates.

8. Certainly Gordon and Slemrod (1988) find that high-income individuals are heavily indebted on average; that indebtedness suggests a substantial ability to borrow.

9. Alternatively the firm can incorporate immediately, and losses can be carried forward and can be offset against future profits. Given the high failure rate of new firms, however, this option is unlikely to be more attractive.

10. Perhaps the fall in wealth simply reflects a capital loss arising from the failure of the firm, not yet reflected in asset values in 1982.

11. If the 37 percent fall in the wealth/income ratio between 1982 and 1988 is entirely due to a change in reported income, then income must have dropped by 37 percent when an entrepreneur.

12. According to the figures in table 3–3, these individuals add 1.45 times their annual income to their assets between 1982 and 1988, assuming no change in income. Since on average they would have been entrepreneurs for only half this period, this figure suggests a 48 percent (1.45/3) savings rate during this period.

13. If I represents true income, I^r represents reported income, and W reflects assets, then under this story the estimates imply that $A/I + 4.5 = A/I^r$. Assuming that the forecasted A/I for a nonentrepreneur of the same demographic characteristics would have been around 4.5, then $I^r \approx 2$.

14. If entrepreneurs save an additional fraction s of their income each year, then after ten years the additional savings, as a fraction of annual income, would equal $\int_0^{10} se^{rt}dt$. If $r = .10$ and the added wealth equals 4.5 times annual income, then $s = .26$.

References

Besley, Timothy, and Costas Meghir. 1998. "Tax-Based Savings Incentives." Mimeographed.

Fazzari, Steven M., R. Glenn Hubbard, and Bruce C. Petersen. 1988. "Financing Constraints and Corporate Investment." *Brookings Papers on Economic Activity*, pp. 141–95.

Gertler, Mark, and Simon Gilchrist. 1994. "Monetary Policy, Business Cycles, and the Behavior of Small Manufacturing Firms." *Quarterly Journal of Economics* 109: 309–40.

Gordon, Roger H. 1998. "Can High Personal Tax Rates Encourage Entrepreneurial Activity." *International Monetary Fund Staff Papers* 45: 49–80.

Gordon, Roger H. and Jeff MacKie-Mason. 1993. "Tax Distortions to the Choice of Organizational Form." *Journal of Public Economics* 55: 279–306.

Gordon, Roger H., and Joel Slemrod. 1988. "Do We Collect Any Revenue from Taxing Capital Income?" *Tax Policy and the Economy* 2: 89–130.

Hoff, Karla. 1994. "The Second Theorem of the Second Best," *Journal of Public Economics* 54: 223–42.

Stiglitz, Joseph, and Andrew Weiss. 1981. "Credit Rationing in Markets with Imperfect Information," *American Economic Review* 71: 393–410.

4

The U.S. Fiscal System as an Opportunity-Equalizing Device

Marianne Page and John E. Roemer

In democracies, at least, it is an axiom that taxation should be fair. What constitutes fairness depends on one's theory of fairness or justice. Most Americans subscribe to some version of an equal-opportunity theory of justice. Recently Roemer (1998) proposed a general conception of what equalizing opportunities requires. In this chapter we apply that conception to the issue of income taxation in the United States. In this first section we review this approach to equalization of opportunities and indicate how the tax-and-transfer system of a country can be viewed as an instrument for equalizing opportunities for income. If fairness requires equality of opportunity,[1] then a fair tax-and-transfer system is one that equalizes opportunities for some objective, which arguably should be income. (An alternative but far more controversial objective would be welfare—more controversial since equalizing opportunities for welfare would require, according to our theory, an interpersonally comparable and measurable index of individual welfare.)

The popular idiom formalized by this theory is leveling the playing field: equal opportunity with respect to acquiring income will have been achieved when the playing field has been leveled. What troughs in the playing field should be leveled in its initial state? They are, we propose, the disadvantages that individuals face by virtue of circumstances beyond their control that hinder their capacity to achieve the objective in question—in our case income. Thus the first step in conceptualizing equality of opportunity is to specify the circumstances beyond the control of individuals that are relevant for the problem at hand. We next partition the population into a set of types, where a type consists of all individuals with the same circumstances.

Besides circumstances what influences the value of the objective (in our case income) that the individual eventually acquires? His own effort and the policy that may be applied to intervene in the achievement of the objective, such as tax policy. Effort should be conceived of as those actions and behaviors of the individual that society wishes to hold him accountable for—basically everything but circumstances and perhaps luck. To be explicit, we view the outcome for the individual as a function of circumstances, effort, policy intervention, and luck.

The philosophy of equal opportunity is this: the achievement of the objective by an individual should be sensitive to his effort, not to his circumstances. That is, the equal-opportunity planner intervenes with policy so that the value of the objective achieved by individuals will reflect their effort but will be independent of their type or circumstances. In brief the playing field is leveled by using policy to compensate those with disadvantageous circumstances.

The language of the theory thus consists of five words: *objective, circumstance, type, effort,* and *policy.* There are many ways of computing equal-opportunity policy: given the objective of opportunities that are to be equalized, many decisions must be made concerning what constitutes the relevant circumstances, effort, and set of policies. For instance, one might advocate using educational investment as the appropriate policy to equalize opportunities for income, rather than the nation's fiscal system.[2] One can study the choice of instrument using economic analysis: what is the cost of achieving a given degree of opportunity equalization with respect to different choices of the policy instrument? We do not address that problem here. We ask to what extent the actual fiscal system in the United States equalizes opportunities for income among citizens.

To summarize in another way, equality of opportunity distinguishes between two sets of factors that influence a person's achievement of an objective: circumstances and effort. Such equality seeks to hold the person responsible for the consequences of effort, not for the consequences of one's circumstances. It is thus to be distinguished from the more radical equality-of-outcome view, which would use policy to equalize so far as possible the degree of the objective achieved by all. That view implicitly holds individuals responsible for nothing about their behavior.

The modern conception of equality of opportunity grew out of a lively debate among political philosophers initiated in the early 1970s by John Rawls's *Theory of Justice*. Rawls's theory discussed the distinction between what we have called *circumstances* and *effort*, but his proposal of "maximin primary goods" inadequately captured the idea that individuals should be held responsible for their effort but not for their circumstances. Other important contributions to the debate were Sen 1980, Dworkin 1981a and b, Scanlon 1988, Arneson 1989, and Cohen 1989. A summary of this intellectual history can be found in Roemer 1996, chapters 5, 7, and 8.

We proceed to formalize quickly the proposal outlined above. (An elaborate presentation can be found in Roemer 1998.) Let Φ be the set of feasible policies, with generic element ϕ. Let the types of individual be denoted $1, 2, \ldots, T$, with generic index t. Let $u^t(e, \phi)$ be the value of the objective achieved on average by individuals of type t who exert effort e under policy ϕ. Assume for the moment that effort is a one-dimensional variable, an assumption we later drop.

Under a given policy ϕ, a distribution of effort among the individuals in each type will be forthcoming. Denote the distribution functions (CDFs) of those probability distributions as $E^t(e; \phi)$. Our aim is to use policy to equalize so far as is possible the average value of the objective achieved across types for a given degree of effort. But we do not wish to equalize the objective value for individuals who expended different degrees of effort. If we could do what has just been proposed, we would have implemented the equal-opportunity view: that the degrees of the objective achieved by individuals are sensitive to their effort, but not to their circumstances (type).

But there is a conceptual problem. How can we compare the degrees of effort expended by individuals in different types? The distributions of effort at a policy ϕ will in general be very different across the types. And the distribution of effort in a type is a characteristic of the type, not of any individual. Because we wish not to hold persons responsible for their type, we should therefore not hold them responsible for being in a type with a "bad" distribution of effort. Consequently we should not use the raw effort e that an individual expends as the appropriate measure of his effort for inter-type comparisons, for it is polluted by characteristics of the type-distribution of effort. We must rather find a measure of effort from which we have purged the characteristics of the effort distribution of the type. The obvious choice is to measure a person's effort by the centile (more generally quantile) of the effort distribution of his type at which he sits. This gives us an inter-type comparable measure of effort in which the degree of a person's effort is assessed by comparing him only to others with his circumstances. For example, those at the medians of their effort distributions in different types will be declared to have expended the same degree of effort (as opposed to the same level of effort).

Given the functions u^t and the distributions E^t, we can compute the indirect objective functions, denoted $v^t(\pi; \phi)$, *which give the average value of the objective among members of type t*, who are located at the πth quantile of their effort distribution, when the policy is ϕ. We assert that all individuals regardless of type who have the same index π have expended the *same degree of effort*, although their levels of raw effort are generally different.

Let us now fix the effort quantile π at some number in the interval [0,1]. If we consider only this slice of the population—all those at degree of effort π in the various types—then our equal-opportunity goal would be to choose ϕ in Φ to

$$\underset{\phi}{\text{Max}} \ \underset{t}{\text{Min}} \ v^t \ (\pi; \phi). \tag{4-1}$$

At the solution to 4–1, the average achievement of the objective across types at the given degree of effort, π, is as equal as possible in the sense that *maximin* is the appropriate substitute for *equalize* when equality leads to Pareto suboptimal allocations. (In economics we always substitute *maximize the minimum value* for *equalize all values* to avoid equalizing at a low level.)

Let us call the solution to program 4–1, ϕ_π. If the policies $\{\phi_\pi\}$ were identical for all π in [0,1], then that well-defined policy would unequivocally be the equal-opportunity policy. Unfortunately this will rarely happen. We will in general have a continuum of policies, one for each π. Thus we must take some second-best approach.

The approach proposed in Roemer 1998 is to create an aggregate objective function that gives the objective function of each π slice—namely, the function $\underset{t}{Min}\, v^t\, (\pi,\phi)$—its per capita weight in the aggregate. That is, we give the objective function of each effort centile of the population a weight of 1 percent in the social objective. Thus our equality-of-opportunity objective becomes

$$\underset{\phi}{Max} \int_0^1 \underset{t}{Min}\, v^t(\pi,\phi)d\pi. \qquad (4\text{--}2)$$

We call the solution to program 4–2 ϕ^{EOp}.

Program 4–2 has two parents: Rawls's maximin and utilitarianism. Our program is egalitarian with respect to individuals across types at the same degree of effort but utilitarian with respect to the π slices of individuals across effort levels. It turns out that the optimal policy ϕ^{EOp} always lies "between" the pure utilitarian policy and the pure Rawlsian policy. To the extent that effort is important and circumstances are unimportant, ϕ^{EOp} is close to the utilitarian policy and far from the Rawlsian policy; to the extent that circumstances are important and effort is unimportant, ϕ^{EOp} is close to the Rawlsian policy and distant from the utilitarian policy. Thus Rawls and utilitarianism are located at two poles: the first ignores differential effort and hence responsibility; the second ignores differential circumstances. The equal-opportunity policy strikes a measured compromise, holding the individual responsible for effort but not for circumstances.

We have not thus far referred to *efficiency*. It is intuitively clear that in many cases if we compensate those from disadvantaged types a great deal, we may lower the average value of the achieved objective (income, for us) in society substantially below what it would have been without the compensatory policy, for disadvantaged types may be relatively "inefficient" at converting resources into the objective. (Here, the "resource" is redistributive taxation.) By *efficiency* many people mean the size of the aggregate pie—this is simply measured by the utilitarian objective, which at policy ϕ is

$$\sum_t p_t \int_0^1 \nu^t(\pi;\phi)d\pi, \qquad (4\text{--}3)$$

where p_t is the fraction of the population in type t. Choosing ϕ to maximize 4–3 is a different problem from the equal-opportunity program 4–2; those concerned with the efficiency cost of 4–2 will be concerned with the decrease in the size of the pie in moving from actual policy to the equal-opportunity policy. Expressing this decrease in average income as a fraction of average income under the current policy, we define the efficiency cost of the equal-opportunity policy relative to the present policy as

$$\epsilon = \frac{(\sum_t p_t \int_0^1 \nu^t(\pi,\phi^{pre})d\pi - \sum_t p_t \int_0^1 \nu^t(\pi,\phi^{EOp})d\pi)}{\sum_t p_t \int_0^1 \nu^t(\pi,\phi^{pre})d\pi}, \qquad (4\text{--}4)$$

where ϕ^{pre} is the present policy. We do not ignore this concern with efficiency in what follows.

The Equal Opportunity Objective

Let $\nu^t(\pi,\phi)$ be the level of the objective reached on average by individuals of type t who are at the πth quantile of the effort distribution of their type when the instrument or policy is ϕ. The equal-opportunity program is, as noted,

$$\underset{\phi\in\Phi}{Max} \int_0^1 \underset{t}{Min}\, \nu^t(\pi,\phi)d\pi \qquad (4\text{--}5)$$

where Φ is the set of admissible policies.

Our objective is income. We shall choose Φ to be the set of affine tax-and-transfer policies specified as functions of pretax income. More specifically a generic element $\phi\in\Phi$ is a function $\phi(x)=b\,x+c$ where x is prefisc income and $\phi(x)$ is postfisc income. Presently we impose some restrictions on Φ.

Let $G^t(\cdot,\phi)$ be the distribution function of postfisc income in type t at policy ϕ. We conceive of effort as all those choices and behaviors of individuals not specified by a person's type. In particular, since income is (by definition of *effort*) a monotone increasing function of effort, we may conclude that the individual at the πth quantile of the effort distribution of a type is precisely one who is at the πth quantile of the prefisc *income* distribution of type. (Recall that income is a function of type, policy, effort, and luck. We assume that luck averages out for a large population; then at a given policy and type, income is a monotone increasing function of effort.) Now impose the restriction that all elements of Φ be monotone increasing functions: then the individual at the πth quantile of the prefisc income distribution is also at the πth quantile of the postfisc income distribution. Thus we have the equation

$$\pi = G^t(v^t(\pi,\phi);\phi). \tag{4-6}$$

Since $G^t(\cdot,\phi)$ is a strictly increasing function it possesses an inverse, and we can write

$$G^{t-1}(\pi,\phi) = v^t(\pi,\phi). \tag{4-7}$$

Substituting into 4–5, our objective becomes

$$\underset{\phi \in \Phi}{Max} \int_0^1 \underset{t}{Min} G^{t-1}(\pi,\phi)d\pi. \tag{4-8}$$

Now there is a simple geometric interpretation of 4–8. For simplicity let there be two types of individuals, and suppose their two distribution functions, $G^1(\cdot;\phi)$ and $G^2(\cdot;\phi)$, for a particular ϕ, are as pictured in figure 4–1. Then the integral in 4–8 is simply the shaded area bounded by the vertical axis, the ordinate axis, the line at the ordinate value one, and the left-hand envelope of the graphs of G^1 and G^2.

In figure 4–1 we have drawn the graphs of $\{G^t\}$ as intersecting in several places for purposes of generality. But in actual empirical work the distribution functions of postfisc income of different types will not cross if we restrict ourselves to monotone policies ϕ. Therefore in our application, 4–8 says to choose ϕ to maximize the area above the postfisc distribution function of the most disadvantaged type, bounded by the axes and line $y = 1$.

Finally, we observe (as is well known) that the area above a distribution function is just the mean value of the distribution. Thus the equal-opportunity program in this case requires us to

FIGURE 4–1
INCOME DISTRIBUTION FUNCTIONS FOR TWO HYPOTHETICAL TYPES

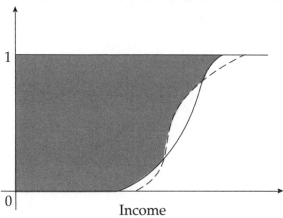

find that policy that maximizes the average postfisc income of the most disadvantaged type.

The Admissible Set of Policies

As we said, we choose the policy space Φ to consist of a subset of monotone affine tax functions. In our initial computations we chose a larger space, namely, all monotone quadratic tax functions, thus allowing for progressive taxation. That choice complicates the computations and adds virtually nothing to the conclusions, for it turns out that both the actual fiscal regime in the United States and the equal-opportunity regimes that we computed are virtually affine. Hence we find the restriction to a domain of affine tax regimes acceptable.

Suppose the present observed policy $\hat{\phi}$ is given by $(\hat{b},\hat{c})$ and the distribution of prefisc income is $\hat{H}$ for the entire sample and $\hat{H}^t$ for type t. Then average postfisc income is given by

$$\int \left(\hat{b}x + \hat{c} \right) d\hat{H}(x) = m, \tag{4–9}$$

while average prefisc income is

141

$$\int x d\hat{H}(x) = \mu. \tag{4-10}$$

The difference $\mu - m$ is government consumption per capita, assuming a balanced budget, which we write

$$\mu - m = (1 - \hat{b}) \int x d\hat{H} - \hat{c}. \tag{4-11}$$

The first restriction we impose on policies is that they be revenue neutral in the sense of holding government consumption constant. Thus for any policy $\phi \in \phi$ where $\phi = (b,c)$, we insist that

$$c = (1 - b) \int x d H(x;\phi) + m - \mu. \tag{4-12}$$

Equation 4–12 gives an expression for c (implicitly, since c is part of ϕ) as a function of b. We may therefore, from now on, specify a policy as b, where it is understood that the associated c is the solution of 4–12.

We insist that φ be monotone increasing in prefisc income, which is the usual incentive-compatibility constraint. This condition simply means that

$$b \geq 0. \tag{4-13}$$

Finally, we insist that the postfisc income of the individual with zero income be nonnegative:

$$c \geq 0. \tag{4-14}$$

Thus Φ is the set of all linear functions satisfying 4–12, 4–13, and 4–14.

Measuring the Degree of Equal Opportunity

At policy b the postfisc income of an individual with income x is $bx + c$ where c is given by 4–12. $\phi(x)$ includes transfers payments that the individual receives but not his consumption of public goods provided by the government. We take a simple approach to allocating government consumption; namely, we assume that everyone consumes his per capita share, $\mu - m$. Thus, we define an augmented postfisc income distribution for type t as $\tilde{G}^t$ where

$$\tilde{G}^t(y + \mu - m;\phi) \equiv G^t(y;\phi). \tag{4-15}$$

We simply add $\mu - m$ to everyone's postfisc income.

Consequently the value of the equal-opportunity objective

at φ is the area above the graph of $\tilde{G}^{t'}(z;\phi)$, where t' is the most disadvantaged type, which may be expressed as

$$\phi(x_{\max}) + \mu - m - \int_{\mu-m}^{\phi(x_{\max}) + \mu - m} \tilde{G}^{t'}(z;\phi)dz \qquad (4\text{--}16)$$

where $x_{\max}$ is maximum prefisc income in type t at ϕ. But this is the same as

$$\phi(x_{\max}) + \mu - m - \int_{\phi(0)}^{\phi(x_{\max})} \tilde{G}^{t'}(y;\phi)dy. \qquad (4\text{--}17)$$

As we have remarked, this is just equal to the average postfisc income of the most disadvantaged type plus $\mu - m$.

Our goal is to measure the extent to which current fiscal policy equalizes opportunities for income. To do so, we compare three situations:

1. the value of the equal-opportunity program without taxation (laissez-faire)—call it V_1
2. the value of the equal-opportunity program at present policy—call it V_2
3. the value of the equal-opportunity program at the optimal solution to the equal-opportunity program—call it V_3

Then we define

$$\nu = \frac{V_2 - V_1}{V_3 - V_1} \qquad (4\text{--}18)$$

as the degree to which present policy equalizes opportunities for income. Note ν will be a number in $[0,1]$, assuming that present policy does equalize opportunity to some extent, compared with laissez faire.

Optimal Taxation

To compute values V_1 and V_3, we need to compute the labor supply responses of individuals to tax policies. We adopt a simple quasi-linear utility function for this purpose. Namely, we assume that all individuals maximize

$$u(x,L) = x - \alpha L^{1+1/\eta} \qquad (4\text{--}19)$$

where x is income and L is labor (α and η are the same for all agents). It is well known that in this formulation η is the labor

143

supply elasticity with respect to the wage. We assume that there is a distribution of wages, F in the population, and F^t in the type t. The wage is the individual's earnings should he work exactly one unit of time, but he may choose to work more or less than that.

Our procedure is to observe the actual relationship between prefisc and postfisc income; for the United States this turns out to be almost exactly affine. Thus we can characterize present policy as $\hat{\phi}(x) = \hat{b}x + \hat{c}$. Then, using the labor supply function, we invert to find the distribution of wages in each type. Then we work with the wage distribution to carry out our calculations of the effect of taxation, with the usual methods of optimal taxation theory.

Our actual individual, of wage w, faces the linear fiscal policy $\hat{\phi}$. Thus he solves the program

$$\underset{L}{\text{Max}}\ \hat{b}(wL) - \alpha L^{1+1/\eta},$$

which gives a labor supply of

$$\hat{L}(w) = \left(\frac{\hat{b}w}{\hat{\alpha}}\right)^{\eta} \tag{4–20}$$

where $\hat{\alpha} \equiv \alpha(1 + 1/\eta)$. Recall that we observe a current aggregate prefisc income distribution of $\hat{H}$ and $\hat{H}^t$ in type t. By 4–20 it follows that the prefisc income, $x(w)$, of a w individual is

$$x(w) = \left(\frac{\hat{b}}{\hat{\alpha}}\right)^{\eta} w^{\eta+1} \tag{4–21}$$

Since x is monotone in w (because $\eta + 1 > 0$), we invert to find the distribution function of wages in type t:

$$F^t(w) \equiv \hat{H}^t(x(w)) \tag{4–22}$$

and, of course, for the aggregate:

$$F(w) \equiv \hat{H}(x(w)). \tag{4–23}$$

We can now easily compute V_1. It is the value of the equal-opportunity program associated with the policy $(b,c) = (1,0)$. Prefisc income and postfisc income are given in this case by

144

$$y = \left(\frac{1}{\hat{\alpha}}\right)^{\eta} w^{\eta+1},$$

and so the postfix income distribution in type t is just

$$G^t(y) = F^t\left((\hat{\alpha}^{\eta}y)^{\frac{1}{1+\eta}}\right). \tag{4-24}$$

Since $\mu - m = 0$ in this case (government consumption is zero), the value of 4–17 is just the average income of the worst-off type.

We next show how to compute the equal-opportunity policy. Labor supply at policy b for a worker of wage w is given by $L(w) = \left(\frac{bw}{\hat{\alpha}}\right)^{\eta}$ and hence prefisc income is given by $wL(w) = \left(\frac{b}{\hat{\alpha}}\right)^{\eta} w^{\eta+1}$. Substituting into 4–12, we can write:

$$c = (1-b)\int \left(\frac{b}{\hat{\alpha}}\right)^{\eta} w^{\eta+1} dF(w) + m - \mu.$$

Now let t denote the most disadvantaged type. Then the average postfisc income of that type at policy b is given by

$$b\int \left(\frac{b}{\hat{\alpha}}\right)^{\eta} w^{\eta+1} dF^t(w) + (1-b)\int \left(\frac{b}{\hat{\alpha}}\right)^{\eta} w^{\eta+1} dF(w) + m - \mu.$$

Consequently our problem is to choose b to maximize this expression. Letting

$$A = \int \left(\frac{1}{\hat{\alpha}}\right)^{\eta} w^{\eta+1} dF^t(w), \quad B = \int \left(\frac{1}{\hat{\alpha}}\right)^{\eta} w^{\eta+1} dF(w),$$

our problem is to

$$\max_b b^{\eta+1}A + (1-b)b^{\eta}B.$$

The solution is given by

$$b^{EOp} = \frac{B\eta}{(\eta+1)(B-A)}.$$

Knowing the equal-opportunity policy, we can now compute the efficiency cost of that policy (4–4) and the degree to which present policy equalizes opportunities for income (4–18).

The Data and Our Typologies

Our analysis is based on data from the Panel Study of Income Dynamics (PSID), a longitudinal survey conducted by the University of Michigan's Institute for Social Research. The PSID began in 1968, when households of a national probability sample were interviewed. Members of those families have been reinterviewed every year since 1968. Thus the PSID contains information on the prefisc and postfisc income of adults in 1990, but because many of these adults were children included in the survey in 1968, it also provides information on the socioeconomic characteristics of their parents. We restrict our sample to the Survey Research Component of the PSID because we want our analysis to be based on a sample that is nationally representative (some necessary sample restrictions prevent our sample from meeting the ideal). Because the Survey of Economic Opportunity component of the PSID includes only low-income households, we do not use it.

Our sample is composed of male heads of households who were between the ages of twenty-five and forty in 1990. We exclude females from our sample because a significant portion of women's work is nonpaid household and child-rearing work; hence our assumption that income is a monotone increasing function of effort is less appropriate for women. Our sample is restricted to household heads because this is the only group for which detailed income/tax/transfer data are available.[3] We chose age twenty-five as our lower age limit because most of the individuals in our sample had completed school in 1990, before we begin to measure their earnings. We chose age forty as the upper age limit to exclude from our sample those who left home at late ages. This exclusion is important because our sample must consist of individuals for whom there is information on parental education. Individuals who are older than age forty in 1990 will have been older than age sixteen in 1968 and therefore will be less likely to have been living at home in 1968.

The PSID contains detailed information on income sources as well as an estimate of family (federal) income taxes. Our measure of prefisc income includes the individual's wages and salaries, labor income from bonuses, professional trades, roomers, gardens, farms and other business practices, and income from assets such as rent or interest and dividends. Starting with our measure of prefisc income we add income from transfers such as aid to families with dependent children, and unemployment and workers' compensation and non–Social Security retirement income. We do not include Social Security retirement benefits (read on). We then subtract the PSID's tax estimate to obtain a measure of postfisc income.[4] We do not subtract Social Security taxes from income. We delete from our sample anyone who is missing income information or for whom a component of income is a major assignment (meaning that a component of income was estimated by the PSID). This leaves us with a sample of 1,196 men.

We do not deduct Social Security taxes paid and do not add any Social Security transfers to income for the following reason. Almost nobody in our sample is at retirement age. If we deducted Social Security taxes paid, no corresponding transfer payment against those taxes would show up in our sample. The simplest solution seems to be to ignore the Social Security fisc entirely for this age group.

To obtain estimates of the actual mapping of prefisc into postfisc income in the United States, we regressed individuals' postfisc income on their prefisc income. Our estimate is that the observed tax-and-transfer policy is $(b,c) = (.790, 3074.6)$; the estimated standard errors are, respectively, .002 and 87.4 The r^2 of this regression is 0.991. Eyeballing the plot shows that linearity is a good assumption.

We next partition the sample into types based on circumstance. We study two different typologies of individuals: one where individuals are typed with respect to their parents' level of education and a second where they are typed according to their race. The first typology is applied by partitioning the sample roughly into thirds, according to whether the head of the household in which the individual was living in 1968 had completed less than twelve years of education, had obtained a high

TABLE 4–1
THREE-TYPE SOCIOECONOMIC TYPOLOGY

η	b^{EOp}	c^{EOp}	ν	ϵ
0.03	.235	18,165	.367	.964
0.08	.544	9,687	.659	.971
0.12	.735	4,392	.951	.991
Present policy	.790	3,074		

school diploma and perhaps some vocational training but no college, or had completed some college. The sample sizes for each of these types are 415, 392, and 389.

We also classified individuals according to their race. For simplicity (and due to small sample sizes) we divide the sample into two types based on whether the survey respondents identified themselves as being white or black. We eliminated from our sample individuals whose primary racial designation was something other than white or black. This reduced our sample to 1,185 men, of whom 69 were black.

The Results

We calibrated the utility function (that is, the value of α) by assuming that the individual of median prefisc income, which is $27,100, supplies one unit of labor time. We carried out the calculations under three different hypotheses concerning the value of the elasticity η.

Table 4–1 presents the results for the typology, which consists of three socioeconomic types, as proxied by the level of education of the respondent's parents. Recall that the effective marginal tax rate is $(1 - b)$. Thus, under the present policy, the effective marginal tax rate is 21 percent. Under the "pessimistic" elasticity assumption, that $\eta = 0.12$, the equal-opportunity policy would raise the effective marginal tax rate only by 5.5 percent. Correspondingly, under that elasticity assumption, present policy achieves equalization of opportunity to a degree of 95 percent. Furthermore, the efficiency cost of implementing equal opportunity would be less than 1 percent. Conversely, if $\eta = 0.03$ (elasticity optimism), then present policy is only 37 percent effective in equalizing opportunities. The optimal policy would

TABLE 4–2
BLACK-WHITE TYPOLOGY

η	b^{EOp}	c^{EOp}	ν	ϵ
0.03	.085	21,649	.273	.935
0.08	.211	17,683	.357	.900
0.12	.301	15,230	.424	.891

institute an effective marginal tax rate of 76 percent. The efficiency cost would be 3.6 percent. Under this policy the lump-sum transfer would be about $18,000.

In sum the degree to which equalization of opportunity is effected by present policy depends massively on assumptions about the labor supply elasticity. This is not surprising. Intuitively, if that elasticity is large, then dead-weight losses preclude our raising taxes to transfer income to disadvantaged types.

Table 4–2 presents the results for the black-white typology. Here we see that, even if $\eta = 0.12$, the present fiscal system achieves equality of opportunity to a low degree, of 42 percent. The optimal regime would raise the marginal tax rate to 70 percent, and the efficiency cost would be high, on the order of an 11 percent diminution in national income. If we are elasticity optimists, then the present system's degree of effectiveness falls to 27 percent, and the EOp solution would raise marginal effective tax rates to more than 90 percent.

It is perhaps elucidating to see the postfisc distributions of income, by type, in the various regimes. Figure 4–2 presents the postfisc distributions of income of the three socioeconomic types under the present regime. Figures 4–3 and 4–4 present the postfisc income distributions by type for the socioeconomic typology, in the laissez-faire and equal-opportunity regimes, respectively, when $\eta = 0.12$. The postfisc income distributions by type are closest together under the equal-opportunity regime: perfect equality of opportunity would hold when the three income distributions by type were identical.

Figures 4–5 through 4–8 present the laissez-faire and equal-opportunity income distributions by type for the cases $\eta = 0.08$ and $\eta = 0.03$. Finally, figures 4–9 through 4–15 present

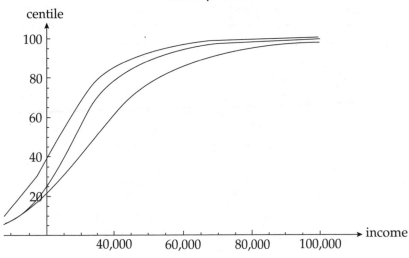

FIGURE 4–2

DISTRIBUTIONS OF POST-FISC INCOME BY TYPE, OBSERVED POLICY

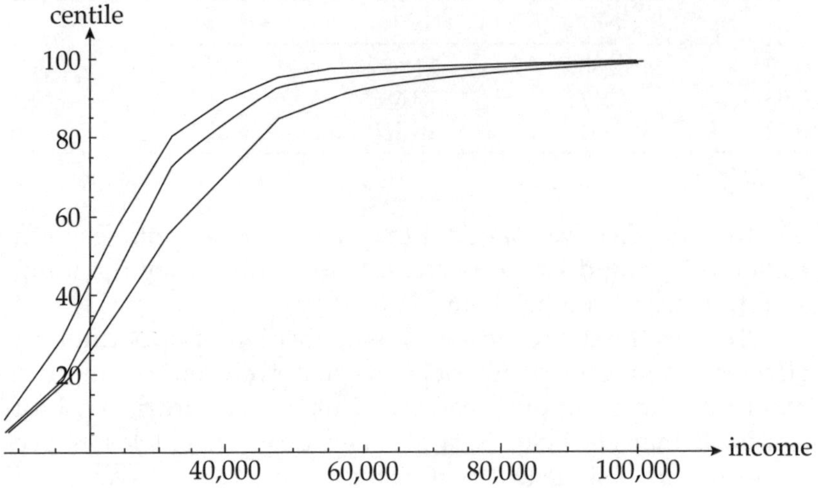

FIGURE 4–3

DISTRIBUTIONS OF INCOME BY TYPE, LAISSEZ-FAIRE REGIME, WHEN $\eta = 0.12$

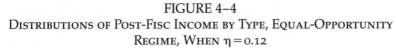

FIGURE 4–4
DISTRIBUTIONS OF POST-FISC INCOME BY TYPE, EQUAL-OPPORTUNITY
REGIME, WHEN η = 0.12

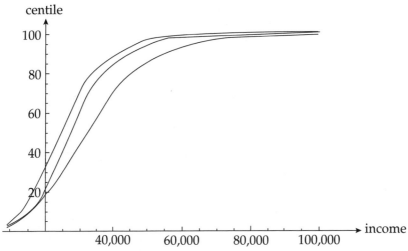

FIGURE 4–5
DISTRIBUTIONS OF INCOME BY TYPE, LAISSEZ-FAIRE REGIME,
WHEN η = 0.08

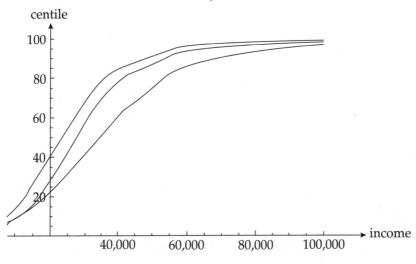

151

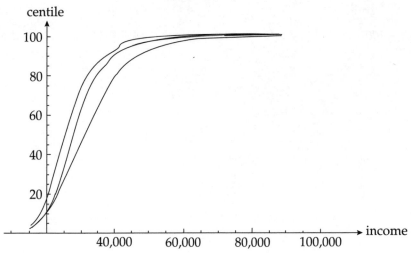

FIGURE 4–6
DISTRIBUTIONS OF POST-FISC INCOME BY TYPE, EQUAL-OPPORTUNITY
REGIME, WHEN η = 0.08

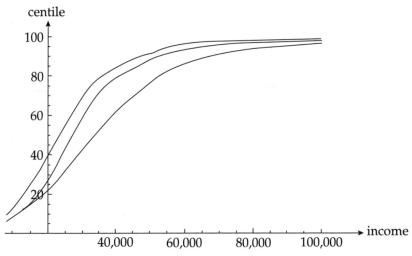

FIGURE 4–7
DISTRIBUTIONS OF INCOME BY TYPE, LAISSEZ-FAIRE REGIME,
WHEN η = 0.03

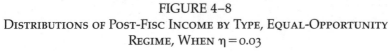

FIGURE 4–8
DISTRIBUTIONS OF POST-FISC INCOME BY TYPE, EQUAL-OPPORTUNITY
REGIME, WHEN η = 0.03

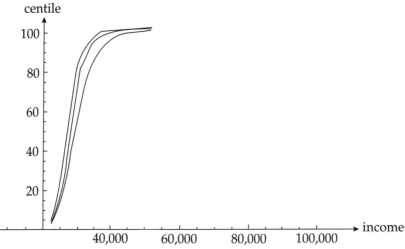

the analogous postfisc income distributions for the black-white typology.

Final Discussion

Two main observations emerge clearly from this exercise:

1. The extent to which the current tax-and-transfer system equalizes opportunities for income among socioeconomically defined types in the United States depends dramatically on one's view about the degree of labor-supply elasticity with respect to the wage.

2. The extent to which the current tax-and-transfer system equalizes opportunities for income depends dramatically on one's definition of the relevant circumstances: while the current regime may do quite well in leveling the playing field with respect to troughs and mounds associated with socioeconomic status, it does badly in leveling the playing field with respect to troughs due to racial background.

One way of putting observation 2 is that the economic disadvantage associated with being black in the United States would be

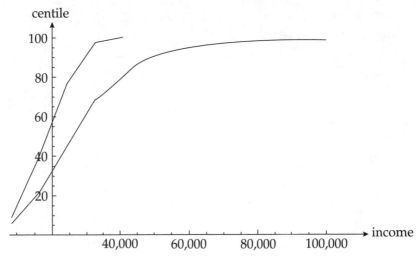

FIGURE 4–9
DISTRIBUTIONS OF POST-FISC INCOME, BY TYPE, OBSERVED POLICY,
BLACK-WHITE TYPOLOGY

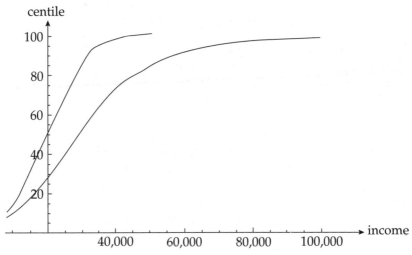

FIGURE 4–10
DISTRIBUTIONS OF INCOME, LAISSEZ-FAIRE REGIME, WHEN $\eta = 0.12$,
BLACK-WHITE TYPOLOGY

FIGURE 4–11
DISTRIBUTIONS OF POST-FISC INCOME, EQUAL-OPPORTUNITY REGIME,
WHEN η = 0.12, BLACK-WHITE TYPOLOGY

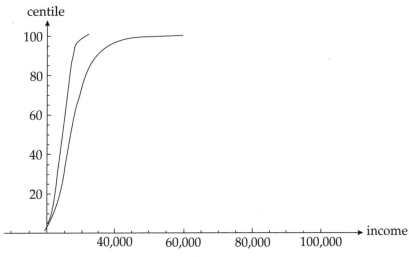

FIGURE 4–12
DISTRIBUTIONS OF INCOME, LAISSEZ-FAIRE REGIME, WHEN η = 0.08,
BLACK-WHITE TYPOLOGY

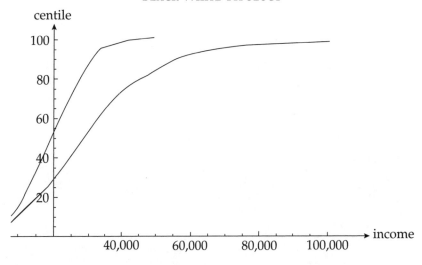

155

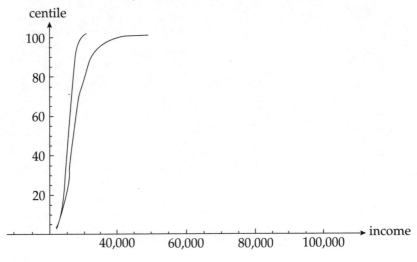

FIGURE 4–13
DISTRIBUTIONS OF POST-FISC INCOME, EQUAL-OPPORTUNITY REGIME,
WHEN η = 0.08, BLACK-WHITE TYPOLOGY

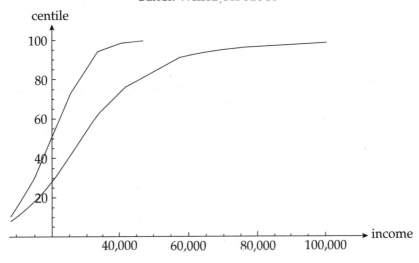

FIGURE 4–14
DISTRIBUTIONS OF INCOME, LAISSEZ-FAIRE REGIME, WHEN η = 0.03,
BLACK-WHITE TYPOLOGY

FIGURE 4–15
DISTRIBUTIONS OF POST-FISC INCOME, EQUAL-OPPORTUNITY REGIME,
WHEN η = 0.03, BLACK-WHITE TYPOLOGY

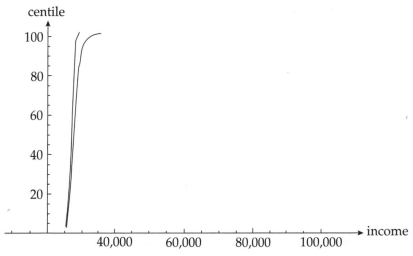

only slightly rectified by compensating individuals with regard to the socioeconomic status of the family in which they grew up. This factor suggests that if compensatory programs are to be successful in rectifying inequality of economic opportunity in our society, they must be predicated on racial as well as socio-economic characteristics of the individuals targeted.

We wish to reemphasize that our analysis has taken perhaps the most conservative possible view of what constitutes effort. We have declared that a person's degree of effort is perfectly calibrated by observing the quantile of the income distribution of his type. Thus family connections, luck, and so on, which may cause income to be higher than otherwise, are here implicitly classified as *effort*. Were we to define *effort* explicitly to consist of measurable behaviors of certain kinds such as the number of years of school attended, we would undoubtedly calculate that present tax-and-transfer policy is less efficient with regard to our goal than is indicated in tables 4–1 and 4–2. That is to say, we should view the values of v reported in those tables as upper bounds on the true values.

Finally, as we wrote in the introduction, other instruments, such as compensatory educational programs, may be both more effective with regard to equalizing opportunities for income, and more politically acceptable, than the tax-and-transfer system. (In fact, with regard to political acceptability, this is almost surely the case.) Nevertheless, it is interesting to know the extent to which our fiscal system equalizes opportunities for income, if, as we said, such equalization is an important component of fairness.

Notes

1. See Young (1994, chapter 6), for a quite different discussion of how income taxation might embody fairness.

2. See Betts and Roemer 1998, in which we compute the distribution of educational finance that would equalize opportunities among citizens for the acquisition of wage-earning capacity.

3. Detailed income/tax/transfer data are also available for wives, but we have restricted our sample to men only.

4. For married couples, the PSID provides an estimate of the joint taxes paid by husbands and wives. We calculate the husband's tax share by multiplying total taxes by the share of the couple's income associated with the husband.

References

Arneson, R. 1989. "Equality and Equality of Opportunity for Welfare." *Philosophical Studies* 56: 77–93.

Betts, J., and J. E. Roemer. 1998. " Equalizing Opportunity through Educational Finance Reform." Working paper, Department of Economics, University of California, Davis, and University of California, San Diego.

Cohen, G. A. 1989. "On the Currency of Egalitarian Justice." *Ethics* 99: 906–44.

Dworkin, R. 1981a. "What Is Equality? Part 1: Equality of Welfare." *Philosophy and Public Affairs* 10: 185–246.

———. 1981b. "What Is Equality? Part 2: Equality of Resources." *Philosophy and Public Affairs* 10: 283–345

Rawls, J. 1971. *A Theory of Justice.* Cambridge: Harvard University Press.

Roemer, J. E. 1996. *Theories of Distributive Justice.* Cambridge: Harvard University Press.

———. 1998. *Equality of Opportunity.* Cambridge: Harvard University Press.

Scanlon, T. 1988. "The Significance of Choice." In *The Tanner Lectures on Human Values,* vol. 8, edited by S. McMurrin. Salt Lake City: University of Utah Press.

Sen, A. 1980. "Equality of What?" In *The Tanner Lectures on Human Values,* edited by S. McMurrin. vol. 1. Salt Lake City: University of Utah Press.

Young, P. 1994. *Equity.* Princeton: Princeton University Press.

Commentary

Casey B. Mulligan

Optimal and Actual Tax Incidence

The Page and Roemer essay is concerned with quantitatively computing the "fair" or "just" distribution of income and comparing that distribution (and the fiscal policies required to achieve it) with the actual distribution of income and actual fiscal policies. The purpose of the comparison is partly to show voters, intellectuals, and whoever else is interested how actual policy deviates from what it ought to be. But the authors also believe that the voters and intellectuals have the basic idea of what policy ought to be and, in democracies at least, actual policies qualitatively coincide with the optimal policies that they compute. Hence, with the qualitative nature of optimal policy widely understood (namely, taxing the rich to finance welfare increases for the poor), their job is to offer quantitative computations of optimal policy and show how they compare with quantitative descriptions of actual policy. This part of their paper is an analysis of tax and spending incidence, in the spirit of Pechman (1985). To summarize, they conclude that actual U.S. policy is progressive—but not progressive enough.

Fiscal and Regulatory Policy as a Package Deal

I believe that the following simple programming problem better represents what voters and intellectuals want from government policies. At first glance, my programming problem may seem basically similar to that of Page and Roemer. But where they differ, many readers will agree that my problem is the more appropriate one. What will be even more clear is that my programming problem can easily represent more of what governments do.

A first impression that my departures from Page and Roemer are just in the details is deceiving. I will solve the programming problem and show how optimal policies require regressive regulations—and I mean *regressive* in the strong sense of the word (Jesse Jackson says it less ambiguously: "reverse Robin Hood"). Progressive fiscal policies may be used and detected by the tax incidence methods of Page, Roemer, Pechman, and others, but I will show that they are only a reaction to the regressive regulations rather than an indicator of a progressive government.

Let's take a look at the model of Mulligan and Philipson (1999). It has two equally sized groups, rich and poor (denoted with the superscripts r and p). Obviously the poor care about themselves, but the rich care about them too. However, the rich are not particularly interested in lump-sum transfers that might be spent by the poor on whatever they choose. Instead the rich prefer the poor to obtain "high-quality" schooling, "high-quality" medical services, retirement wealth, and other "merit goods" rather than tobacco products, alcohol, vacations, "low-quality" medical care, "low-quality" schooling, television viewing, pornography, and other nonmerit goods.

This basic idea can be expressed mathematically by displaying utility functions for rich and poor people. The utility of the rich V^r depends on their enjoyment of their own consumption $u^r(c^r, m^r)$ and their enjoyment of the consumption of merit consumption by the poor $v(m^p)$. The utility of the poor V^p depends only on their enjoyment of their own consumption $u^p(c^p, m^p)$.

$$V^r = u^r(c^r, m^r) + v(m^p), \quad u_c^r, u_m^r, v' > 0 \qquad (4C\text{–}1)$$
$$V^p = u^p(c^p, m^p), \quad u_c^p > 0$$

The quantity consumed of merit goods is denoted m, and the consumption of other goods, c. Subscripts denote partial derivatives. The "altruism" of the rich can be seen mathematically as $\partial V^r / \partial m^p > 0$, but the merit–good nature of their altruism is seen in the unwillingness of the rich to substitute c^p for m^p—as compared with the willingness of the poor to make such a substitution.

Now consider a laissez-faire allocation, where rich and poor are endowed with incomes y^r and $y^p < y^r$, both types of goods are produced at constant marginal cost 1, and each type chooses his own consumption. The laissez-faire allocation satisfies:

laissez-faire allocation

$$1 = \frac{u_m^r}{u_c^r} = \frac{u_m^p}{u_c^p} \qquad (4C\text{--}2)$$

Now consider a planner's problem for this economy. The planner chooses consumption for all agents, taking as his objective a weighted average of the utilities of both types of agents.

efficient allocation

$$\max_{c^r,\, m^r,\, c^p,\, m^p} \alpha V^r + (1 - \alpha)V^p$$

$$\text{s.t. } c^r + m^r + c^p + m^p \le y^r + y^p \qquad (4C\text{--}3)$$

$$=> 1 = \frac{u_m^r}{u_c^r} = \frac{u_m^p}{u_c^p} + \frac{\alpha}{1 - \alpha} \frac{v'}{u_c^p} > \frac{u_m^p}{u_c^p}$$

The laissez-faire allocation is inefficient because it equates the merit-nonmerit marginal rate of substitution of the poor with the selfish merit-nonmerit marginal rate of substitution of the rich, that is, the MRS computed from the function u^r. In other words the poor allocate their resources between merit and nonmerit goods without concern for the preferences that the rich have for the allocation of the poor's resources.[1] A lump-sum payment from the rich to the poor and a reallocation of the poor's consumption toward merit goods could make both the rich and the poor better off. But the inefficiency remains when lump-sum transfers are made from the rich to the poor without requiring the poor to reallocate their consumption.

The inefficiency can be seen graphically with respect to a utility possibility frontier (UPF), as shown in figure 4C–1. The UPF is the solid curve and graphs the feasible combinations of (V^p, V^r) attained from solutions to the planner's problems indexed by $\alpha \in [0,1]$. The allocation A, representing laissez faire, is on the interior of the utility possibility set because of the inefficiency noted above.

Suppose that the laissez-faire allocation produces $m^r > m^p$.[2] Now, as a substitute for the planner, consider introducing a regulation or "mandate" $\underline{m}$ requiring all to consume $m > \underline{m}$. This is

FIGURE 4C–1

Utility Possibility Frontier in a Merit Good Economy

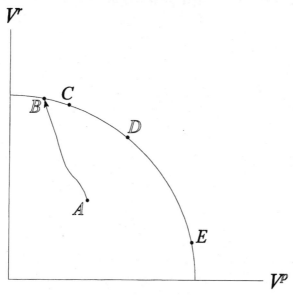

an "unfunded mandate" in the sense that no resources are taken from or given to either the rich or poor. If $\underline{m}$ is less than or equal to the merit consumption by the poor under the laissez-faire regime, then the allocation is the same under the mandate and denoted A in figure 4C–1. As we increase $\underline{m}$, the poor consume more m^p and less c^p, and the resulting allocation moves to the northwest in figure 4C–1. Small increases in $\underline{m}$ make the rich better off because, from their point of view, too little m^p is consumed at A. Increases in $\underline{m}$ make the poor worse off because their choices are further constrained. If we rule out the case where the rich would prefer to see $m^p > m^r$, then an unfunded mandate achieves a Pareto optimum such as the allocation B in the diagram.

The unfunded mandate achieving B is "regressive" because it makes the rich better off and the poor worse off according to their own preferences.

In addition to regulating, suppose that the government makes lump-sum transfers from rich to poor. Then the government can combine the transfer with a mandate to achieve allocations on the *UPF* to the southeast of *B*. The transfer is from rich to poor—and hence might be called "progressive" by Page and Roemer. But the mandate-transfer combination could well be regressive in the sense of making the poor worse off relative to laissez faire—as is the case with allocation *C* in figure 4C–1. An important quantitative question about a mandate-transfer combination is whether the transfer is enough to compensate the poor for submitting to regulation.

Consider an example: Medicare. Because Medicare taxes workers and uses those taxes to purchase medical goods and services, Medicare can be interpreted as a mandate: a program requiring citizens to spend a minimum amount of their resources on medical care. Medicare (perhaps when combined with Medicaid) may also have an income-transfer component— the rich may pay more in taxes than they receive in benefits while the poor receive more in benefits than they pay in taxes[3]— but the important quantitative question is whether the transfer is enough to compensate the poor for submitting to the mandate.[4]

Conclusions

Implicit in Page and Roemer's acceptance of existing policy instruments as a means for redistribution (and explicit in some of Roemer's other work) is a paternalistic rejection of the typical economist's practice of respecting the preferences of others. In the paternalistic view, the poor are better off at an allocation like *C* for two reasons: they are getting a subsidy and they are being forced to do what is "good for them." Paternalism may or may not be "just," but Philipson and I would like to bring paternalism to the foreground of tax incidence analysis rather than leaving it hidden from the unsuspecting individualist.

The merit goods model suggests that progressive fiscal policy is only a byproduct of another policy objective, namely, to distort the consumption of the poor. The merit-good model is not my preferred model of government, but this lesson from it is quite general. Whether or not the merit-good model is correct, I find it hard to accept that "Robin Hood" type redistribution is or ever will be a primary policy objective. The more realistic view finds that government policy is about other things—taking

from the young and giving to the old, taking from the urban and
giving to the rural, discouraging nonmerit consumption, taking
from nonveterans and giving to veterans, and maybe even providing public goods—and that any redistribution from rich to
poor is just an accidental byproduct of these other policies.
Being explicit about this process would not only facilitate an
understanding of the causes and effects of policy, but maybe
even help the poor.

Notes

1. Certainly a variety of other ways can model the same inefficiency. A
Good Samaritan problem is one possibility, with the poor choosing c^p first and
then choosing m^p while knowing all along that the rich will offer to help if
resources available for m^p are inadequate. Another possibility is to allow the
rich to have some concern for c^p, as long as the rich and poor have different
willingness to substitute c^p for m^p. Yet another possibility is to allow for positive
(negative) externalities of m^p (c^p) in the budget constraint of the rich. All that
matters for the main results is that laissez faire leads to a misallocation of
resources between c^p and m^p.

2. A sufficient condition has identical functions u^p and u^r for which merit
goods are normal.

3. McClellan and Skinner (1997) question this for Medicare.

4. See Mulligan and Philipson (1999) for a review of the literature showing
that the poor do in fact prefer to spend less on medical care than provided to
them by Medicare (and Medicaid).

References

McClellan, Mark, and Jonathan Skinner. 1997. "The Incidence of Medicare." NBER Working Paper 6013. April.

Mulligan, Casey B., and Tomas Philipson. 1999. "Regulation and the
Income Incidence of Government Policy." Working paper, University of Chicago. January.

Pechman, Joseph. 1985. *Who Paid the Taxes 1965–85*. Washington, D.C.:
Brookings Institution.

5
Balanced-Budget Restraint in Taxing Income from Wealth in the Ramsey Model

Edmund S. Phelps

The past two decades mark a swing in Western political economy back to several traditional values. Welfare reform in the Netherlands and the United States clearly rests on the principle of individual responsibility: the moral premise that those who choose not to help themselves are not entitled to help from the state and might even do better without it. The wave of privatization, sweeping from the United Kingdom to the Mediterranean and points east, rests on the value of capitalism, the premise that people need and seek the stimulation and progress achievable by private enterprise.

When it comes to individual responsibility and private enterprise, I am fully on board. My book *Rewarding Work* would extend and intensify the integration of the less-advantaged in the capitalist economy—as much to buttress capitalism against its opponents as to widen the opportunity for self-support and personal growth that capitalism can uniquely provide. Yet some new policy talk deals with more than individualism or capitalism. Whether these added precepts are on solid ground is unclear.

The new proposals regarding tax policy offer an obvious example. Is a budgetary surplus looming up? Cut taxes—surpluses are anathema, deficits are good (as discussed in the editorial "King Solomon's Tax Cut," *Wall Street Journal*, July 27, 1998). Is there wage inequality? Cut the taxes of those whose incomes are low (Kemp 1998). Slow growth of productivity? Cut tax rates to spur investment and entrepreneurship (Reynolds

1998). A slump coming? Cut taxes to boost incentives to supply and demand labor (Foster 1998) (also discussed in the editorial "Tax Cuts for Growth," *Wall Street Journal*, October 16, 1998). Pragmatists advocate such policies simply on the empirical belief that all current tax rates are higher than any reasonable cost-benefit analysis can justify, and hence the best tactic is to cut any tax whenever possible as long as the optimum is not remotely in sight. These pragmatists do not apparently have a conception of some "best" tax policy to which society could gravitate.

A few advocates of new tax policies have views on fiscal structure: the best tax mix and budgetary balance. For Robert Hall (and Steve Forbes)[1] the right tax mix would exempt interest, dividends, and capital gains, while for Jude Wannicki (1978) fiscal reform must emphasize lightening the burden on labor. In response to a structural slump—some nonmonetary shock (foreign or domestic) imparting a contractionary impulse directly to the real economy—Robert Barro (1974) favors steadiness in tax rates to allow the budget balance to move only into a passive deficit, while Robert Mundell (1971) favors an activist response of cutting marginal tax rates to insulate or cushion economic activity from the contractionary force. But these views are not visibly derived from models of taxation for some kind of social optimum—although conceivably some can be grounded in such a model.

Many members of the new fiscal movement conversely invoke as their standard what they call the ideal of the free market. Yet no delineation of the free-market tax structure and the free-market budget deficit has ever appeared, and its existence is doubtful. The free market cannot serve as the basis for fiscal policy: the notion of the free market is fatally problematic. Some important truths *do* reside among the propositions of free-market thought: there is a presumption that in general the freedom to buy and sell, to borrow and lend is crucial for prosperity. (Laws inhibiting capital mobility and the flow of goods will typically cause welfare losses for which the gainers cannot compensate the losers.) And individual freedoms of various kinds are a valuable restraint on government in general. (Free capital flows can be useful as a discipline on governments tempted to get out of jams or to pander to populist demands by raiding profits or enterprises; free trade is one of the best disciplines available to impede the organization of interest groups.) The trouble is that some political economists—Friedrich Hayek and Milton Friedman among them—so extended the meaning of the term *free market* that it has become a neologism for laissez faire. And laissez faire cannot offer a coherent basis for fiscal policy: the deficit and the tax mix.

In its laissez-faire conception the only perfectly free market is one without any government regulations, expenditures, and subsidies at all. But without some interventions there could be no market at all: government, hence some tax revenue, is needed to support well-running markets and to defend property. (Seeing this, Hayek makes concessions driven by common sense—even concessions, such as the safety net, that are *not* necessary for markets to function.) Capitalism could not survive either: today's technologies demand expensive employment subsidies to ensure that the capitalist economy can offer self-support through full-time earnings to a broad-based workforce. If an economy were to realize the ideal of the free market, it would have only nomadic producer-traders: nomads because they would have to keep moving to avoid predators and independent traders because, deprived of contract enforcement and regulation, their exchanges would be confined to self-enforcing contracts. Tough-minded, yet typically rather expensive, interventions in the marketplace fortunately benefit virtually everyone—or would if enacted.

A "social welfare" approach to optimum fiscal structure seems to have no alternative. The main basis of that approach is still the neoclassical public finance theory.[2] Taking up this approach and using what must be the simplest model fit for the purpose, I want to study the "optimal" *mix* of the tax rates on wealth and wages, given one or more requirements for tax revenue, notably, the social entitlements of the welfare state. The bulk of this analysis supposes that the government adheres to the policy of a continuously balanced budget, but I comment at the end on the optimality of a budgetary *surplus*. My main aim is to investigate whether taxation of the income from private savings deserves to be the sacred cow that policy discussions make it. For decades in most Western countries labor has generally paid high tax rates while in practice the income from wealth pays at a far lower rate. Recently the European Commission under the leadership of Mario Monti has taken up the challenge of devising reporting requirements that would reduce the enormous interest income that escapes taxation by going outside national borders. Clearly such efforts cannot succeed unless they are widely multilateral. But neither can they succeed unless and until a case is made for taxing the income from wealth at rates comparable to (and perhaps exceeding) tax rates on earned income.

A related aim is to examine the response of the mix of tax rates to changes in the current stock of private wealth and in the constant commitments of the government. If the government has committed itself to a certain social entitlement into the future, would the effects of financing it through taxing labor on incentives to work and to save then create a case for taxing the income from private wealth? If the state borrowed for a time before finally adopting the policy of tax financing, does the inherited government debt push up only the tax rate on labor? As net wealth grows, what levels do the tax rates on wage and nonwage income approach?

These questions I addressed before in a series of papers with Janusz Ordover in which we postulated a sequence of two-period overlapping generations of worker-savers operating in a closed economy (Ordover and Phelps 1975, 1979). It turned out that if the government were *not* bound by a balanced budget and if existing wealth held by the elderly were exempt from income taxation, our results sustained the classic proposition of Corlett and Hague (1953): the income from wealth should be subject to a positive tax rate if and only if future consumption is more complementary to present work effort than present consumption is. Conversely, if the government is bound to balance the budget, the taxation of income from wealth cannot generally be excluded; but the conditions for a positive tax rate on the income from wealth did not look broad or intuitive. However, this life-cycle model had no bequests, not even by a subset of the population. If the desire to bequeath is too important to omit, the subject of the optimal tax mix in intertemporal models needs reopening.[3]

The theoretical setting for the analysis here is an extension of the model of national saving and national effort—wealth accumulation and labor input in today's terminology—built some seventy years earlier by the British philosopher and amateur economist Frank Ramsey (1928). The legendary status of that contribution is well earned: in one paper he introduced the single agent, the infinite horizon, the aggregate production function, and more. One extension made to this basic model is the introduction of a fixed entitlement to a cash income: a stylized representation of the returns from social wealth. The other alteration is to make the Ramsey economy a small open economy—for reasons of realism more than the slight simplicity gained. The global capital market at all times allocates just enough capital to the country to equate capital's marginal productivity to the invariant and unchanging real-world rate of interest. The nationals, all in the same situation and with similar preferences, supply labor to the domestic market and supply saving to the global capital market so as to maximize their infinite-lifetime utility. (Thus wealth will not generally equal domestic capital.) The national government must service the constant public debt, pay the constant entitlement to all nationals, and possibly make needed government purchases.

The first part of this analysis lays out the model and conducts the analysis. The second part asks how the results change if we suppose that the government feels free to deviate far from a balanced budget.

Optimal Taxation in the Ramsey Model

In the model here the representative agent at every time t plans to follow the path of consumption and work effort that maximizes the indefinite integral of remaining lifetime utility, discounting future utility rates back to time t at utility discount rate ρ, and chooses the current consumption rate c and effort l accordingly. Suppressing time subscripts except where clarity requires, the integral may be written

$$J = \int [u(c) - m(l) - (\hat{u} - \hat{m})]e^{-\rho t}dt \qquad (5\text{--}1)$$

where u is the instantaneous rate of utility from consumption and m is the instantaneous disutility from effort. To accommodate the special case of a zero utility discount in which Ramsey was particularly interested, the utility functions must have the property that the current rate of utility deriving from consumption approaches an upper bound $\hat{u}$ as current consumption goes to infinity, and the rate of disutility from work approaches some lower bound $\hat{m}$ as current effort goes to zero.[4] In forming the integral to be maximized, the "bliss" rate of net utility is subtracted from the current rate of net utility, as Ramsey and von Weizsäcker did, so that a maximum exists in the case $\rho = 0$.

The representative agent's maximization is subject to the differential equation expressing the agent's saving, which is the time-rate of change of the agent's private wealth, as the excess of income—wage income, income from wealth, and entitlement receipts—over consumption. Let a denote the agent's private wealth, v^h the after-tax wage rate, r^h the after-tax interest rate, and b (>0) the constant entitlement paid to every agent. Then

$$\dot{a} = v^h \ell + r^h a + b - c \qquad (5\text{--}2)$$

In the present version of the model, the government wants the greatest possible value of the same objective function, J, and uses its instruments, the two proportional tax rates, to that end subject to the constraint on them. It is notationally convenient to view the two rates as *specific* taxes rather than ad valorem taxes: a tax per unit of effort, $v - v^h$, which is the wedge between the before-tax and the after-tax wage per hour, and the analogous tax per unit of wealth, $r - r^h$, which is the wedge between the before-tax real-world interest rate and the after-tax interest rate available to the country's private citizens. (The corresponding ad valorem rates are obtained upon dividing by v and r, respectively, so that nothing substantive is entailed by this formulation of the tax rates.) The government's constraint is that its algebraic *public* saving must be exactly zero throughout. Let A denote wealth per worker, equivalently per head, L the labor effort per worker, and C consumption per worker. Then, letting g (>0) denote government purchases per head, Δ the public debt, and thus $r\Delta$ the debt service and recalling that r and b are also constants, we have the balanced budget relation[5]

$$(v - v^h)L + (r - r^h)A = b + r\Delta + g = const. > 0. \qquad (5\text{--}3)$$

The analysis below usually takes v^h as the sole decision variable of the government and uses the above balanced-budget equation to solve for the resulting value of r^h.

A basic postulate of the model is that the agents planning their work and saving correctly forecast the path of the tax rates that the government will impose, and the government correctly forecasts the path of consumption, work, and assets that the representative agent will choose. Thus the economy is in a remarkable expectational equilibrium in which each party correctly anticipates the unfolding of the economy. Also in a Nash equilibrium, given the path taken by the others, no individual player could do better than what he is doing and planning to do since he has correctly anticipated the course chosen by others. Perhaps the unrealism of the framework in this respect is so great that it would prove critical in any real-world application, but this cannot be deduced beforehand; we have to know something about the implications of the model as structured here before reaching such a conclusion.

The appeal of the equilibrium premise is that we can at least imagine the representative agent exploiting the special stationary structure of the dynamic system—that the other agents are going to be accumulating and working at the same rates he is and that the government's tax rates at each moment are a stationary function of the current state of the system, which is captured by the current value of the state variable A.[6] Hence the representative agent understands that his lifetime utility depends not only on his own wealth a but also on the wealth per head of the others, which is effectively average wealth, A, since every agent's own wealth is negligibly small. The motion of the latter variable is given by

$$\dot{A} = v^h L + r^h A + b - C \tag{5-4}$$

and, by virtue of the balanced budget relation above, by

$$\dot{A} = vL + rA - r\Delta - g - C \tag{5-5}$$

In optimizing, every individual entertains the possibility of choosing a path of a that diverges from the path of A. For intertemporal equilibrium, though, the path of A that the individual expects and thus the path of the fiscal parameters that A governs must cause him to choose a path of a that exactly matches the path of A that he is figuring on.

A solution to the problem must therefore meet two basic requirements. The first is the *optimality requirement* that each identical agent in the choice of c and l and the government in its choice of v^h are maximizing the agent's utility integral, subject to the differential equations giving the rate of change of a and of A.[7] This leads to equation 5–6, which involves an unknown function j giving the maximized utility integral (net of the bliss level) as a function of the two current state variables, a and A, both of which are initially equal to the given A_o:[8]

$$pj\,(a,A) = \max_{v^h}\max_{c,l}\{\{u(c) - m(l) - (\hat{u} - \hat{m})$$
$$+ \{v^h l + A^{-1}[rA - r\Delta - b - g + (v - v^h)L]a + b - c\}j_a(a,A) \qquad (5\text{–}6)$$
$$+ [vL + rA - r\Delta - g - C]j_A(a,A)\}\}$$

The second basic requirement is the *equilibrium requirement* that the agents' (shared) *expectation* of the growth of A, which each plans on when calculating his own effort and consumption, is precisely equal to the actual growth of A, which arithmetic decrees as equal to the growth of an agent's a. Similarly the L expected by the agent equals the agent's l, and the C expected equals the agent's c. Hence

$$v^h l + r^h a + b - c = vL + rA - r\Delta - g - C; \, l = L, \, c = C, \, a = A.$$
$$(5\text{–}7)$$

Thus each identical agent, facing the current tax rates and other parameters—hence the current v^h and r^h—chooses c and l to maximize the sum of current net utility of the bliss level *plus* the consequent saving times the marginal utility of the agent's wealth, a, taking as *given* his expectation of the others' saving (the rate of change of A) and its implications for the rate of change of v^h and r^h. Because that expectation is correct, the actual L, C, and dA/dl may be substituted for those expectations. There is an external effect on the individual's lifetime utility from the saving of the *others* (more on that issue follows); however, the agent takes that saving as a given, since he cannot hope that acting alone, he can change their saving. With interior solutions assumed, this maximization leads to the familiar first-order marginal-utility conditions in equations 5–8 and 5–9:

$$u'(c) = j_a(A,A),$$ (5–8)

$$m'(l) = v^h j_a(A,A)$$ (5–9)

Thus consumption per head is given by a demand function $Ç(j_a)$, which is decreasing in the marginal utility of private wealth, that is, $Ç'(j_a) > 0$; effort per head is given by a labor supply function $£(v^h \cdot j_a)$, which is increasing in the marginal utility of wealth times the after-tax wage.

As for the government, it chooses v^h (thus r^h) to maximize the sum of the agent's aforementioned maximand (its maximized value) *plus* the contribution external to the individual agent, namely, the average saving by the others times the marginal utility to the individual of *their* wealth per worker, A. In this calculation the government does not take the path of A as given but instead, using equation 5–7, takes average saving dA/dt to be the agent's saving da/dt and hence dependent on v^h. Thus the government's optimal tax-mix policy maximizes the right-hand side of equation 5–6 while taking into account both equation 5–7 and the utility-maximizing behavior of the agents in equations 5–8 and 5–9.[9] The first-order condition for the government's maximum is therefore characterized by setting equal to zero the derivative of the expression in curly braces on the right-hand side of equation 5–6 with respect to v^h and makes use of equation 5–7 and the workers' first-order conditions in equations 5–8 and 5–9. This gives

$$0 = -dC/dv^h[-u'(C) + j_a(A,A) + j_A(A,A)] + dL/dv^h$$
$$[-m'(L) + vj_a(A,A) + vj_A(A,A)] = -dC/dv^h j_A(A,A)$$ (5–10)
$$+ dL/dv^h[(v - v^h)j_a(A,A) + vj_A(A,A)]$$

This equation simplifies further. The first-order conditions in equations 5–8 and 5–9 imply the following responses of C and L to a small increase of v^h:

$$dC/dv^h = 0,$$ (5–11)

$$dL/dv^h = j_a(A,A)/m''(L)(>0).$$ (5–12)

Current consumption is independent of the current after-tax wage since there is no cross-substitution effect; since the variation in v^h is only for a vanishing duration (a length of time of measure zero), there is no income effect either. The former is not true of effort supplied, however, which is strictly increasing in the current wage rate because of the substitution effect. These results and the previous equation 5–10 give

$$0 = (v - v^h)j_a(A,A) + vj_A(A,A). \tag{5–13}$$

Before a discussion of this result, it may be noted that the government obtains the same condition if it maximizes the right-hand side of

$$pj(A,A) = u(C) - m(L) - (\hat{u} - \hat{m}) \tag{5–14}$$
$$+ [vL + rA - r\Delta - g - C][j_a(A,A) + j_A(A,A)].$$

The last bracketed expression is the marginal social utility of economywide wealth per worker, which may be greater or smaller than the marginal private utility of the agent's own wealth.

The result in equation 5–13 says that there are two distinct external effects from the increased effort induced by a cut in the tax on labor, even though the tax on (the income from) wealth makes up for any net revenue shortfall. The first is the external benefit that occurs if there is a positive wedge between the marginal product of labor, v, and the after-tax wage rate, v^h; the induced increase in effort by others, in generating a temporary increase in the tax base, makes possible a temporary cut in current tax rates, which increases the disposable income of the individual agent, which is valued at the marginal utility of the agent's private wealth, j_a. The second benefit is the consequent increase in saving per worker, which is the whole of the increase in the output rate since no change in the consumption rate occurs; the increase in saving is valued at the marginal utility for the representative agent of the others' wealth per worker, j_A. The latter, so far as we know at present, may be positive or negative.

Following from equation 5–13, the sign of the optimal current tax rate on labor is opposite to the sign of the marginal utility of the wealth of others.[10] If we have $j_A(A, A) > 0$, then $v - v^h < 0$, thus a *negative* tax on labor.[11] Were the labor tax nonnegative in that situation, the marginal welfare effect of a small *reduction* of the tax rate would be positive on both counts. First, the resulting increase in the amount of labor supplied

175

would have a marginal product on national income exceeding its private marginal product because of the tax wedge. Second, with $j_A (A, A) > 0$, the individual agents would be working too little and failing to take account that if they could enter into a pact to increase their current rate of effort to *save more*, the faster addition to national wealth would produce a beneficial external effect, represented by $j_A(A, A)$, though not a benefit that an agent acting alone could afford since the benefit would be diffused over the population. In this situation a negative tax on labor is the instrument to provide agents the incentive to do the extra work, and thus the extra saving that will benefit everyone since consumption is not stimulated. The external effect from the added wealth of others is indeed *positive* if and only if the income from wealth is being positively taxed; then and only then, under the balanced budget restraint, the added wealth increases the r^h corresponding to a given v^h , and this increase in r^h increases agents' disposable income and thus increases their current rate of utility. Such an increase in r^h occurs if and only if the optimal tax rate on the income from wealth is positive: hence the government's total outlay (entitlements plus debt service plus purchases) exceeds the tax revenue raised by the optimal tax rate on wages.[12]

To investigate the sign and the size of the external effect and thus the optimal tax structure, we need to study the intertemporal behavior of the functional equation implied by equation 7–6 and the optimal policies of workers and the government. This procedure gives the following equation in the unknown function and its derivatives, where the motions of the two state variables a and A are identical along an equilibrium path:

$$pj(a,A) = u(c) - m(l) - (\hat{u} - \hat{m})$$
$$+ \{v^h l + A^{-1}[rA - r\Delta - b - g + (v - v^h)L]a + b - c\}j_a(a,A) \quad (5\text{–}15)$$
$$+ [vL + rA - r\Delta - g - C]j_A(a,A)$$

Since this equality holds for all a and A , the partial derivative of the left-hand side with respect to each must equal the partial derivative of the right-hand side. Thus, differentiating with respect to a yields equation 5–16 and differentiating with respect to A yields equation 5–17:

$$pj_a(a,A) = r^h j_a(a,A) + j_{aa}(a,A)\dot{a} + j_{Aa}(a,A)\dot{A} \qquad (5\text{--}16)$$

$$
\begin{aligned}
pj_A(a,A) = \{&-[-r\Delta - b - g + (v - v^h)L]\, A^{-2}a \\
&+ (v - v^h)(\partial L/\partial A)\}j_a(a,A) + (r + v\partial L/\partial A - \partial C/\partial A) \qquad (5\text{--}17) \\
&j_A(a,A) + j_{aA}(a,A)\dot{a} + j_{AA}(a,A)\dot{A}
\end{aligned}
$$

where use has been made of the individual agent's first-order conditions.[13] The derivatives with respect to A are partial in the sense of holding a constant, but they are total derivatives in the sense that they include the indirect effects of a change in A that arise as v^h and the marginal utilities j_a and j_A vary with A. (The whole effect of current A on current C and L arises through these indirect impacts.)

In equation 5–16 the last two terms add up to the time-rate of change of the marginal utility of the individual's private wealth, j_a, thanks to the proposition on continuous functions that the symmetrical cross-partial derivatives are equal to one another. (In equation 5–17 the last two terms can be seen as analogous.) Hence this equation implies that the marginal utility is declining at a *proportionate* rate equal to the excess of r^h over ρ. In equation 5–17 the expression in the curly braces is the derivative of the budget-balancing r^h with respect to A. Here the expression in square brackets taken with the minus sign equals $(r - r^h)a$ by the budget-balance equation so that after canceling the a with the A, one is left with $r - r^h$. Hence the entire expression in the curly braces equals the total derivative of tax revenue per worker (coming from the other agents) with respect to the others' wealth per worker, A; that is, it equals $r - r^h + (v - v^h)$ $\partial L/\partial A$. Therefore the external effect of increased A is positive—of benefit to the individual agent—if the income from wealth is taxed and labor is either subsidized or taxed only weakly; the external effect is negative—of harm to the individual agent—if labor is taxed and wealth is subsidized or taxed only weakly.

Let us denote the two shadow prices, $j_a(A, A)$ and $j_A(A, A)$, by q and p, respectively; thus q is the marginal utility of the individual's private wealth, p the marginal utility to him of the wealth of others, positive or negative. Then, recalling the discussion in the preceding paragraph, we have the two differential equations 5–18 and 5–19:

$$dq/dt = -(r^h - \rho)q \tag{5-18}$$

$$dp/dt = -\{[r + v\partial L/\partial A - \partial C/\partial A] - \rho\}p - \{r - r^h \\ + (v - v^h)\partial L/\partial A\}q \tag{5-19}$$

In terms of p and q, equation 5–13 in the optimal v^h gives equation 5–20:

$$v^h/v = (q + p)/q \Leftrightarrow v - v^h = -v(p/q) \tag{5-20}$$

We may use the latter relationship to substitute for $v - v^h$ to obtain equation 5–21:

$$dp/dt = -[r - \partial C/\partial A - \rho]p - (r - r^h)q \tag{5-21}$$

To work with p/q instead of p we will need equation 5–22:

$$d(p/q)/dt = (p/q)\{-(r - r^h - \partial C/\partial A) - (r - r^h)(q/p)\} \tag{5-22}$$

Using equations 5–20 and 5–22, we can go on to derive equation 5–23:

$$dv^h/dt = -[r - .r^h - \partial C/\partial A]v^h - \partial C/\partial A\ v \tag{5-23}$$

The differential equations in v^h and in q together with the original differential equation in dA/dt, which is a function of C and L, constitute a three-equation dynamic system in the three unknowns, A, q, and v^h. In this system L and C are functions of the underlying three variables. (The partial derivatives of L and C with respect to A, given q and v^h, are zero, but with equations 5–8 and 5–9, L is increasing in q, v^h, and C is decreasing in q so that A has an indirect effect on both C and L. The derivatives with respect to A above are total derivatives, with only a being held constant.)

Some Implications. Since $r > \rho$, a nonvanishing shortfall of the utility rate from its modified bliss rate would occur if fiscal policy were to truncate the accumulation of wealth rather than allow savers' incentive to accumulate without bound. That is obvious in the case $0 = \rho < r$ no matter how small r, and it is no less true when $0 < \rho < r$. The argument is straightforward.[14] (It would be optimal for wealth not to explode only if r is endogenous and driven asymptotically to equality with ρ as in a closed economy or if utility satiation were attainable with a finite income.) This situation has implications for the asymptotic versions of the trio of differential equations (both the one with equation 5–23 and the one with equation 5–21). Substituting from the budget equation for r^h gives r less the excess of government interest obligations and entitlements over revenue from taxation of wages as a *ratio* to A. In the limit as A goes to infinity, the ratio goes to zero. Therefore r^h goes to r in the limit. Even if taxation of the income from wealth always gives a nonvanishing revenue, the *rate* of tax in the sense of $r - r^h$ vanishes.

The justly famous result of Corlett and Hague is a powerful influence limiting the extent to which fiscal policymakers countenance heavy taxation of nonwage income. The Corlett-Hague analysis suggests that nothing is gained from the introduction of a second distortion, namely, a tax on future consumption in exchange for lighter taxation of present consumption, unless the consequent change in the intertemporal terms of trade between present and future consumption has a complementarity effect that boosts the supply of effort and thus reduces the distortion from the existing tax on labor. The present model possesses no such complementarity (real economies have no well-accepted evidence of such complementarity). But the usual tax analysis does not contain some features of the model here, such as budget balancing and unbounded wealth accumulation arising from the economy's openness. It is of interest to investigate whether the optimality of exempting nonwage income from tax extends to the present model.

Under the Corlett and Hague policy of $r^h = r$, the implied differential equation system using equation 5–21 rather than equation 5–23 contains no obvious contradiction. When we consider the system with equation 5–23, however, the latter equation becomes

$$dv^h/dt = -(v-v^h)\partial C/\partial A. \qquad (5\text{–}24)$$

To raise the required revenue under the Corlett-Hague policy, the tax on labor must always be positive: thus dv^h/dt is nega-

179

tive. There are two cases to consider. If $\partial C/\partial A$ is nonvanishing as A goes to infinity, v^h must hit zero. That situation violates and contradicts the budget constraint. In general the marginal propensity to consume with respect to wealth tends to equal the after-tax interest rate. If the model implies that conclusion, no force tends to make the marginal propensity vanish as wealth goes to infinity.

If $\partial C/\partial A$ is vanishing, then the declining after-tax wage might remain bounded above zero. But such an equilibrium trajectory need not exist. To go to an extreme, suppose that labor approaches zero as wealth approaches infinity; the model as written implies this direction, although introducing positive utility from a modest level of effort would be trivial. At some point the revenue from wage taxation would cease to cover the government's obligations. In short the Corlett-Hague policy is not generally feasible. With such foreknowledge the optimal policymaker would presumably deviate from the Corlett-Hague policy from the outset.

Would instead taxing only income from wealth be optimal—a sort of *anti*–Corlett-Hague policy? In that event $v - v^h = 0$, and hence $(r - r^h)A = r\Delta + b + g$. Further, according to equation 5–20, $p = 0$. The latter implies that the right-hand side of equation 5–21 is negative, since private wealth always has positive marginal utility ($q > 0$). But that implication contradicts $p = 0$. This policy cannot be optimal.

We can broaden our set of impossibility results by rewriting differential equation 5–22 in a more user-friendly way:

$$d/dt(v - v^h) = (r - r^h)v^h + (v - v^h)\partial C/\partial A. \qquad (5\text{–}25)$$

We can take for granted that the optimal fiscal policy will not cause the unit tax on labor, $v - v^h$, to rise or fall without bound. Further, the motion of $v - v^h$ must be monotone, the system being driven by a single-state variable whose motion is itself monotone. Hence the left-hand side of equation 5–25 must be vanishing or zero to begin with. As established, $r - r^h$ will equal or approach zero as A approaches infinity. Therefore, for the right-hand side to approach zero along with the left-hand side, $v - v^h$ must also approach zero. This situation leads to the interpretation that as wealth approaches infinity, the government can afford asymptotically to face the worker-saver with rewards to both work and saving equal to their respective marginal social productivities: wealth is growing to such levels as to render negligible the burden of meeting the government's constant social commitments.

This fruitful result implies that if both taxes were positive, the tax on labor would be growing. But since the labor tax must be shrinking sooner or later as wealth goes to infinity, the labor tax rate must switch direction, a move that violates the property that the motions of the variables must be monotone in this model since it has a single-state variable, wealth. At any time two positive tax rates would be inopportune. To raise the needed positive revenue, at least one of the tax rates must be positive: thus the two tax rates must have opposite signs.

Therefore two classes of paths appear to be candidates for optimality. One candidate is negative taxation of labor with the algebraic unit tax on labor rising (toward zero) and the tax per unit of nonwage income positive and always large enough so that $r - r^h$ outweighs the negative $v - v^h$ so that the right-hand side is positive. Hence the negative labor tax is shrinking in absolute value.

The other candidate is positive taxation of labor with the unit labor tax falling (toward zero) and the tax rate on the income from wealth negative and large enough in absolute value so that $r - r^h$ outweighs the negative $v - v^h$ so that the right-hand side is negative. Hence the positive labor tax is shrinking. Thus either labor is subsidized and the subsidy shrinks and vanishes in the limit, or wealth is subsidized and its unit subsidy shrinks and vanishes in the limit.

But in this model wealth optimally goes to infinity and thus causes the labor supply function steadily to shrink—to nothing in the classic case in which no amount of effort brings positive utility. In that case the revenue obtained from taxing labor must also vanish while the present model features a positive level of government commitments to be tax financed. So as long as the (constant) level of required revenue is positive, the second candidate—a positive and falling tax rate on labor—is not eligible. More generally, taking into account asymptotic labor supply rates that are greater than zero, as long as the asymptotic effort supplied when multiplied by the revenue-maximizing labor tax is short of financing the sum of the government's net obligations, $r\Delta + b + g$, the second scenario is infeasible. That scenario would be feasible only in the reverse case in which the government's net commitments were negative, thanks to a negative net public debt, or at any rate smaller than the asymptotic maximum revenue from labor taxation.

Conclusions

There is an optimal level of government entitlements and debt service to subsidize labor, with the total outlay financed through a positive, though falling, tax on the income from wealth. With government commitments high—higher than what can be financed asymptotically through taxation of labor—society has an available welfare gain from boosting saving to spread the burden of the government's commitments over a larger amount of wealth, which is a potentially large element of the tax base. Because the individual worker-saver does not internalize this welfare effect, we cannot look to the marketplace to do so when unassisted by government. Even if initially as a trial policy all tax revenue were collected from wealth and none from labor, the general welfare would improve by a move to subsidize labor and to tax the income from wealth more heavily—though not to the point of making the after-tax rate of return to wealth negative (which would raise tax evasion problems)—to generate a current stimulus to work, earning, and thus saving. This channel, from after-tax wage to work to saving despite the rise of the tax rate on interest income, is a special feature of the Ramsey model, although a few other models offer a diminished, modifed variation of that feature.

This finding fits a subsidiary theme in my extensive arguments for low-wage employment subsidies. I have sometimes pointed out that the more mature advanced economies today tend to be awash with wealth—much of it in the form of social wealth, that is, entitlements, although private wealth has also increased considerably in several Western countries over the past two decades, following the great slowdown in growth. Unfortunately the hugely enlarged volume of private wealth still is lightly taxed on average, with inevitable consequences for the tax rate on labor. By stepping up the rate of tax on the income from wealth, the structure of taxation ought to neutralize some ill-effects that this artificial nonlabor income has on morale and the resulting resource allocation.

Since the model here is not always easy to understand and the analysis has been rather informal on the whole, some readers might question whether my results can be correct. I have delved into a more formal mode of analysis with phase diagrams, but the complexity of the dynamic system makes a persuasive analysis difficult. However, I can comment on the literature that seems to reach a different conclusion and thereby hope that the reconciliation of those findings with mine will bolster confidence in my findings.

Christophe Chamley has shown that without a policy of continuous budget balance and with only the intertemporal constraint on the government to pay its bills with interest sooner or later, the optimal policy is an initial interval of sustained budgetary surplus in which income from wealth is taxed to the highest limit, with that interval followed by a policy of zero taxation of the income from wealth and positive taxation of labor. I have two comments on the relation of his work to mine. First, Chamley's initial budgetary surpluses are clearly doing the job that heavy taxation of nonwage income does in my model. In both models, taxation of nonwage income is initially heavy. But the budget surplus in Chamley's model at some point eliminates the need for taxation of nonwage income, while that need is moderated only progressively in my model. Second, it is not clear that Chamley would have obtained a zero tax rate on interest income after the initial interval had he admitted entitlements into his model. My own calculations, using his equations, suggest not. However, the questions of the comparative impact of government purchases, interest income from abroad, and entitlements on tax policy deserve study.

Notes

1. Forbes's plan is cited in the editorial "Marginal Rates Reemerge," *Wall Street Journal*, September 24, 1998. The original proponents of the flat tax also

envision making interest income tax exempt but explain that they would end the tax deductibility of interest costs as well (Hall and Rabushka 1995).

2. The early architects are A. C. Pigou (1928) and Frank P. Ramsey (1927). The latter is not the Ramsey model of 1928, cited below.

3. In another paper, with Kumaraswamy Velupillai, I struggled with aspects of the question (1988). An early book of mine deals with signaling households a fiscal burden of the right size (1965).

4. The elasticity of the marginal utility of consumption with respect to the consumption level is greater than 1 (at least asymptotically). This elasticity is conceptually orthogonal to and thus independent of the coefficient of relative risk aversion, which pertains to the willingness to risk wealth, lifetime wage rate, etc.

5. There is no contradiction between one or more episodes of deficit spending in the past, saddling the present with a burdensome debt, and a plan not to run deficits in future.

6. If the agent tentatively expects a certain path of wealth accumulation and associated path of tax rates, he tests that expectation by checking to see whether it will cause his own wealth accumulation to follow the same path.

7. In the expression for the agent's saving, the balanced budget constraint has been used to substitute for r^h.

8. This is Bellman's equation, which Isaacs calls the "main equation" in differential games. However, the present problem has the added dimension of many private agents.

9. A departure from the optimal tax-mix policy (making the tax rates an optimal function of A) will make the right-hand side smaller than the left-hand side.

10. One cannot argue from the result that with a positive wedge, there would be a gain from a temporary reduction of it to any conclusion about whether the wedge ought to be positive.

11. The above equation equally implies that if $j_A(A, A)<0$, $v - v^h>0$, a positive tax on labor. A possible source of the negative externality from wealth in the present model would seem to be the loss of tax revenue that results from the decrease of effort induced by the wealth increase in combination with a positive tax rate on labor. However, the latter effect cancels out below in the derivation of equation 5–21.

12. Even before the analysis below, it is clear that a tax policy with negative taxation of labor income forever could *not* be optimal *if* through budget balancing it required r^h to be nonpositive. A policy keeping the after-tax rate of return to saving nonpositive would end wealth accumulation, which cannot be optimal if, as here, the social rate of return to saving, r, exceeds the social time preference rate ρ. Further, empirically it seems likely that total reliance on wealth taxation *would* leave no return on wealth: if the ratio of total private wealth to national income is less than 8 as in the United States, taxing even as much as 3 percent of it would raise revenue of less than 24 percent of the national income—not enough to finance our "welfare state."

13. The procedure here appears in Bellman 1956, p. 264, and in Sargent 1987, p. 21, where the literature is surveyed.

14. Assume that the economy approaches or reaches a rest point where $r^h = \rho$ though $\rho < r$. Then by lowering r^h for a brief time, and thus raising v^h, more effort is temporarily induced, and the extra income from that effort is saved. By then restoring r^h and v^h, the government can permit households to enjoy the fruits of the extra saving in the future. Since their time preference rate is less than the market interest rate, a net addition to lifetime discounted utility ought to be feasible.

References

Barro, Robert. 1974. "Are Government Bonds Net Wealth?" *Journal of Political Economy* 82 (November–December): 1095–1118.

Bellman, Richard. 1956. *Dynamic Programming.* Princeton: Princeton University Press.

Chamley, Christophe. 1986. "Optimal Taxation of Capital Income in General Equilibrium with Infinite Lives." *Econometrica* 54 (May): 607–22.

Corlett, W. J., and D. C. Hague. 1953. "Complementarity and the Excess Burden of Taxation." *Review of Economic Studies* 21 (January): 21–30.

Foster, J. D. 1998. "U.S. Economy Slowing Down? Cut Taxes." *Wall Street Journal*, July 22.

Hall, Robert, and Alvin Rabushka. 1995. *The Flat Tax: A Simple Progressive Consumption Tax.* Stanford: Hoover Institution Press.

Kemp, Jack. 1998. "We Need Liquidity, Mr. Greenspan." *Wall Street Journal*, August 17.

Mundell, Robert A. 1971. "The Dollar and the Policy Mix." *Essays in International Finance* 85 (May).

Ordover, J. A., and E. S. Phelps. 1975. "Linear Taxation of Wealth and Wages for Intragenerational Lifetime Justice." *American Economic Review* 65 (September): 660–73.

———. 1979. "The Concept of Optimal Taxation in the Overlapping-Generations Model of Capital and Wealth." *Journal of Public Economics* 12 (January): 1–26.

Phelps, Edmund S. 1965. *Fiscal Neutrality toward Economic Growth.* New York: McGraw Hill.

Phelps, Edmund S., and Kumaraswamy Velupillai. 1988. "Optimum Fiscal Policy When Monetary Policy Is Bound by a Rule." In *The Economics of the Public Debt*, edited by K. J. Arrow and M. J. Boskin. London: Macmillan.

Pigou, A. C. 1928. *A Study in Public Finance*, 3rd ed. rev. New York: St. Martins (1956).

Ramsey, Frank P. 1927. "A Contribution to the Theory of Taxation." *Economic Journal* 37 (January): 47–61.

————. 1928. "A Mathematical Theory of Saving." *Economic Journal* 38 (December): 543–59.

Reynolds, Alan. 1998. "Japan Should Cut Taxes to Spur Investment." *Wall Street Journal*, September 11, 1998.

Sargent, Thomas J. 1987. *Dynamic Macroeconomic Theory*. Cambridge: Harvard University Press.

Wannicki, Jude. 1978. *The Way the World Works*. New York: Basic Books.

Commentary

N. Gregory Mankiw

Edmund Phelps addresses a classic question: How should society allocate the tax burden between capital and labor? This question is increasingly important. Despite claims that the era of big government is over, taxes as a percentage of the national income are now at a historic high. How we choose to allocate that tax burden is likely to have major impact on the welfare of current and future generations.

Phelps has adopted the framework of the Ramsey growth model. I have mixed feelings about using the model for this purpose. The standard assumption used to justify this kind of model is that the world is populated by infinite-horizon households with operative intergenerational bequest motives, as suggested by Robert Barro in his 1974 paper on government debt. This stretch is implausible if the Ramsey model is intended to be a theory of the typical consumer. Anyone who has looked at the microdata on wealth accumulation cannot help but be struck by the fact that many Americans live paycheck to paycheck with almost no savings at all. Many people seem to live with planning horizons closer to four weeks than to infinity.

Conversely the Ramsey model may be a good starting point if we are trying to model wealth accumulation. It is a well-known fact that wealth is highly concentrated. It is also well established that a high percentage of wealth is bequeathed from generation to generation. Wealthy Americans apparently do have operative bequest motives, and their behavior may well be described by the Ramsey model. In other words even though the Ramsey model may not describe the typical consumer well, it may describe the typical wealth holder. For the purpose of analyzing capital taxation, therefore, the Ramsey model may be quite useful.

The question that motivates this chapter is whether capital taxation is desirable if the alternative—labor taxation—is distorting the labor-leisure trade-off. In a 1986 *Econometrica* essay, Christophe Chamley examined the issue of optimal taxation in this kind of model and proved that optimal tax rates on capital income are asymptotically zero. Phelps has drawn a somewhat different conclusion, apparently because he rules out the possibility of the government's running a budget surplus. I prefer Chamley's set of assumptions.

Chamley shows that a zero tax on capital income is optimal only asymptotically. In the short run things are different because there is always a desire to tax "old capital" in these models. This is one manifestation of the time-inconsistency problem. To encourage accumulation, the government wants to announce that it will not tax capital, but once capital is in place, it wants to impose a one-time capital levy. As a result of this time-inconsistency problem, the government should want to commit itself to a zero capital tax in the long run.

Based on my reading of Chamley's results, here is my guess about optimal policy in the kind of economy that Phelps is studying: the government should immediately confiscate all capital since this is a perfect nondistortionary tax. The government should then commit itself to never taxing capital again. If the government needs revenue beyond the capital levy, it should rely only on wage taxes (or equivalently consumption taxes). Phelps's balanced-budget assumption rules out this possibility because this policy requires large initial budget surpluses. But there is scant justification for ruling it out.

What is the intuition for a zero optimal capital tax? It goes roughly as follows. The deadweight loss of a tax is convex in the tax rate. Thus, when different commodities are taxed, uniform taxation is optimal absent any differences in elasticities or cross-elasticities of supply or demand. In an intertemporal context, where the different commodities are consumption at different dates, uniform taxation means a uniform consumption tax, which can be shown to be equivalent to a uniform wage tax. Taxing capital income is undesirable because it means taxing future consumption more heavily than current consumption, which violates the presumption for uniformity.

One dimension of the problem that Phelps and much of the other literature ignore but might be worth exploring is heterogeneity in saving behavior. Many people live paycheck to paycheck, and wealth accumulation is highly concentrated. As a result, most of the population directly pays no capital taxes at all. Although the true incidence of any tax cannot be inferred from who writes the check to the government, one should be naturally suspicious of any model that fails to take account of these basic microeconomic facts regarding heterogeneity in saving behavior.

To see what such a model might look like, let me sketch out a simple example. Imagine that the economy is populated by two sorts of people. One group, the *capitalists*, exhibits behavior that is well described by the Ramsey model. We can view these people as having operative intergenerational bequest motives. A second group, the *workers*, lives paycheck to paycheck. Their consumption equals their after-tax wage income in every period. In essence this is the consumption model that John Campbell and I examined empirically in several papers.

Suppose that the workers are in the majority and therefore control tax policy. They have to pay for a level of government spending g, which can either be a public good or a transfer payment and which I consider exogenous. The choice that this majority faces is how much to tax labor income and how much to tax capital income: the goal is to maximize after-tax wages. Thus the worker majority ignores the welfare of the capitalist minority. To keep things simple, I start by comparing alternative steady states and ignoring all issues of transition.

Given this assumption, the issue of tax policy boils down to the following optimization problem:

maximize $\quad (1-\tau)w$
τ,θ

subject to

$$w = f(k) - f'(k)k$$
$$\tau w + \theta f'(k)k = g$$
$$(1-\theta)f'(k) = \rho$$

where w is the wage, k is the capital stock per worker, $f(k)$ is output per worker, g is government spending per worker, τ is the tax rate on labor income, θ is the tax rate on capital income, and ρ is the subjective discount rate for the capitalists in the economy.

The objective here is simply maximizing the after-tax wage, $(1 - \tau)w$. In pursuing this goal, the worker majority faces three constraints. The first constraint says that labor earns its marginal product, which by Euler's theorem equals output left over after capital is paid its marginal product. The second constraint is a government budget constraint that says that revenue from labor taxes plus revenue from capital taxes must equal government spending. The third equation states that the after-tax marginal product of capital equals the subjective discount rate of capitalists; this condition follows from the intertemporal first-order condition for the capitalists and the assumption that we are in a steady state. This equation is a standard result in Ramsey-like models.

The result of this problem is interesting: $\theta = 0$. That is, the optimal tax on capital income is zero. This is true even though we have been solving the optimal tax problem from the standpoint of the workers in the economy.

Why do workers want to exempt capital income from taxation? The reason is that the supply of capital is highly elastic in this model: in the long run, it is infinitely elastic at rate ρ. Thus, when capital is taxed, the quantity falls precipitously and in turn depresses the real wage. This effect is sufficient to make any tax on capital income undesirable, even from the perspective of people who own no capital.

Given this result, one might wonder: Why isn't the AFL-CIO clamoring for the elimination of the capital income taxation? There are many possible answers. Perhaps this model is not the right way to analyze capital accumulation. Or perhaps it is the right model, but the AFL-CIO does not know that.

The most appealing answer, however, is that the AFL-CIO is plagued by the time-inconsistency problem already discussed. In the short run it is tempting for workers to confiscate all capital and enjoy a temporary consumption binge. Offsetting this desire is the understanding that imposing a capital levy regularly eliminates any incentive for the capitalists to save and thus cripples the economy in the long run. Once we acknowledge this problem, we immediately move the analysis into the realm of game theory. We have to model the situation as an interaction between workers and capitalists as they play a repeated game, with workers choosing tax rates and capitalists choosing saving rates. Clearly multiple equilibriums will occur. Some equilibriums will resemble the commitment case with zero capital tax rates and economic prosperity, and others will resemble the no-commitment case with high capital tax rates and depressed living standards. Obviously the zero capital tax equilibrium is in the long run better for both workers and capitalists.

What are the implications of all this for public policy? If this class of models is useful for policy analysis, the clear implication is that zero tax rates on capital income are optimal. In practice this could be accomplished in a variety of ways. One would be the adoption of a Hall-Rabushka–style flat tax. Although this tax reform is often advocated on the grounds of "flatness," an equally notable feature is that it integrates the corporate and personal income taxes and allows full immediate deduction of investment expenses. As a result the Hall-Rabushka flat tax is more like a consumption tax than an income tax.

One could accomplish much the same thing in a somewhat less radical way. For U.S. tax policy, this means eliminating the corporate income tax, eliminating the estate tax, and greatly expanding the role of IRAs and other tax-exempt savings accounts. To a small extent tax policy has been heading in this direction; indeed President William Clinton called for an expansion in tax-advantaged savings accounts in his 1999 state-of-the-union speech. Yet the idea of reducing capital taxation is most often a partisan issue. To put it simply, if Frank Ramsey were alive today and if he took his model seriously as a guide for tax policy, he would probably be a Republican.

6

Growing Inequality and Decreased Tax Progressivity

Joel Slemrod and Jon M. Bakija

For at least two decades the average real income of the bottom four deciles has stagnated, while the real income of those at the top of the income distribution has grown sharply. Income inequality has sharply increased.

During the same period the progressivity of the tax-and-transfer system has not increased and has arguably declined. In the 1980s the progressivity of the federal tax system first declined and then increased: in 1990 it was not substantially different from what it was in 1980.[1] Arguably the top rate increases of 1990 and 1993 increased progressivity, but the expansion of capital gains tax preferences in 1997 and possibly after offset the higher top rates. The generosity of transfers to the poor has declined too.

This chapter explores the links between these two phenomena. We emphasize the causal link going from inequality to progressivity and note that optimal taxation theory predicts the opposite of what has occurred: growing inequality should increase progressivity. We discuss public choice alternatives to the optimal progressivity framework. The chapter also addresses the opposite causal direction—that changes in taxation have caused the (apparent) increase in inequality—and also the possibility that the two phenomena are causally unrelated but instead are caused by a common set of exogenous factors.

We make two empirical contributions to this debate. First,

We are grateful for helpful comments from Jim Poterba, Bill Gale, and other participants in the AEI conference and at a presentation of the paper at the Georgetown Law Center.

we argue that standard measures of income distribution ignore the implications of the large recent runup in stock prices, and we attempt a crude calculation of what this impact might be. We calculate the distribution of income while taking account of the stock market runup, and compare it against more standard measures that ignore it. In addition the effective tax rate on these gains is arguably quite low and reduces the progressivity of the tax system much below what standard measures suggest. Finally, we investigate the "nonevent study" offered by the major changes in the distribution of income beginning in 1996 and discuss its implications for the issues addressed in this chapter.

Should Increased Inequality Reduce Tax Progressivity?

Optimal Progressivity Theory. For the sake of argument, the modern theory of optimal progressivity accepts the right of government to redistribute income through the tax system (and other means), sidesteps the ethical arguments about the value of a more equal distribution of economic outcomes, and instead investigates the implications of various value judgments and parameters of the economic system for the design of the tax system. Front and center comes the fact that greater redistribution of income requires higher marginal tax rates, which may provide disincentives to work, save, take risks, and invest in human and physical capital. The essential problem then is to describe the inherent trade-offs between the distribution of income and economic performance.

Mirrlees (1971) initiated the modern literature formalizing this trade-off. In his formulation the government must choose an income tax schedule to raise a given amount of total revenue, with the goal of maximizing a utilitarian social welfare function. This function implicitly trades off the welfare of individuals at different income levels but assumes that social welfare increases when any member of society (including the richest) is better off, with the welfare of others held constant. It therefore precludes envy as the basis of tax policy.[2] Mirrlees first investigated what characterizes the optimal income tax[3] for any set of assumptions about the social welfare function, the distribution of endowments, and the behavioral response (utility) functions. He concluded that in this general case only very weak conditions characterize the optimal tax structure, conditions that offer little concrete guidance in the construction of a tax schedule.

In the absence of general results, the approach has been to make specific assumptions about the key elements of the model and then to calculate the parameters of the optimal income tax system. This approach is meant to suggest the characteristics of the optimal income tax under reasonable assumptions and to investigate how these characteristics depend on the elements of the model. Mirrlees also pioneered this approach in his 1971 article and concluded that the optimal tax structure is approximately linear (that is, it has a constant marginal tax rate and an exemption level below which tax liability is negative) and has marginal tax rates that are quite low by then current standards, usually between 20 and 30 percent and almost always less than 40 percent.[4] This result was stunning and unexpected even, it seems, to Mirrlees himself, especially in an era where top rates of 70 percent or more were the norm.

Subsequent work investigated the sensitivity of the optimal income tax to the parametric assumptions. Of particular interest to the topic at hand, Mirrlees presented an example in which widening the distribution of skills, assumed equal to wage rates, increased the optimal marginal tax rates, although he considered the dispersion of skills necessary to imply much higher rates to be unrealistic. In his baseline numerical simulation he set the value of σ (the standard deviation of the associated normal distribution) in the assumed logarithmic distribution of skills to be equal to 0.39, derived from Lydall's (1968) figures for the distribution of income from employment for various countries. When Mirrlees repeats the simulation with $\sigma = 1.0$, a much wider dispersion of ability, he reports (p. 207) that the optimal tax schedule

> is in almost all respects very different. Tax rates are very high: a large proportion of the population is allowed to abstain from productive labor. The results seem to say that, in an economy with more intrinsic inequality in economic skill, the income tax is a more important weapon of public control than it is in an economy where the dispersion of innate skills is less. The reason is, presumably, that the labour-discouraging effects of the tax are more important, relative to the redistributive benefits, in the latter case.

Stern (1976), examining only flat-rate tax systems, corroborates the Mirrlees finding. For his base case featuring an elasticity of substitution between goods and leisure of 0.4 when $\sigma = 0.39$, the optimal marginal tax rate is 0.225, but it rises to 0.623 when $\sigma = 1$. Cooter and Helpman (1974) perform a variety of numerical simulations, and find that for all of them the optimal marginal tax rate increased as the constant-mean ability distribution spreads out.[5]

The dispersion of skills is not the only determining parameter. Atkinson (1973) explored the effect of increasing the egalitarianism of the social welfare function. Even in the extreme case of Rawls's (1971) "maximin" social welfare function, where social welfare is judged solely on the basis of how well off the worst-off class of people is, the model generated optimal tax rates not much higher than 50 percent. Stern (1976) argued that Mirrlees's assumption about the degree of labor-supply responsiveness was excessive and thereby overstated the costs of increasing tax progressivity. This is true because the greater the responsiveness, the greater the social waste (in this case people whose labor productivity exceeds their valuation of leisure but who do not work) per dollar of revenue raised. Stern showed that with a more reasonable estimate of labor-supply responsiveness (an elasticity of substitution of 0.4 instead of 1.0), the value of the optimal tax rate exceeds 50 percent, approximately twice as high as what Mirrlees found.

In sum, simple models of optimal income taxation do not necessarily point to sharply progressive tax structures, even if the objective function puts relatively large weight on the welfare of less-well-off individuals. This conclusion does, though, depend critically on the sensitivity of the labor supply to the after-tax wage rate and the subject of this essay, the distribution of endowments.

The last point suggests an apparent inconsistency between the theory of optimal income taxation and the actual U.S. income tax-and-transfer policy of the past two decades: the degree of progressivity has hardly budged, may have decreased, and certainly has not increased substantially in the face of apparently massive increases in the degree of pretax income inequality. There are many ways, not mutually exclusive, to reconcile this inconsistency. The optimal progressivity models may not be rich enough to give accurate predictions about appropriate tax-and-transfer policy. Other changes in the U.S. economy, either unrelated to the increasing inequality or structurally related but distinct from it, may explain the policy response. Finally, the political system may produce outcomes in a way that is unrelated to, or even opposite from, what the artificial construct of constrained social welfare maximization would predict. We next consider each of these possible explanations of the inconsistency between the theory and the practice of income tax progressivity. We begin by looking more closely at the models of optimal progressivity.

"Richer" Models of Optimal Tax Progressivity. In the standard formulation of the optimal progressivity problem, the rich are different from the poor in only one way: they are endowed with the ability to command a higher market wage rate, which is presumed to reflect a higher real productivity of their labor effort. But a variety of other reasons account for why some people become affluent and others do not, with vastly different policy implications.

The rich may have been lucky. The influential study of Jencks and his colleagues (1972) concluded that in addition to on-the-job competence, economic success depended primarily on luck[6] but that "those who are lucky tend, of course, to impute their success to skill, while those who are inept believe that they are merely unlucky"[7] (p. 227). If there is income uncertainty that is uncorrelated across individuals and for which private insurance markets do not exist, then taxation becomes a form of social insurance; a more progressive system, by narrowing the dispersion in after-tax income, provides more social insurance than a less-progressive tax system. The optimally progressive tax system then balances the gains from social insurance (and perhaps also redistribution) against the incentive costs. Varian (1980) argued that in the presence of substantial uncertainty and luck, the optimal marginal tax rate should in all likelihood be high because high realized income is probably due to a good draw of the random component of income and because taxing an event probably largely due to luck has minimal disincentive effects.

The rich may have different tastes, either for goods compared with leisure (working harder) or for future consumption. In the former case even with homogenous wage rates, some people have higher incomes by virtue of working more, but the higher income is offset by less leisure time. In this case a progressive tax system is not necessarily redistributing from the better-off to the worse-off, but does so capriciously according to tastes. Sandmo (1993) investigates a model with heterogeneous tastes but offers no unambiguous conclusions about optimal progressivity.

The rich may have inherited more either in terms of financial resources or in terms of human capital. If inherited endowment is the principal source of inequality (so that *inter alia* people do not differ in what they make of their endowments), from a one-generation perspective a tax system that redistributes the fruits of this endowment has a slight potential economic cost. A longer horizon is required, however, because such taxation would arguably affect the incentive of parents to leave an endowment and so could affect the incentive of potential benefactors to work and to save.

The rich may have different skills than everyone else, rather than more of the same kind of skills. This characterization certainly rings true, as the affluent tend to supply "skilled" rather than "unskilled" labor, that is, entrepreneurs, professionals, or the "symbolic analysts" of Reich's (1991) terminology.

Why does this matter for optimal progressivity? For one thing, as Feldstein (1973) first addressed, when two distinct types of labor exist, the relative wage rate depends on the relative supply to the market of the two kinds of labor, which in turn depends on the tax system chosen. Thus the tax system redistributes income directly through differential tax liabilities and also indirectly by alterations in the wage structure. Although Feldstein argued that this redistribution did not substantially alter optimal progressivity, Allen (1982) disagreed and argued that an increase in the statutory progressivity of an income tax system could actually make members of the lower-ability, lower-income group worse off because it reduces their before-tax wage rate.

But what if the affluent offer a particularly essential ingredient to the economy? Gilder (1990, 245) maintained that "a successful economy depends on the proliferation of the rich, on creating a large class of risk-taking men who are willing to shun the easy channels of a comfortable life in order to create new enterprise." If the market appropriately prices entrepreneurial talent, then the standard optimal progressivity framework still applies: the extent that taxes discourage its supply is a social cost. But more may be involved if important spillovers of information result from entrepreneurial activity whose social value cannot be captured by the entrepreneurs themselves. In economics jargon, positive externalities of innovation exist. These kinds of externalities are the building blocks of many "new growth" theories, propounded by Romer (1990) among others, who argue that policy can have persistent effects on economic growth rates, not just on the level of economic performance. Gilder appears to believe this and asserts that "most successful entrepreneurs contribute far more to society than they ever recover, and most of them win no riches at all" (p. 245).

Any positive externalities from the activities of the affluent because of their entrepreneurial nature argues for lower taxation at the top than otherwise. But the argument is not crystal-clear. Although a larger fraction of the rich than the general population classify themselves as professional or managerial (48.5 percent compared with 27 percent in 1982, according to Slemrod 1994), a larger than average fraction (12 percent compared with 1 percent) are lawyers and accountants, professions that some have argued deter economic growth because they are concerned with rent-seeking rather than income creation. Magee, Brock, and Young (1989) present evidence that countries with more lawyers grow more slowly.

Why Increased Inequality Matters for Optimal Progressivity. This discussion suggests that the cause of the increased inequality matters in determining the appropriate policy response. But no one knows why the dispersion of pretax incomes has surged. Changing inheritance patterns or tastes are unlikely to be important and, as we discuss later, the weight of the evidence suggests that labor-supply changes are not a major factor either.

That leaves a change in the relative return to skills and luck as the two relevant factors to consider. The two are not necessarily mutually exclusive factors. After all, because the widening dispersion of the return to skills—often summarized as the return to education—was not completely anticipated, to some extent the extraordinary recent earnings of those endowed with the right skill type is just a good draw. If so, the taxation of these earnings will have a relatively small efficiency effect over the long run. Any such tax would have an (inefficient) impact on skill-acquisition decisions. In any event a progressive tax system does provide some degree of social insurance against uncertainty in the distribution of the return to skill, whether caused by unpredictable technological advances or developments in the global economy. We return to this issue later when we discuss the implications of globalization.

The Public Choice Perspective
on Increased Inequality and Progressivity

Up to this point we have addressed the appropriate, or optimal, degree of progressivity, given a specified social-objective function and a characterization of how the economy works. In this section we put aside that normative question and focus on a question of public choice: Given the political institutions and mechanisms for social choice in the United States, does an increase in inequality trigger the kinds of policy changes that would increase progressivity?

According to the standard theory of optimal progressivity, a more unequal wage distribution should increase the amount of redistribution because it increases the weight placed on the equity gain from redistribution relative to the efficiency losses. This is also the prediction of the "rational" (public choice) theory of the size of government proposed by Meltzer and Richard (1981), in which increased inequality increases mean income relative to the income of the decisive voter and thus makes redistribution more attractive to him. Persson and Tabellini (1994) and Alesina and Rodrik (1994) incorporate versions of this result in constructing models of why greater pretax-and-transfer inequality is bad for economic growth.

Peltzman (1980), stimulated by his observation that in prac-

199

tice greater inequality seemed to lead to less redistribution, constructed a model in which the total support for redistribution increases if income differences among beneficiaries narrow. Because inequality tends to increase both within-group and between-group inequality, its net effect on redistribution is indeterminate. Kristov, Lindert, and McClelland (1992) developed a pressure-group model of individuals with "social affinity" (that is, in which people care more about the well-being of people like themselves), which predicts that progressive redistribution is fostered by greater proximity and intermobility between the middle and poorest income ranks and is reduced by greater proximity and intermobility between the middle- and top-income ranks. They also suggest that economic growth affects the political will to provide income support for the poorest: depressions awake sympathy for persons with low income and reinforce the opinion that poverty arises because of bad luck. Lindert (1996) explains that this "Robin Hood paradox" occurs because greater inequality between lower- and middle-income classes means less commonality of identity, which weakens the inclination of middle-class voters to redistribute income toward lower-income families.

In sum, models of public choice do not speak with one voice as to how policy would actually respond to an increased dispersion of earnings. Empirical investigation has not yet succeeded in identifying which set of conceptual models best captures the key features of the U.S. political system with regard to fiscal progressivity.

Did Tax Changes Cause the Increased Inequality?

Maybe the process works the other way around. Maybe changes in the tax system have driven the increase in inequality. The reduced tax rates on high-income families may have induced them to expend more effort, which increases measured incomes (as opposed to the income net of the value of forgone leisure). The reduced tax rates may also have caused a host of other behavioral responses, ranging from substitution away from tax-preferred activities such as charitable contributions, investment in tax-exempt bonds, and compensation as fringe benefits to less investment in tax-avoidance strategies to less tax evasion. The labor-supply response to increased progressivity would show up as increased inequality of labor income, and all responses would show up as increased inequality of taxable incomes.

A sizable empirical literature has attempted to measure the magnitude of these responses. With some exceptions the profession has settled on a value for the compensated labor-supply elasticity close to zero for prime-age males, although for married women the responsiveness of labor force participation appears to be significant. Overall, though, the compensated elasticity of labor supply appears fairly small. In models with only a labor-leisure choice, that elasticity implies that the efficiency cost of income taxation is bound to be low as well.

Some intriguing evidence suggests that the response to taxes of total reported taxable income may not be small, at least for high-income families. Lindsey (1987) was one of the first to point out that the 1981 top rate cut in the Economic Recovery Tax Act of 1981 (ERTA) from 70 percent to 50 percent coincided with a major increase in the share of income reported to the IRS by the top 1 percent of the income distribution. He argues that the tax cut was a principal cause of this increase, as it reduced the penalty for receiving (or, to be precise, reporting) taxable income, and he estimates the elasticity of taxable income with respect to the net-of-tax share at 1.6–1.8.

Feenberg and Poterba (1993) use tax-return data to calculate a time series of inequality measures that focuses on high-income households. Using interpolations of published Statistics of Income (SOI)–aggregated data, they calculate the share of U.S. adjusted gross income (AGI) and several components of AGI received by the top 0.5 percent of households arranged by income. After being approximately flat at about 6.0 percent from 1970 to 1981, the share of AGI received by this group begins in 1982 to increase continuously to 7.7 percent in 1985, then jumps sharply in 1986 to 9.2 percent. There is a slight increase in 1987 to 9.5 percent, then another sharp increase in 1988 to 12.1 percent.

Feenberg and Poterba argue that this pattern is consistent with a behavioral response to the reductions over this period in the tax rate on high-income families. They also report that among the top income earners, the largest increase in share could be attributed to the top one-fifth of 1 percent. This fact, they assert, "casts doubt on the view that the factors responsible for the increase in reported incomes among high-income taxpayers, especially in the 1986–1988 period, are the same factors that were responsible for the widening of the wage distribution over a longer time period" (p. 161). Rather, they argue, "it reflect[s] other factors including a tax-induced change in the incentives that high-income households face for reporting taxable income" (p. 170).

Comparing cross-sectional slices of income distributions has serious and well-known problems because it entails comparing different groups of households across years. Analyzing longitudinal, or panel, data on an unchanging set of taxpayers can mitigate the potential hazards of inferring behavioral response from comparing the behavior of two distinct groups of taxpayers. Thus analysis of panel data characterized the next wave of investigations of the taxable-income elasticity.

Feldstein (1995) investigates the high-income response to the Tax Reform Act of 1986 (TRA86) by using tax-return panel data that follow the same set of taxpayers from 1979 to 1988. Feldstein analyzes married couples with available tax returns for both 1985 and 1988. He groups taxpayers by their 1985 marginal tax rate, calculates group means for taxable income and the net-of-tax rate for each group, and then calculates the percentage change in the mean between the years, with the difference of these percentages used to obtain elasticities. After making several adjustments to the data, he concludes that the 1985–1988 percentage increase in various measures of income (particularly taxable income excluding capital gains) was much higher, compared with the rest of the population, for those high-income groups whose marginal tax rate was reduced the most. Based on this finding, he estimates that the elasticity of taxable income with respect to the net-of-tax rate is high, between 1 and 3 in alternative specifications. To put this into perspective, an elasticity greater than $\frac{(1-t)}{t}$, where t is the tax rate, produces a Laffer-type inverse revenue response; thus the upper-end range of Feldstein's estimates suggests that tax increases might decrease revenue collected.

Unfortunately Feldstein's data set contained only few high-income observations; for example, the top income class on which Feldstein focuses most of his attention (nonelderly couples in the 49–50 percent tax brackets in 1985) contains only fifty-seven observations. The wide variation among this group in financial situations and in income changes over time makes generalizing from such a small sample problematic.

Auten and Carroll (1999) use a much larger longitudinal data set of 14,102 tax returns for the same set of taxpayers for 1985 and 1989. Because their data oversamples, it contains 4,387 taxpayers in the 49 percent or 50 percent tax rate bracket in 1985. Rather than rely on group means, Auten and Carroll employ a multivariate regression approach and regress the change in AGI between 1985 and 1989 against the change in marginal tax rate and a set of demographic variables. The regression approach allows them to control for occupation as a proxy for demand-side nontax factors that affected the change in compensation over this period. They conclude that changes in tax rates appear to be an important determinant of the income growth of the late 1980s, although the results are somewhat sensitive to the choice of sample and weighting. Their central estimate of the net-of-tax price elasticity is 0.6.

Moffitt and Wilhelm (2000) also investigate behavioral response to TRA86, but they use panel data from the 1983 and 1989 Survey of Consumer Finances (SCF). Because of data limitations, they study an income concept closer to AGI than to taxable income. They replicate the sizable tax elasticities for AGI found by Feldstein and conclude that the elasticities arise from the behavior of the extreme upper tail of the income distribution.

All studies discussed so far focused on the effect of ERTA or TRA86 on taxpayer behavior. For reasons elaborated on below, a study of tax changes that increased tax rates would be especially helpful. Carroll (1998a) uses a panel of taxpayers spanning the tax increases of the 1990 and 1993 acts to consider to what extent taxpayers change their reported incomes in response to changes in tax rates. The tax-rate response is identified by comparing the change of higher-income taxpayers with those of moderate-income taxpayers when the relative taxation of these two groups changes, with many nontax factors such as the taxpayer's age, occupation, and industry being controlled. Carroll concludes that the taxable-income price elasticity is approximately 0.4, smaller than the earlier studies of the tax reductions in the 1980s but nevertheless a response that is positive and significantly different from zero.

Measuring and interpreting taxable income elasticities present several methodological problems, which are discussed at length in Slemrod 1998. A key issue is the difficulty of controlling for underlying trends in income inequality that are unrelated to the tax changes. In both ERTA and TRA86 the largest rate cuts applied to the highest tax brackets, so that a positive taxable-income elasticity implied larger increases in reported taxable income among affluent Americans and thus an increase in the apparent inequality of income. One obvious methodological problem is separating out the influence of the tax changes from nontax factors affecting the steadily increasing dispersion of (taxable) income. A voluminous literature (much of it summarized in Levy and Murnane 1992) has documented an increase in inequality in the United States. Karoly (1994) presents Census Bureau data showing that inequality among families, after reaching a postwar low in 1967–1968, began to increase during the 1970s and continued to rise through the 1980s. Although the trend toward greater inequality began in the late 1960s, about two-thirds of the increase in the Gini coefficient between 1968 and 1989 occurred between 1980 and 1989. Despite the widespread acknowledgment of these basic facts, the origin of the increase in inequality remains highly controversial. The two leading explanations, which are not mutually exclusive, are technological change, which increased the relative return to skilled labor, and increased globalization of the U.S. economy, which increased the effective relative supply of unskilled labor and thereby lowered its relative return.

For the most part, what we know about this phenomenon comes from data sets that are either top-coded or include few of the highest-income families. Thus the evidence is generally about the growing percentage differential in the earnings of people at, say, the tenth percentile compared with the ninetieth percentile. However, the publicly available tax-return data are not top-coded and in fact oversample high-income people; they suggest a similar trend since 1970. As discussed earlier, Feenberg and Poterba (1993) document that the share of income reported by the top 0.5 percent of the population increased slowly but steadily beginning in 1970, accelerated around 1980, and shot up in 1986. They contend that this trend is consistent with the pattern of declining effective tax rates on affluent Americans that began in 1970 and picked up steam with the rate cuts of 1981 and 1986. Indeed as the top individual marginal tax rate has been monotonically declining since the early 1960s, there is an a priori case that tax changes are a factor in the growing inequality.

Slemrod (1996) attempts to separate out the tax and nontax causes of inequality by performing some time-series regression analyses of the Feenberg and Poterba high-income shares for 1954 to 1990, with the data for the post-1986 years adjusted to correspond to a pre-TRA86 definition. (This adjustment reduces the measured increase in the shares after 1986, but the increase remains substantial.) Included as explanatory variables are the contemporaneous, lagged, and leading tax-rate measures, a measure of earning inequality between the ninetieth and tenth percentiles, and some macroeconomic variables that might differentially influence incomes at different percentiles. Based on the evidence up to 1985, the demand-side earnings-inequality variable is the dominant explanation. However, the regression using data up to 1990 assigns almost all the increase in the high-income share of AGI to the decline in the top tax rate on wage income. These findings imply either (1) that in the mid-1980s there was a break in the relationship between the nontax factors affecting the top 0.5 percent of the population and the factors affecting earnings dispersion more generally or (2) that the increase in the taxable income of the high-income families was primarily tax-driven. I suspect that the second explanation applies, although Fullerton (1996) argues that because TRA86 involved extensive tax definition as well as rate changes, it is difficult to conclude confidently that the change in rates was the critical factor.

Another post-TRA86 empirical strategy called for praying for tax increases on the rich in the hope that whatever biases were creeping into the estimates of the taxable-income elasticity based on the 1981 and 1986 tax-cut experience would be offset in analyses of tax increases. The tax increases of 1990 and 1993 answered these prayers, and Carroll (1998a) has emphasized the possibility that his lower estimates of the taxable-income elasticity are at least partly due to this offsetting bias.

Another empirical strategy used by both Auten and Carroll (1999) and Carroll (1998a) is to include in the analysis variables that measure the nontax factors that might have differentially affected income growth over the period spanning the tax change. Dummy variables for census regions are an uncontroversial example. More problematic is the use of dummy variables for occupation. The rationale for doing so is that a differing occupational mix may explain why a given income group may have experienced a different percentage change in taxable income. As Auten and Carroll discuss, this strategy is sensible to the extent that the dummy variables account for relative increases in labor productivity due to technological advances or higher demand due to more global integration. However, to the extent that they reflect differences in the flexibility to alter work schedules or compensation arrangements in response to tax rate changes, that is, different elasticities, the inclusion of such variables may bias downward the estimated elasticity. This problem could be avoided by replacing the occupational dummies with independent estimates of wage rate growth for the taxpayer's occupational category; this replacement would restrict the explanatory power of occupation to demand-side factors.

Goolsbee (2000) notes that the analyses of both the 1981 and the 1986 tax cuts look across samples where the stock market increased dramatically, corporate profits rose, and GDP growth increased and that these factors are associated with relative increases in the compensation of top executives, holding tax influences constant.

In sum, a considerable body of evidence supports the notion that the changes in the pattern of marginal tax rates did induce behavioral responses that would make the distribution of reported taxable incomes more unequal. To the extent that this is true, the increased inequality of taxable incomes overstates the growth in inequality of welfare because much of it is a substitution away from untaxed and generally unmeasured welfare-producing activities by those who formerly had much higher marginal tax rates. However, the extent of these induced behavioral responses remains controversial. Especially in light of new developments discussed later, tax changes are unlikely to be responsible for all or most of the observed increase in the inequality of income.

Changing Third Factors

The correlation between changing inequality and progressivity might be purely coincidental,[8] although such an assertion cannot be proven. A more interesting (and falsifiable) possibility is that the same third factor causes both trends. An intriguing candidate for this factor is the increasing globalization of national economies. That globalization is an important cause of the increased inequality in the United States and other industrialized countries is taken quite seriously, although it is highly controversial; we have nothing to add to this debate. Instead we are interested in its implications. Suppose that globalization is at least partly responsible for the growth in inequality. Can it also explain the flight from progressivity?

For this question the prediction of optimal taxation models is fairly clear: absent the ability of national or supernational governments to tax individuals on a worldwide basis, openness increases the cost of government and of progressivity because it increases the elasticity of taxed activities. In particular, capital has more alternatives than to locate within a country's own borders, people have more opportunities to purchase goods outside their country of residence, and some firms and groups of people have increasing flexibility about their country of residence. The higher the elasticity of taxed activities, the greater is the social cost per dollar raised.

If countries react to the increasing cost of government caused by globalization, then the size of government and the extent of progressivity should be shrinking. Thus in principle globalization could explain both the trend increase in inequality and the decline in progressivity. However, this line of reasoning flies in the face of empirical studies that claim that across countries and across time within countries, greater openness has led to larger, not smaller, governments. Cameron (1978) first discovered this relationship; he found that openness, measured as exports and imports of goods and services as a percentage of GDP in 1960, was the best single predictor of the growth of public revenues relative to output from 1960 to 1970 for eighteen member-nations of the Organization for Economic Cooperation and Development (OECD). Rodrik (1998) has updated this finding with a sample of more than 100 countries that establishes a strong and robust positive association between an economy's exposure to trade and the size of its government in both cross-sectional and longitudinal settings.[9] Myrdal (1960) had predicted this conclusion: he argued that "all states have felt compelled to undertake new radical intervention" (p. 702) in response to more chaotic economic relations following openness. Likewise, Lindbeck (1995, p. 56) observed that overt social insurance and tax systems represent built-in stabilizers that maintain full employment despite the uncertainties of demand inherent in an open economy.

Thus, globalization may increase both the cost and the benefits of at least some kinds of government: both the supply and the demand curves shift upwards. Interpreting progressivity as one aspect of government implies that the change in progressivity is indeterminate but the price of progressivity certainly increases. Some of this cost increase occurs because tax revenues are more difficult to raise in a world of mobile tax bases, but some of it occurs because citizens are more willing to tolerate a costly social insurance in a world that is vulnerable to economic forces generating uncertainty and inequality. The consequence for progressivity is thus not entirely clear.

The leading alternative to globalization as an explanation for growing inequality is skill-biased technological change. What is its impact on taxation? On the tax collection side, it has facilitated computer checks of tax returns against information reports provided to the Internal Revenue Service by employers, banks, and other financial institutions and thus has lowered the cost of collecting revenue in an equitable way. Conversely the growth of electronic commerce and the diffusion of sophisticated financial instruments has undoubtedly facilitated certain kinds of tax avoidance. In principle technological change could be a third factor affecting both inequality and progressivity, but we are far from any quantitative understanding of this relationship.

Two Recent Developments

Two recent developments shed some fascinating new light on the growth in inequality and its relationship to the tax system.

The Impact of the Stock Market Runup on Inequality and Progressivity. Between January 1, 1995, and December 31, 1997, broad-based indexes of the stock market more than doubled. Accounting for this phenomenon certainly increases the measured inequality of income, in particular the share of total income received by the top, say, 1 percent of families ranked by income. Depending on the incidence assumptions that one makes, it can also sharply decrease the measured degree of tax progressivity.

Illustrating the impact of this extraordinary burst of accrued income, table 6–1 shows the results of three alternative methodologies for computing the distribution of income. All three are based on the 1995 Survey of Consumer Finances, which includes detailed income and wealth information for 4,299 households. The sample is stratified with a heavy over-sampling of high-income and high-wealth households. A nonresponse-adjusted weight provided by the SCF is used to make the results nationally representative.[10]

Three different definitions of income—each corresponding to an alternative assumption about the income derived from the ownership of corporate equities—are used to illustrate the distribution of income in the United States. The first definition, what we call self-reported income, is the answer to "How much was the total income you received in 1994 from all sources, before taxes and other deductions were made?" This amount generally equals the sum of answers to questions about the various components of income, which treat capital income on a nominal realization basis. For instance, the survey asks about capital gains from sales of assets such as stocks and real estate but does not ask about accrued capital gains on assets that were not sold during the year.

TABLE 6-1
DISTRIBUTION OF INCOME UNDER ALTERNATIVE DEFINITIONS OF INCOME

Income Rank	Mean Income (in $000)			Share of Total Income (%)			
	SCF self-reported income	SCF income definition (1)	SCF income definition (2)	Treasury's family economic income	SCF self-reported income	SCF income definition (1)	SCF income definition (2)
Top 1%	627.7	695.3	1,013.8	14.3	14.3	14.2	17.8
95–99%	159.7	196.6	242.5	13.9	14.6	16.0	17.0
90–94%	93.3	107.3	127.3	10.7	10.7	10.9	11.2
80–89%	68.2	75.5	83.4	16.0	15.6	15.4	14.7
Top quintile	120.8	138.7	172.7	54.9	55.2	56.5	60.7
60–79%	45.4	50.1	53.2	21.5	20.7	20.4	18.7
40–60%	29.6	31.4	32.7	13.3	13.5	12.8	11.5
20–39%	17.2	18.6	19.2	7.8	7.9	7.6	6.7
Bottom quintile	5.9	6.2	6.4	2.9	2.7	2.5	2.2
Overall	43.8	49.1	56.9	100	100	100	100

NOTES: Households are sorted separately for each income definition.
Income definitions:

Family economic income is the income concept used by the Treasury Department in its distributional tables. It is based on the Haig-Simons definition of income and imputes accrued capital income to tax return and census data using a variety of data sources.

Self-reported income is the response to the SCF question on income, which counts income on a realization basis.

(1) Replaces reported capital income with a 6.4 percent real return to publicly traded corporate equities, and a 3 percent real return to net worth other than business equity but includes closely held business income as reported.

(2) is the same as 1 but assumes a 28 percent real return to publicly traded corporate equities.

SOURCE: 1995 Survey of Consumer Finances, unpublished distributional tables provided by the Treasury Department's Office of

We construct two other income definitions to approximate an accrual-based measure of income under two different assumptions about the rate of return to corporate equity. For each definition we replace reported realized nominal capital income (except for closely held business income) with imputed accrued capital income. The capital income imputations are derived by applying uniform real rates of return to publicly traded corporate equities and nonbusiness net worth. All other income items are included as reported. These cover wages and salaries; income from a closely held professional practice, business, or farm; pension income; Social Security income; unemployment insurance benefits; public assistance such as AFDC, food stamps, and SSI; and other miscellaneous forms of income such as gains from gambling. Reported dividends, realized capital gains, interest income, and rent, trust, and royalty income are all excluded from income and replaced with imputed measures of capital income. No attempt is made to replace reported income from closely held businesses with an imputed measure based on accrued capital income because closely held business income cannot be reliably divided into returns to labor and capital in the data. The real rate of return to nonbusiness net worth is assumed to be 3 percent, which is the rate used by the Treasury Department's Office of Tax Analysis for interest-bearing assets and debts in its distributional tables (Cilke et al. 1994, 3–26).

For our first alternative definition, the real rate of return to publicly traded corporate equities is assumed to be 6.4 percent, which is intended to approximate the rate of return implied by corporate earnings in 1995. The 6.4 percent figure was calculated by dividing $371.8 billion, the National Income and Product Accounts measure of corporate profits after inventory valuation, capital consumption adjustment, and profit taxes for 1995 (August 1998 Survey of Current Business, table 1.16), by $5.85 trillion, the total corporate equity holdings in the 1995 SCF. The $5.85 trillion denominator includes all C- and S-corporation equity held either directly or through IRA, Keogh, or defined-contribution pension accounts. For the second alternative definition, we use a rate of return to publicly traded corporate equities of 28 percent. This is the annualized total real rate of return on the Standard & Poor's 500 index between December

211

1994 and December 1997, with monthly reinvestment of dividends (President 1996, 1997, 1998). The CPI-U is used to deflate the total S&P 500 return to a real rate of return. Our measure of publicly traded corporate equities includes both equities held directly and those held in IRA, Keogh, and defined-contribution pension accounts, such as 401(k)s.[11] Table 6–2 shows the distribution of net worth and equity holdings by the alternative definitions of income.

Table 6–1 shows the results of this exercise. Comparing the columns labeled *self-reported income* with those labeled *income definition 1* reveals that replacing realized corporate-source income with a constant 6.4 percent accrual rate of return does not materially affect the estimated distribution of income. Also shown for comparison purposes is the income distribution under the Treasury Department's concept of family economic income, which follows a similar approach to our income definition 1, but makes more detailed imputations using a variety of data sources, including tax return data. The distribution of income in the Treasury calculations is also quite similar to that found in the SCF under either self-reported income or income definition 1. However, as the columns labeled *income definition 2* indicate, using the actual 1995–1997 rate of return to publicly traded equities of 28 percent causes dramatic changes. Relative to income definition 1, the share of income received by the top 1 percent of the weighted sample rises from 14.3 percent to 17.8 percent, an increase of almost one-fourth; the share of the ninety-fifth to the ninety-ninth percentile group increases by about one-sixth, from 14.6 percent to 17.0 percent. Conversely, when the actual accrual rate of return is imputed to be 28 percent, the share of the bottom quintile falls from 2.7 percent to 2.2 percent, and that of the second lowest quintile declines from 7.9 percent to 6.7 percent.

We do not mean to imply that the rate of accrued capital gain during this period is likely to persist and make the more dispersed income distribution a steady state. But neither should the rate be ignored, as it represents an enormous amount of income that is highly skewed even in light of the recent diffusion of stock ownership. Ranked by income definition 2, households in the top percentile of the income distribution on

TABLE 6–2
EQUITY AND NET WORTH OF HOUSEHOLDS, RANKED BY ALTERNATIVE DEFINITIONS OF INCOME

Income Rank	Mean Equities (in $000)			Net Worth (in $000)			Equities as a Share of Net Worth		
	Self-reported income	Income definition (1)	Income definition (2)	Self-reported income	Income definition (1)	Income definition (2)	Self-reported income	Income definition (1)	Income definition (2)
Top 1%	992.9	1,273.0	1,569.2	5,078.2	5,430.4	5,581.9	0.196	0.234	0.281
95–99%	204.3	214.2	230.3	1,021.2	1,146.6	1,200.7	0.200	0.187	0.192
90–94%	85.0	91.0	79.3	452.5	504.4	573.3	0.188	0.180	0.138
80–89%	53.4	39.4	33.8	297.7	266.6	248.8	0.179	0.148	0.136
Top quintile	138.5	148.9	161.3	720.1	760.3	787.0	0.192	0.196	0.205
Next highest quintile	22.8	19.4	13.5	173.4	151.4	142.0	0.131	0.128	0.095
Middle quintile	9.8	8.2	4.3	105.9	104.0	95.2	0.093	0.079	0.045
Next lowest quintile	8.8	3.7	1.7	83.6	77.7	70.9	0.105	0.048	0.025
Bottom quintile	1.7	0.9	0.3	51.3	39.2	37.8	0.034	0.023	0.009
Overall	36.3	36.3	36.3	227.0	227.0	227.0	0.160	0.160	0.160

SOURCE: Survey of Consumer Finances, 1995, and authors' calculations (discussed in text).

average owned $1.5 million in publicly traded corporate equities in 1995. At an annual real rate of return of 28 percent, these households received an extra $1.2 million in income on average over the course of three years due to the stock market boom.[12]

Depending on what tax burden one attributes to the income accrued by shareholders from 1995 to 1997, the runup also may have had a substantial impact on the progressivity of the tax system. If one attributes to this income only an accrual-equivalent capital gains tax—arguably only about 5 percent once one accounts for the benefit of deferral and the carryover of basis at death—the effective progressivity is much lower than official estimates would suggest.

If, though, the stock market runup were due to an increased expected present value of corporate earnings, then this situation would normally be accompanied by a concomitant increase in corporate tax payments so that the effective tax rate on this income is the average corporate tax rate plus any additional tax due at the individual level on dividends and capital gains. If one attributes this tax in proportion to either the owners of corporate equity or, as is standard in incidence analysis, to the owners of all wealth, then the estimated progressivity would not be substantially altered.

The "Taxpayer Didn't Notice" Act of 1995 and the 1996 and 1997 Surge in Inequality: A Nonevent Study. Most of the recent evidence concerning the effect of taxes on taxpayer choices as reflected in reported taxable income comes from analyses of the 1981, 1986, 1990, and 1993 tax changes. The first two lowered the top marginal tax rate, and the latter two increased it. Because one of the most difficult empirical tasks is to separate out the effect of the tax changes from nontax-related trends in income inequality, the fact that the latter two tax changes increased rather than decreased rates is helpful.

It is also insightful to analyze trends in income inequality over periods when there is no important tax change. One fascinating period began in 1996, immediately after the passage of an exceptionally uneventful tax bill of 1995, which among things did *not* change the tax rate structure. Striking developments soon followed this nonevent.

The first sign that something extraordinary was happening was the unexpected surge in federal individual income tax revenues. Individual income tax receipts for fiscal year 1997 turned out to be $61 billion, or about 9 percent, higher than the Congressional Budget Office had estimated in January 1997.[13] About half this increase was due to capital gains realizations. Roughly $20 billion was due to an unexpectedly high level of capital gains reported on returns for tax year 1996. Another $14 billion represented unexpectedly high estimated tax payments for 1997, much of that also probably due to capital gains. Total capital gains realizations increased by 45 percent between 1995 and 1996, and preliminary estimates suggested another 45 percent increase in 1997. Although the higher 1997 estimated tax payments may have partly reflected a response to the capital gains rate cut implemented on May 7, 1997, the 1996 realizations would have been expected to be *lower* due to anticipation of the following year's rate cut. Another factor was the increasing share of income reported by higher-income, and therefore higher marginal tax rate, individuals. The CBO calculated that the effective income tax rate (total income taxes paid divided by total adjusted gross income) increased from 13.7 percent to 14.0 percent from 1994 to 1995 and to 14.6 percent in 1996. Taxpayers with income of $200,000 or more (in 1996 dollars) accounted for 17 percent of total AGI in 1996, up from 16 percent in 1995 and 14 percent in 1994. In a July 1998 report, the CBO (1998b) mentions that actual revenues for 1998 were also running higher than anticipated, but it did not have enough information to discuss the sources.

In its January 1998 report the CBO (1998a) speculated that another component of the surge of incomes at the top was bonuses and stock options. Rapid growth in both stock prices and grants of employee stock options has caused the taxable value of exercised options to increase dramatically. The CBO referred to data that suggested that the taxable value of exercised options doubled in 1995, doubled again in 1996, and continued to grow rapidly in 1997.

Carroll (1998b) documents that the share of total income reported by taxpayers with more than $200,000 (in 1989 dollars) in total income jumped from 14.0 percent in 1995 to 16.0 percent

TABLE 6-3
DISTRIBUTION OF MODIFIED ADJUSTED GROSS INCOME, 1991–1997

Totals

Modified AGI ($000)	1991	1992	1993	1994	1995	1996	1997
<0	−61,597	−60,698	−62,524	−63,942	−65,906	−65,446	−49,630
0–5	40,560	40,444	42,171	44,462	46,898	49,748	50,345
5–10	114,245	117,865	124,042	125,589	130,826	134,879	140,298
10–20	373,865	382,839	400,343	418,819	444,590	460,068	478,709
20–30	442,024	445,290	463,651	481,937	494,658	520,349	551,227
30–50	815,366	837,520	853,684	886,855	928,310	960,354	1,012,945
50–75	669,210	686,697	702,786	732,854	757,710	793,323	840,676
75–100	301,365	314,214	316,007	340,703	365,098	390,341	427,707
100–200	324,790	341,398	353,776	374,579	420,201	463,083	506,622
200–300	99,534	102,240	109,707	118,529	129,673	145,659	160,638
300–500	87,334	100,210	95,461	103,851	118,588	131,768	144,908
500–1,000	73,656	85,497	80,640	83,565	97,934	111,271	128,571
Over 1,000	103,138	139,973	121,234	127,086	153,162	183,772	227,327
Total	3,383,490	3,533,489	3,600,978	3,774,887	4,021,742	4,279,169	4,620,343
Over 200	363,662	427,920	407,042	433,031	499,357	572,470	661,444

Shares
(%)

Modified AGI ($000)	1991	1992	1993	1994	1995	1996	1997
<0	-1.82	-1.72	-1.74	-1.69	-1.64	-1.53	-1.07
0–5	1.20	1.14	1.17	1.18	1.17	1.16	1.09
5–10	3.38	3.34	3.44	3.33	3.25	3.15	3.04
10–20	11.05	10.83	11.12	11.09	11.05	10.75	10.36
20–30	13.06	12.60	12.88	12.77	12.30	12.16	11.93
30–50	24.10	23.70	23.71	23.49	23.08	22.44	21.92
50–75	19.78	19.43	19.52	19.41	18.84	18.54	18.20
75–100	8.91	8.89	8.78	9.03	9.08	9.12	9.26
100–200	9.60	9.66	9.82	9.92	10.45	10.82	10.97
200–300	2.94	2.89	3.05	3.14	3.22	3.40	3.48
300–500	2.58	2.84	2.65	2.75	2.95	3.08	3.14
500–1,000	2.18	2.42	2.24	2.21	2.44	2.60	2.78
Over 1,000	3.05	3.96	3.37	3.37	3.81	4.29	4.92
Total	100.00	100.00	100.00	100.00	100.00	100.00	100.00
Over 200	10.75	12.11	11.30	11.47	12.42	13.38	14.32

NOTES: Income classifier is modified AGI in 1991 dollars. All totals are expressed in nominal dollars (in $ millions).
Modified AGI is defined as AGI minus capital gains in AGI and Social Security in AGI, plus tax-exempt interest income.
Data for 1997 are preliminary and are particularly subject to error at the bottom (modified AGI<0) and the top of the income distribution.
SOURCE: Office of Tax Analysis, U.S. Treasury Department. We are grateful to Bob Carroll for providing us with this information.

in 1996. Even more strikingly, the share received by those with more than $1 million jumped from 5.1 percent to 6.4 percent, or by more than one-quarter.

Table 6–3 gives a seven-year perspective on the recent surge in incomes at the top. In this table the income figures are based on a concept of modified adjusted income, which excludes real-ized capital gains. The share of total income received by those returns with greater than $200,00 (in 1991 dollars) of income in-creased from 11.47 percent to 14.32 percent, or more than one-fourth, between 1994 and 1997. Even more striking, the share received by those with an income exceeding $1 million increased from 3.37 percent to 4.92 percent, or nearly 50 percent. Some of this increase is certainly due to a larger number of returns in this category, but certainly not all.

The increase between 1994 and 1997 in the share of income received by high-income taxpayers is of at least the same order of magnitude as the increase between 1985 and 1988, which con-vinced nearly all observers, including Slemrod (1996), that be-cause nontax factors could not explain this surge, the Tax Reform Act of 1986 must have been a major influence. It is less convincing to ascribe such a role for the "Taxpayer Didn't No-tice" Act of 1995 or any tax change passed in 1994.

Table 6–4 explores the sources of income growth between 1995 and 1996 in greater detail. Here taxpayers are ranked by adjusted gross income, which includes capital gains. In just one year the number of returns with incomes greater than $1 million increased by 27.5 percent, while AGI going to millionaires in-creased by 38.1 percent. Although in this case capital gains was the fastest-growing source of income (71.2 percent) for this group, there was also tremendous one-year growth in all other forms of income, such as a 29.9 percent increase in wages and salaries. By contrast the total number of returns for people at all income levels increased only 1.6 percent, and overall AGI regis-tered only a 5.1 percent increase.

Some fascinating information from state income tax returns also sheds light on this trend. Table 6–5 uses data from 1995 and 1996 New Jersey income tax returns. While overall growth in New Jersey gross income was 7.6 percent, it was double-digit for all annual income classes exceeding $250,000 and was nearly 50

TABLE 6–4
Changes in Adjusted Gross Income and Income Sources, by Income Group in the United States, 1995–1996
(in $ billions, except for number of returns column)

Size of Adjusted Gross Income ($000)	Tax Year	Number of Returns	Adjusted Gross Income	Salaries and wages	Interest and dividends	Capital gains	Partnership and S-corporation income
				Income Sources (in $ billions)			
Under $200	1995	116,954,819	3,549.30	2,896.05	213.29	64.79	24.53
	1996	118,827,802	3,729.36	3,009.93	221.13	81.52	26.37
	Growth (%)	1.6	5.1	3.9	3.7	25.8	7.5
$200–500	1995	1,007,136	292.12	174.56	31.75	24.93	32.18
	1996	1,198,671	347.40	204.71	35.97	35.72	36.66
	Growth (%)	19.0	18.9	17.3	13.3	43.3	13.9
$500–1,000	1995	178,374	120.35	60.21	15.99	15.99	20.34
	1996	213,823	144.81	70.48	17.78	23.78	23.79
	Growth (%)	19.9	20.3	17.1	11.2	48.7	17.0
More than $1,000	1995	86,998	227.58	70.64	36.86	64.71	48.70
	1996	110,912	314.40	91.75	43.26	110.80	59.96
	Growth (%)	27.5	38.1	29.9	17.4	71.2	23.1
Total	1995	118,218,327	4,189.35	3,201.46	297.89	170.42	125.75
	1996	120,351,208	4,535.97	3,376.87	318.14	251.82	146.78
	Growth (%)	1.8	8.3	5.5	6.8	47.8	16.7

NOTE: Interest and dividends includes taxable interest, taxable dividends, and tax-exempt interest. *Capital gains* is defined here as taxable net gain less taxable net loss on Schedule D, plus capital gain distributions reported on Form 1040. Partnership and S-corporation income is net income less net loss.
SOURCE: Internal Revenue Service, *Statistics of Income Bulletin*, fall 1998, and *Individual Income Tax Returns 1995*.

TABLE 6-5
CHANGES IN GROSS INCOME SOURCES, BY INCOME GROUP IN NEW JERSEY, 1995–1996

Size of Gross Income ($000)	Tax Year	Number of Returns	Gross Income (in $ billions)	Income Sources (in $ billions)				
				Employee compensation	Interest and dividends	Capital gains	Partnership income	S-corporation income
Under $250	1995	3,326,133	130.38	109.21	6.663	2.230	1.075	0.623
	1996	3,337,510	136.36	113.37	6.812	2.895	1.103	0.765
	Growth (%)	0.3	4.6	3.8	2.2	29.8	2.6	12.3
$250–500	1995	31,260	10.54	6.92	0.651	0.634	0.657	0.355
	1996	36,085	12.17	7.91	0.703	0.894	0.716	0.434
	Growth (%)	15.4	15.5	14.3	8.0	41.0	9.0	22.2
$500–1,000	1995	9,737	6.55	3.88	0.488	0.569	0.479	0.446
	1996	11,083	7.45	4.37	0.497	0.780	0.556	0.486
	Growth (%)	13.8	13.7	12.6	1.8	37.0	16.1	9.0
$1,000–3,000	1995	3,615	5.58	2.81	0.503	0.765	0.370	0.693
	1996	4,394	6.74	3.32	0.514	1.087	0.485	0.827
	Growth (%)	21.5	20.8	18.1	2.2	42.1	31.1	19.3
More than $3,000	1995	689	4.50	1.30	0.505	1.112	0.349	1.013
	1996	987	6.74	2.04	0.504	1.794	0.660	1.348
	Growth (%)	43.3	49.8	56.9	−0.2	61.3	89.1	33.1
Total	1995	3,371,434	157.55	124.12	8.81	5.31	2.93	3.13
	1996	3,390,059	169.46	131.01	9.03	7.45	3.52	3.86
	Growth (%)	0.6	7.6	5.6	2.5	40.3	20.1	23.3

SOURCE: State of New Jersey, Department of the Treasury, *Statistics of Income*, summer 1997 and fall 1998.

percent for those families fortunate enough to have more than $3 million in gross income. To be sure, much growth in the income of the highest class can be traced to the fact that the number of tax returns increased by more than 40 percent, from 689 to 987, but the increase in the size of this group itself is a remarkable phenomenon.[14]

The source of the large gains at the top of the income distribution is also of interest. The total gross income increase of returns exceeding $250,000 was $5.93 billion. Of that almost none was in the form of interest and dividends. A total of 46.0 percent was employee compensation, 24.9 percent was capital gain, 9.5 percent was in partnership income, and 11.1 percent was in S-corporation income.

Conclusions

> There's something happenin' here.
> What it is ain't exactly clear.
>
> —Stephen Stills

Our analysis in the last section suggests an extraordinary increase in the income, both realized and unrealized, of the already affluent beginning around 1996. What new light does this development shed on the chicken-and-egg ruminations of the first part of this essay?

First of all, it casts some doubt on the hypothesis that the top tax rate cuts of 1981 and 1986 were the key factor in generating the increases in measured inequality of the last two decades. A decade passed between 1986 and 1996, with two top tax rate *increase* episodes in between, so it is difficult to link the recent surge in incomes at the top to tax-cutting policy. If the 1996 surge is not tax related, it makes more plausible the case that the surge of 1986, of a similarly large magnitude, was not primarily tax driven.

More important, the recent evidence suggests that the increase in inequality that began in the 1980s has not abated. If anything, the rate of increase dramatically accelerated in the mid-1990s. Standard models suggest that the appropriate response to this development is an increase in the progressivity of the tax-and-transfer system. Models of public choice suggest that this may not happen. The recent uncertainty in the economic situation reminds us that the demand for progressivity as social insurance has not abated and may be increasing.

Notes

1. The Congressional Budget Office has calculated a consistent series of tax distribution for about two decades. This series uses a definition of *income* somewhat broader than adjusted gross income, includes all federal taxes, and assumes that the burden of the corporate income tax falls on capital income generally. Under these assumptions the average tax rate on the top 1 percent of income earners fell from 34.9 percent to 26.2 percent between 1980 and 1985, rose to 36.5 percent by 1995, and then fell slightly to 34.4 percent by 1999. Average tax rates were changed little between 1980 and 1999 for most of the rest of the income distribution. The average rate on the second lowest quintile fell slightly from 15.0 percent to 13.7 percent between 1980 and 1999. In the middle quintile the average rate edged down from 19.1 percent to 18.9 percent. In the second highest quintile the average rate was 22.2 percent in both 1980 and 1999. The rate for the top quintile went from 28.2 percent to 29.1 percent. The bottom quintile did experience a substantial decline in average federal tax rates, from 7.7 percent to 4.6 percent, largely due to an increased personal exemption and standard deduction after 1986 and to an expansion of the earned income tax credit. However, this analysis does not take into account reductions in transfers such as food stamps and welfare payments. The combined tax-and-transfer system is thus probably not much different in its progressivity in 1999 than it was in 1980 (Kasten, Sammartino, and Toder 1994; CBO 1998c).

2. Feldstein (1976) offers an excellent review of these issues.

3. Because a tax schedule may feature rebates rather than taxes at some levels of income, the optimal tax-and-transfer system is really at issue in the optimal progressivity literature.

4. Although the marginal tax rate is approximately constant, the average tax rate (tax liability divided by income) increases with income due to the presence of the positive exemption level. Mirrlees (1971) assumed that the government needed to raise 20 percent of national income in taxes.

5. Helpman and Sadka (1978) claim that this result is not general, but offer only a trivial counterexample with a Rawlsian (maximim) social welfare function and a fixed lowest-ability level of zero. They argue that there should be counterexamples with more general social welfare functions but admit that they were unable to identify such an example.

6. The authors of this study admit, though, that their conclusions do not apply to the *very rich*, defined as those with assets exceeding $10 million (in 1972 dollars).

7. Thurow (1975) offers a similar view.

8. For example, the declining progressivity might simply be due to a declining aversion to inequality at least as expressed through the political system.

9. Lindert (1996) argues that openness fails to explain patterns of social spending for OECD countries from 1960 to 1981.

10. In the case of missing or incomplete answers to certain questions, SCF imputes answers based on other information in the survey. Several different "replicates" of the data—each representing a different set of imputations—are included in the SCF. We use the first replicate.

11. For the retirement accounts the SCF does not provide exact information on the share of the account held in each type of asset but does ask what combinations of assets are held in the accounts. Respondents who reported investing their IRA and Keogh accounts "mostly in stocks or mutual funds" are assumed to keep 100 percent of their IRA or Keogh assets in corporate equities. Those who report investing their IRA or Keoghs in a combination of stocks and bonds, a combination of stocks and interest-bearing accounts, or in a brokerage or cash management account are assumed to keep 50 percent of their IRA or Keogh assets in equities. Those who report a combination of stocks, bonds, and interest-bearing accounts are assumed to keep 33 percent of their IRA or Keogh assets in equities. For defined-contribution accounts, respondents who report that the account is "mostly or all stock" are assumed to have 100 percent of their defined contribution pension assets in equities. Those who report keeping a "split between stock and interest earning assets" are assumed to have 50 percent of their defined contribution assets in equities. Because only limited information on defined-benefit pension plans is available in the 1995 SCF, these plans are excluded from all measures of net worth and equity holdings.

12. Table 6–2 shows equity holdings and net worth by income class. The $1.2 million figure is calculated as $((1 + (.28 - .064))^3 \times (1.5 \text{ million}) - 1.5$ million.

13. This episode is described in Congressional Budget Office 1998a.

14. The income groups are defined in nominal dollars, but little inflation occurred in this period.

References

Alesina, Albert, and Dani Rodrik. 1994. "Distributive Politics and Economic Growth." *Quarterly Journal of Economics* 109: 465–90.

Allen, Franklin. 1982. "Optimal Linear Income Taxation with General Equilibrium Effects on Wages." *Journal of Public Economics* 17: 135–43.

Atkinson, Anthony B. 1973. "How Progressive Should Income Tax Be?" In *Essays in Modern Economics*, edited by M. Parkin and A. R. Nobay, pp. 90–109. London: Longman.

Auten, Gerald, and Robert Carroll. 1999. "The Effect of Income Taxes on Household Behavior." *Review of Economics and Statistics* 81 (4) (November): 681–93.

Cameron, D. 1978. "The Expansion of the Public Economy: A Comparative Analysis." *American Political Science Review* 72: 1243–61.

Carroll, Robert. 1998a. "Do Taxpayers Really Respond to Changes in Tax Rates?" U.S. Department of the Treasury, Office of Tax Analysis Working Paper 78.

————. 1998b. "Tax Rates, Taxpayer Behavior, and the 1993 Tax Act." Paper presented at the Ninety-first Annual Conference of the National Tax Association, Austin, Tex.

Cilke, James, with Bob Gillette, C. Eric Larson, and Roy A. Wyscarver. 1994. "The Treasury Individual Income Tax Simulation Model." Mimeo. U.S. Department of the Treasury, Office of Tax Analysis.

Congressional Budget Office. 1998a. *The Economic and Budget Outlook: Fiscal Years 1999–2008*. Washington, D.C.: GPO, January.

————. 1998b. *The Economic and Budget Outlook for Fiscal Years 1999–2008: A Preliminary Update*. Washington, D.C.: GPO, July.

————. 1998c. *Estimates of Federal Tax Liabilities for Individuals and Families by Income Category and Family Type for 1995 and 1999*. Memorandum. May.

Cooter, Robert, and Elhanan Helpman. 1974. "Optimal Income Taxation for Transfer Payments under Different Social Welfare Criteria." *Quarterly Journal of Economics* 88: 656–70.

Feenberg, Daniel, and James M. Poterba. 1993. "Income Inequality and the Incomes of Very High-Income Taxpayers: Evidence from Tax Returns." In *Tax Policy and the Economy*, edited by James Poterba, pp. 145–77. Cambridge, Mass.: MIT Press.

Feldstein, Martin. 1973. "On the Optimal Progressivity of the Income Tax." *Journal of Public Economics* 2: 357–76.

————. 1976. "On the Theory of Tax Reform." *Journal of Public Economics* 6: 77–104.

————. 1995. "The Effect of Marginal Tax Rates on Taxable Income." *Journal of Political Economy* 103: 351–72.

Fullerton, Don. 1996. "Comment on 'High-Income Families and the Tax Changes of the 1980s: The Anatomy of Behavioral Response'." In *Empirical Foundations of Household Taxation*, edited by Martin Feldstein and James Poterba, pp. 189–92. Chicago: University of Chicago.

Gilder, George. 1990. *Wealth and Poverty*. New York: Basic Books.

Goolsbee, Austan. 2000. "It's Not about the Money: Why Natural Experiments Don't Work on the Rich." In *Does Atlas Shrug? The Economic Consequences of Taxing the Rich*, edited by Joel Slemrod, pp. 141–58. Cambridge: Harvard University Press.

Helpman, Elhanan, and Efraim Sadka. 1978. "The Optimum Income Tax: Some Comparative Static Results." *Journal of Public Economics* 9: 383–93.

Jencks, Christopher, with Marshall Smith, Henry Avlands, Mary Jo Bane, David Cohen, Herbert Gintis, Barbara Heyns, and Stephan Michelson. 1972. *Inequality: A Reassessment of the Effect of Family and Schooling in America.* New York: Basic Books.

Karoly, Lynn. 1994. "Trends in Income Inequality: The Impact and Implications for Tax Policy." In *Tax Progressivity and Income Inequality,* edited by Joel Slemrod. Cambridge: Cambridge University Press.

Kasten, Richard, Frank Sammartino, and Eric Toder. 1994. "Trends in Federal Tax Progressivity, 1980–93." In *Tax Progressivity and Income Inequality,* edited by Joel Slemrod. Cambridge: Cambridge University Press.

Kristov, Lorenzo, Peter Lindert, and Robert McClelland. 1992. "Pressure Groups and Redistribution." *Journal of Public Economics* 48: 135–63.

Levy, Frank, and Richard Murnane. 1992. "U.S. Earnings Levels and Earnings Inequality: A Review of Recent Trends and Proposed Explanations." *Journal of Economic Literature* 30: 1333–38.

Lindbeck, Assar. 1995. "Hazardous Welfare State Dynamics." *American Economic Review* 82: 53–68.

Lindert, Peter. 1996. "What Limits Social Spending?" *Explorations in Economics History* 33: 1–44.

Lindsey, Lawrence. 1987. "Estimating the Behavioral Responses of Taxpayers to Change in Tax Rates: 1982–1984. With Implications for the Revenue-Maximizing Tax Rate." *Journal of Public Economics* 33: 173–206.

Lydall, H. F. 1968. *The Structure of Earnings.* Oxford: Oxford University Press.

Magee, Stephen P., William Brock, and Leslie Young. 1989. *Black Hole Tariffs and the Endogenous Policy Theory.* Cambridge: Cambridge University Press.

Meltzer, Allan H., and Scott F. Richard. 1981. "A Rational Theory of the Size of Government." *Journal of Political Economy* 89: 914–27.

Mirrlees, James A. 1971. "An Exploration in the Theory of Optimum Income Taxation." *Review of Economic Studies* 38 (114):175–208.

———. 1976. "Optimal Tax Theory: A Synthesis."*Journal of Public Economics* 6 (4):327–58.

Moffitt, Robert, and Mark Wilhelm. 2000. "Taxation and the Labor Supply Decisions of the Affluent." In *Does Atlas Shrug? The Economic Consequences of Taxing the Rich,* edited by Joel Slemrod, pp. 193–234. Cambridge: Harvard University Press.

Myrdal, Gunnar. 1960. *Beyond the Welfare State.* New Haven: Yale University Press.

Peltzman, Sam. 1980. "The Growth of Government." *Journal of Law and Economics* 23: 209–87.

Persson, Torsten, and Guido Tabellini. 1994. "Is Inequality Harmful for Growth? Theory and Evidence." *American Economic Review* 48: 600–621.

Rawls, John. 1971. *A Theory of Justice*. Cambridge, Mass.: Harvard University Press.

Reich, Robert B. 1991. *The Work of Nations: Preparing Ourselves for Twenty-first Century Capitalism*. New York: Alfred A. Knopf.

Rodrik, Dani. 1998. "Why Do More Open Economies Have Bigger Governments?" *Journal of Political Economy* 106: 997–1032.

Romer, Paul. 1990. "Capital, Labor and Productivity." *Brookings Papers on Economic Activity*, sp. is., pp. 337–367.

Sandmo, Agnar. 1993. "Optimal Redistribution When Tastes Differ." *Finanzarchiv* 50: 149–63.

Slemrod, Joel. 1994. "On the High-Income Laffer Curve." In *Tax Progressivity and Income Inequality*, edited by Joel Slemrod. Cambridge: Cambridge University Press.

———. 1996. "High-Income Families and the Tax Changes of the 1980s: The Anatomy of Behavioral Response." In *Empirical Foundations of Household Taxation*, edited by Martin Feldstein and James Poterba, pp. 169–88. Chicago: University of Chicago.

———. 1998. "Methodological Issues in Measuring and Interpreting Taxable Income Elasticities." *National Tax Journal* 51: 773–88.

Stern, Nicholas H. 1976. "On the Specification of Models of Optimum Income Taxation." *Journal of Public Economics* 6: 123–62.

Thurow, Lester. 1975. *Generating Inequality*. New York: Basic Books.

U. S. President. 1996. *Economic Report of the President, 1996*. Washington, D.C.: GPO.

———. 1997. *Economic Report of the President, 1997*. Washington, D.C.: GPO.

———. 1998. *Economic Report of the President, 1998*. Washington, D.C.: GPO.

Varian, Hal. 1980. "Redistributive Taxation as Social Insurance." *Journal of Public Economics* 14: 49–68.

Commentary

James M. Poterba

This chapter cogently describes the interplay between the pretax distribution of earnings capacity, the tax system, and the reported distribution of taxable incomes. It emphasizes the important two-way relationship between pretax income inequality and redistribution through the tax system. While the degree of pretax income inequality can affect the design of the tax code, the tax code can also affect the measured distribution of pretax income.

The first part of the essay states that two economic phenomena of the past two decades are difficult to reconcile in the standard neoclassical theory of optimal income taxation. These are (1) the growth of pretax income inequality and (2) the stable or possibly declining progressivity of the income tax system. What can explain the difficulty? There are three broad classes of explanations: (1) mismeasurement of progressivity or income inequality, (2) changes in social tastes for equality, and (3) changes in the actual or perceived distorting effects of progressive tax schedules. I discuss each of these possibilities in turn.

The first possibility is that standard measures of progressivity fail to capture the actual changes in tax progressivity during the past two decades. While there is broad agreement that the wage distribution has become more unequal during that period and that the share of pretax income reported by the highest income households has increased, there is less consensus regarding changes in progressivity. Progressivity is a notoriously difficult concept to measure. Except in special circumstances it is not possible to make unqualified statements about whether one tax system is more or less progressive than another when the two tax systems exhibit different degrees of redistribution at different points in the income distribution. While reductions in the top marginal income tax rates have worked in the direction of reducing progressivity since 1980, other changes, notably the base-broadening of the 1986 Tax Reform Act and the expansion of the earned income tax credit (EITC), partly offset this tendency. For many low-income households the tax system has actually become more progressive in the sense that it is today a more important source of redistribution than it was two decades ago. The chapter notes these issues in a cautious footnote.

Two sets of statistics highlight these developments. The first is the percentage of individuals in the population who are moved into, or out of, poverty as a result of the income tax system. Data reported by the Committee on Ways and Means (1998) show that in 1983 the income and payroll tax systems pushed 4.2 percent of the population into poverty, when poverty is computed on the basis of net-of-tax cash and noncash income. By 1993 the expansion of the earned-income tax credit and other reforms had changed this situation, and the tax system's net impact was to *remove* 0.3 percent of the population from poverty. By 1996 the tax system was a substantial *antipoverty* program, raising 3 percent of the population above the poverty line. These changes should not be viewed in isolation, since other changes in antipoverty programs occurred over this time period. Nevertheless these changes highlight the difficulty with making broad statements about the progressivity of the income tax system. It is also not clear how broadly one should define the tax-and-transfer system for the purposes of addressing progressivity.

A second set of statistics that present a similar picture of *rising* progressivity can be derived from Congressional Budget Office tabulations of average tax rates on families at different points in the income distribution. These statistics, which William Gale shared with me, can be derived from historical data in Committee on Ways and Means 1998 and current information on the CBO website. They show that in 1980 the average tax rate on families in the bottom quintile of the income distribution was 8.1 percent. This rate rose to 10.4 percent by 1985; then declined to 8.9 percent by 1990, primarily as a result of marginal tax rate reductions. It fell sharply to an estimated 4.6 percent in 1999 as a result of EITC expansion. For the second quintile, the 1980 value was 15.6 percent. It rose to 15.9 percent in 1985 but fell to 13.7 percent by 1999. At the top of the income distribution, for families in the top fifth of the income distribution, the average tax rate was 27.6 percent in 1980. Following the Tax Reform Act of 1986, it declined to 26 percent in 1988, but subsequent tax changes raised this average rate to a value of 29.1 percent in 1999. This pattern is also evident for families in the top 1 percent of the income distribution, where average tax rates have varied from 31.9 percent (1980) to 26.9 percent (1988) to 34.4 percent (1999). These summary measures suggest that if anything, progressivity has increased in the past two decades. Clearly the progressivity of different parts of the tax system changed in different ways over this period.

The authors present some intriguing calculations to suggest that standard measures of household income, such as those on which the CBO average tax rate calculations are based, significantly misstate the inequality of pretax incomes in recent years. In particular they emphasize that the unequal pattern of corporate stock ownership, coupled with the rapid rise in share values in the past few years, has generated much greater accruing capital gains at the top of the income distribution than elsewhere. Although the basic point about the distribution of capital gains is undeniable, I am reluctant to replace the standard measure of household income with this expanded version. My primary concern is that corporate stock is only one of many assets on the household balance sheet. If one were to move to an accrual-accounting measure of family income, it would also be appropriate to revalue human capital, owner-occupied housing, and many other components of wealth. The daunting empirical undertaking probably explains a significant part of the popularity of more standard realization-based measures of household income.

If we accept the premise that progressivity has declined or stayed roughly constant, however, we need to find alternative explanations for the comovement in pretax income inequality and tax progressivity. The next two explanations that I consider focus on shifts in tastes and shifts in technology, both with respect to tax design. The explanation of shifting tastes would focus on changes in social preferences for equality over the past two decades. The crucial factors that influence optimal income tax rates in simple theoretical models are the degree of inequality aversion in the social planner's social welfare function and the effect of changes in marginal tax rates on household behavior. Changes in inequality aversion could therefore explain changes in the structure of the income tax that the standard neoclassical analysis would describe as optimal. If one takes the extreme view that the neoclassical theory of optimal income taxation constitutes a *positive* theory of what determines income tax rates, then it is even possible, as in Gabaix (1998), to try to recover social welfare function parameters from the observed structure of income tax rates.

Documenting changes in social preferences about equality is difficult. Tastes for redistributing resources toward low-income households may have declined, perhaps because the long economic expansion of the 1990s has reduced the likelihood that low-income households are in the low-income group because of their inability to find employment. The rise of a new class of rich households, many of whom are young and tied to high-technology industries, may also have affected social preferences about redistribution away from those with high incomes and substantial wealth. The new rich have typically earned rather than inherited their wealth. Because they are associated with a set of industries that are transforming broad components of American society, there may correspondingly be a limited desire to tax them heavily. One bit of evidence that suggests a greater tolerance for income inequality, even when it is clearly visible in the public eye, is the widening gap between CEO pay and the pay of average workers at many firms.

If the social welfare function that a social planner might optimize when designing an income tax system has shifted in this period, accounting for a decline in tax progressivity is not difficult even while the pretax income distribution has become more unequal. This statement begs the question of how individual preferences about equality are aggregated to define a social welfare function. This is an important stumbling block to analyzing how tastes for inequality might affect the progressivity of the income tax.

There is a third potential explanation for the pattern that the authors note. High-income households may have become more sensitive over time to tax incentives, or policymakers may think that they have become so. To evaluate this issue, one must ask whether the labor supply today is more responsive to after-tax wages than it was two decades ago and whether there is any greater sensitivity of saving to after-tax rates of return. If the answers to these questions are yes, then even with a stable social welfare function, marginal tax rates could decline because tax writers would recognize greater marginal distortions associated with a given tax rate.

Whether taxpayer behavior is now more sensitive to taxes is an open question. A solid case can nevertheless be made for the claim that policymakers today have much clearer evidence suggesting that taxes affect behavior. The past twenty years witnessed an outpouring of research suggesting that taxation affects a variety of dimensions of household behavior. Work on the labor supply of secondary earners after the 1986 Tax Reform Act, on changes in hours of work among EITC-eligible households, on how tax incentives affect the allocation of saving between IRA-type accounts and other accounts, and on the sensitivity of capital gains realizations with respect to current and future marginal tax rates suggests that taxpayers respond to clearly defined tax incentives. Although the effects today may not be larger than in the past, perhaps because they are better documented and more widely discussed there is greater reluctance to enact tax systems with high marginal tax rates on those with high pretax incomes. The United States is not alone in having reduced marginal tax rates in the post-1980 period. This has been a coincident development in most developed nations.

There is a fourth and final possibility for explaining the comovement of progressivity and pretax income inequality: the neoclassical theory of optimal income taxation has scant bearing on actual tax policies. The theory is derived in a world with only labor income, while actual income tax schedules devote much of their complexity to the measurement and taxation of capital income. The theory also sidesteps the fundamental political economy issues that surround actual policy design. Slemrod and

Bakija correctly note the lack of agreement on how to model the political economy process that leads to the enactment of an income tax schedule. Few observers of the political process would want to characterize the process as the simple implementation of textbook optimal tax formulas. Conversely the basic insights from the theory, in particular the role of preferences for equality or views about taxpayer behavioral responsiveness, are still relevant for the analysis of actual policy outcomes. One lesson that emerges from this chapter is the need to develop a firmer political economy foundation for analyzing tax policy.

The authors do not limit their analysis to the links between pretax income inequality and the structure of the income tax; they also consider the possibility that the tax system affects the level and distribution of pretax incomes. This is a natural possibility in light of the growing body of evidence on how taxation affects taxpayer behavior. Slemrod and Bakija provide a useful overview of the rapidly growing literature on the impact of marginal tax rates on the taxable income reported by taxpayers, and they add to the debate on this aspect of behavioral response. Previous studies have debated the extent to which changes in the observed income distribution, particularly the fraction of income reported by high-income households in the late 1980s and early 1990s, could be attributed to changes in the tax law during these periods. Undoubtedly a secular trend has increased the concentration of incomes at the top of the distribution. Such a trend tends to magnify the apparent effect of tax reductions, as in 1986, and to reduce the apparent effect of tax increases, as in 1993.

The authors draw on new data sources to document a substantial increase in the concentration of income among high-income households during the 1995–1997 period. They conclude that because no federal income tax changes occurred during this period, one must be suspicious of the claim that the rising share of income received by high-income households in the 1986–1989 period was a result of tax-induced behavioral changes. I conclude that the findings post-1995 weaken the evidence from the 1980s, but I nevertheless believe that the previous evidence should not be dismissed.

Recent experience adds new data to a signal extraction

232

problem. We are trying to estimate the sensitivity of taxable income to tax rates from a time series on income shares accruing to different income groups. Before 1986 the income share accruing to different deciles of the income distribution had not fluctuated much. Against this background, changes in the tax rate seemed responsible for the stark changes between 1986 and 1989, when the income tax system was in flux. Today, with new data that suggest that income shares are in fact more fluid than the pre-1986 data suggested, the claim that tax reforms alone sparked the experience of the mid-1980s must be viewed with more caution. Substantial fluctuation in income shares complicates evaluating any particular change or attributing it to a particular external factor.

One can take issue with the authors' claim that because of the absence of any marginal tax rate changes in the 1995–1997 period, tax factors did not cause the changing income distribution pattern over this period. Previous work on the link between taxes and reported taxable income has employed highly stylized models of taxpayer adjustment. Many studies implicitly view changes within a year or two of a tax change as steady-state responses to the variation in the tax code. Studies with a more sophisticated approach to adjustment dynamics have typically allowed for a one- or two-year period of taxpayer timing adjustments. Yet taxpayers might adjust gradually to a new tax regime. Some behaviors that take advantage of a new configuration of tax rates may take time to adjust. These include shifting from C-corporation to S-corporation status after 1986, shifting assets from income-producing vehicles to capital gain–producing vehicles after 1997, and the expansion of occupations that offer particularly high after-tax returns in a world of reduced marginal tax rates. As the messages from financial advisers and other tax planners diffuse over time, the set of taxpayers affected by these messages can grow. At least in principle some shifts in the pretax income distribution observed even in the 1990s might have been a delayed response to the tax changes enacted in the 1980s.

The experience of the mid-1990s is a wake-up call for further research on the determinants of pretax income inequality and particularly for further analysis of what determines the reported incomes of the highest-income households. Previous work on this question has focused on information from tax returns. Although tax returns contain accurate information on income sources, they contain little information about how particular income flows were earned. If economists and policy analysts are to understand the determinants of the recent changes in the income distribution, analyzing new and nonstandard data sources such as information from firm employment records may be necessary. This is a fertile direction for further work.

References

Gabaix, Xavier. 1998. "Making Cardinal Welfare Judgments by Inferring Distributional Preferences from the Tax System." Mimeo. Harvard University.

U.S. House of Representatives, Committee on Ways and Means. 1998. *1998 Green Book: Background Material and Data on Programs within the Jurisdiction of the Committee on Ways and Means*. Washington, D.C.: GPO.

Index